REAL
ESTATE
SELLING
MAGIC

Real Estate

Gael Himmah
Publishing Company

Selling
Magic

GAEL HIMMAH

P.O. Box 4591
Walnut Creek, Calif. 94596

REAL ESTATE SELLING MAGIC

Portions of this book previously appeared in THE
GAEL HIMMAH SYSTEM FOR INCREASING REAL
ESTATE SALES, 1967, Prentice-Hall, Inc., and are
reproduced here with permission of Prentice-Hall, Inc.

Library of Congress
Catalog Card Number: 74-79854
ISBN 0-9600488-2-0

Fourth Printing . . . . October, 1977

DEDICATION

For my many friends in real estate.

Other Books By Gael Himmah

REAL ESTATE LISTING MAGIC

THE LISTING MASTER

THE GAEL HIMMAH SYSTEM FOR INCREASING REAL
ESTATE SALES   (Extensively revised September, 1974
and re-published with much new material added as REAL
ESTATE SELLING MAGIC)

A WORD FROM THE AUTHOR

Real estate is a magnificent profession. It can make you rich. But sales deficiencies prevent many licensees from realizing their maximum potential. A system of sales procedures which produces volume sales is described in this book.

Careful attention to these pages will reveal the secrets of real estate success. The procedures you must follow are precise, but they are easily mastered. Study the material in this book, learn it, put it to use, and you will be an outstanding success.

Gael Himmah
Walnut Creek, California

CONTENTS

APPENDIX A

Policy Book

APPENDIX B

The Reference Book

APPENDIX C

A Visual Listing Presentation Book   231

TABLE OF FIGURES

REAL ESTATE SELLING MAGIC

INTRODUCTION TO
SELLING

1

If you want to make money, sell real estate!

Selling is our nation's highest paid profession, and real estate is its greatest dollar producing industry. As population grows, land is rapidly becoming the scarcest commodity on earth. Scarcity makes value increase.

Hence, real estate is where the money is and selling is the vehicle which lets you get it.

Real estate is a profession desperately in need of well trained, dedicated salesmen. With application and thought you can become a skilled, money making real estate salesman. I'll show you how to do it.

Don't be intimidated by the number of real estate salesmen already working in your area. Believe me, they won't bother you. The competition you've heard about certainly exists in real estate, but you will be able to rise above your competitors as if they didn't exist.

THE THEOREM OF MEDIOCRITY   Before entering any competitive situation, it is wise to learn all you can about your competition. Real estate is no exception. I want to describe a fact of life I have observed over the years, a condition which will work to your advantage and make your job much easier. It will allow you to

1

outdistance your competitors with speed and ease. I call it my
THEOREM OF MEDIOCRITY.

I have found 80% of people are only average in their business, job, or profession. They are adequate but not outstanding.
They are mediocre in their skills and dedication. These people
are willing to just get by in their jobs. They are satisfied with
their level of performance. They have neither the interest nor
enthusiasm to excel.

I believe 10% of people are below average in job performance, and 10% are highly skilled.

My theorem of mediocrity isn't restricted to any particular
job or profession. It applies to people in every walk of life. I
believe 80% of physicians are only mediocre in their skills and
abilities, 10% are sub-par, and 10% are experts. The same is
true of lawyers, carpenters, accountants, nurses, engineers,
truck drivers, business executives, and salesmen.

If you think this judgment too harsh, consider how difficult
it is to find a house painter who doesn't leave paint splattered
all over your windows, or a gardener who knows why your prize
camellia is failing and how to treat it, or an attorney who has
your contracts properly prepared on the date he promised them.

Doctors mis-diagnose, druggists mis-label prescriptions, auto-
mobiles are poorly engineered and badly assembled. Few
politicians have statesman quality. It's nearly impossible to find
a restaurant that prepares food well, let alone expertly. Business
executives are afraid to make decisions. Hardware salesmen
don't know their product line. Mediocrity is all about us.

We have become so immersed in mediocrity in our everyday
lives we have come to expect it. We're actually surprised when
we encounter the rare individual who excels in his job. It's a
pleasure to watch a skilled bricklayer work, or a good door-to-
door salesman make his sales presentation. Rest assured, my
Theorem Of Mediocrity is valid.

When we apply this theorem to your potential competitors
in real estate, we make a startling discovery. Although many
people have real estate licenses, 80% of them are merely
mediocre, and 10% are poor at their jobs. Hence, 90% of them
aren't going to have much influence on your potential for
success. You have to be concerned only with the highly skilled

salesmen, and they constitute barely 10% of the licensee population. By using the sales techniques detailed in these pages, you'll be in that top 10% yourself, so your competition will be even less.

Don't ever underestimate your own ability or overestimate your competitor's. I know how easy it is for a newly licensed salesman to be intimidated by anyone who has a broker's license.

I remember one of my first sales contract presentations. My sales manager couldn't go with me and my broker was unavailable. I had to go by myself. When I learned the listing agent was a broker, I was horrified. I envisioned all manner of embarassing things happening to me while I tried to muddle my way through a presentation of my contract to the homeowners.

To my great surprise, I discovered that the broker knew less than I about FHA sales. He didn't know what the current point quotes were nor which lender had the lowest quotations. He didn't know the payoff penalty regulations of FHA nor the appraisal fees being charged. And I did!

That presentation caused me, for the first time in my real estate career, to believe in myself as a professional. I was able to answer the homeowners' questions, and did an acceptable job of closing the sale. It did wonders for my ego to realize the broker needed my help. He needed my knowledge. He needed my expertise.

From that day on, I have never abdicated my position of being a knowledgeable real estate agent merely because someone else was a broker, or held a license for more years than I, or worked out of a large office with many branches. Each individual must be assessed on his own merits.

THE "CLIENT RESISTANT" SALESMAN I remember one day not long ago when my wife and I walked into one of the largest real estate offices in one of the largest towns in the Southwest. (I am not licensed as a real estate agent in that state.) It was a Sunday morning and we wanted to look at houses with the intention of purchasing one if we found one we liked.

I intentionally chose that particular office as we didn't have much time and I assumed such a large office would have the best trained salesmen.

Upon entering the office, the floor man looked up from his desk with nary a smile on his lips. He looked up, and looked . . . and looked. He didn't say a word as I walked up to his desk. He didn't rise. He offered neither his name nor his hand. I saw that if we were going to progress, I would have to be the catalyst. I smiled, introduced myself (although I didn't tell him I was a real estate broker from California), and told him we wanted to buy a house. I expected this information to fire him into action.

My wife and I sat down and waited for him to begin his client interview. We sat, and he sat, and we looked at each other. He opened several listing binders, turned a few pages, but didn't say a word. Finally, out of desperation, I said, "Ask me some questions." (See Chapter 7, Qualifying The Buyer, for a description of how to properly interview a walk-in client.)

This was no young boy just graduated from a real estate school. As I learned later, he was a retired Air Force officer, an intelligent, mature man who had been a real estate salesman for seven years.

I'm telling this story to give you self confidence. As you read what happened to my wife and I when we presented ourselves as home buyers, you will be able to compare this salesman's performance to your own. I'm certain the comparison will convince you the competition isn't nearly as acute as you imagined it to be.

The first question he asked was, "How many children do you have?"

He didn't ask how to spell my name. He didn't get my address nor telephone number. It was obvious he didn't have a set pattern for interviewing clients which is an absolute necessity for successful salesmen. He seemed to be struggling for something to say. (See Chapter 5, Introduction To The Buyer, for a discussion of this important subject.) He returned to his listing binders, thumbing rapidly through the pages.

"One," I answered, and waited for his next question. Again, I was disappointed. I saw he wasn't going to ask any more questions.

Again I started the conversation. "We would like to find an attractive home in a good neighborhood," I began. "Two or three bedrooms are sufficient. We would like approximately two thousand feet of living area. The condition of the home is unimportant. If a run-down home has the potential for being remodeled into a showy home, we would like to see it." I told him the price range we would consider.

"We can live anywhere in the country," I went on, "and we want to look at your city. We heard it's beautiful, an ideal place to live."

He looked at me earnestly and said, "If I had my choice, I'd live in Seattle. Good people up there!"

My wife almost fell off the sofa. I couldn't believe a real estate salesman making such a negative comment about the city he works in.

While we were talking, the telephone rang often and although there were other salesmen in the office, he grabbed it each time as if he were thankful for the interruption. He continued riffling through his listing books but seemed never to remove any pages. I knew if we were going to inspect any properties, I would have to push this man.

"Let's go," I said. "We want to see some homes."

He obviously hadn't a clue as to what to show us. He turned desperately to another salesman who, by now, was hanging over the partition behind the floor man's desk. He was an immaculately groomed, middle aged man with polished fingernails and a peculiar grin permanently scrolled across his face.

He minced around the partition and up to the desk, his eyes flashing. "I've got a marvelous home," he bubbled, all smiles and batting eyelashes. "I helped decorate it," he announced with pride. He described it, then, in a burst of enthusiasm, bounded suddenly across the floor, grabbed my hand in both of his and gave me a little squeeze. He threw his head back for emphasis and lisped, "and for the double whammy, it's located just right so it gets television reception from one hundred miles away." He seemed immensely proud of himself as he twirled away and swished back to his desk. He startled me. I wasn't prepared for him out there in the western desert.

By now, my patience was at an end. "Show us some homes,"

I insisted, and walked out the door, hoping to lead our salesman toward his car. This was one of the most "client resistant" salesmen I had ever seen.

Eventually we got him to pick a few homes from his listing books. As we drove off in his Toyota, he turned toward me and said pensively, "If I'd known this was going to happen, I would have brought my station wagon." He made it sound as if this was the first time he had ever shown homes to walk-in clients.

As we pulled up in front of the "double whammy" house he discovered he had no key. "Sorry I can't get you in," he said. "Look in the windows if you like."

"Let's look at something else," I said. My wife was having a hard time not laughing. She knew my temperament and was certain this salesman was stretching my patience to its limits. Actually, he was such a study that he fascinated me. I had never seen anything quite like him.

After the "double whammy" house he drove us four times around a ten block circle. As we cruised past the same cactus time and time again we began to recognize them as old familiar landmarks.

He got himself oriented after a few more circuits and brought us to another home. As we finished our inspection we told him we liked it. At that he informed us that if he was the builder he'd never put such a large home on such a small lot. "Did you notice how small your backyard would be?" he asked. "It's a terrible lot."

I wanted to ask him why he showed us the home if the lot was so bad, but I didn't say anything. Perhaps we wanted a small backyard, a low maintenance lot. Many buyers prefer just such a property. Rather than pointing out the benefits of a small lot, he was victimized by his negative attitude.

We saw another home we liked. When we told him, he immediately said something to discourage a potential sale. "It might look good now," he advised us, "but wait till the first rain. That gully will wash out half your driveway."

Some time later he turned suddenly off a paved street onto an old, rutted, dirt road. Dust swirled into the car in choking billows. "You like dirt roads?" he chirped as we crashed off into the desert.

What a vacant question, and this after I had told him we wanted to live in an attractive neighborhood in town.

I asked if there were rattlesnakes in the area. "Don't think so," he said. As we rounded a hillock of spiny cactus, we saw a young man twirling a four foot rattlesnake round and round by its tail while his dog barked excitedly from his car window. "Well, maybe a few," our hero offered as he sped us deeper into the dusty hills.

For four hours this bewildered real estate salesman drove us around his town and the country surrounding it. He physically exhausted us, another cardinal sin of effective salesmanship.

Finally, he turned from the highway into a country club. "I've saved the best for last," he said proudly. "I know you'll like this. It's my favorite house."

We inspected his prize, and it was lovely. "How much is it?" I asked.

He scratched his chin. "Darned if I know," he said as he led us back to his car and the long ride into town, "but I knew you'd like it."

It was an incredible performance. Needless to say, we left the salesman and his town, never to return again.

Someday I'm going to send that salesman a plaque for his desk. On it I will have engraved

YOU NEVER GET A SECOND CHANCE
TO MAKE A GOOD FIRST IMPRESSION.

SUCCESS
REQUIRES
SKILL
The basic tenets of salesmanship are as true today as they were one hundred years ago. If all salesmen, the prosperous and the poor, were questioned as to their knowledge of sales procedures in their particular industries, most would be aware of the same procedures. But some make a poor living while others earn substantial incomes. If these salesmen have the same basic information about their profession, if they have the same general understanding of sales procedures, if their ability is equal, why then should some be successful and others be unsuccessful?

The answer is not found in a single deficiency nor in one favorable characteristic. To be successful in his profession, the salesman must not only be aware of certain facts of salesmanship, but he must develop his personal sales skills so he can compete favorably with his competitors.

The successful salesman must have a detailed knowledge of his own industry. A general knowledge won't do anymore. Competition is too severe. In addition, he must dissect the structure of his industry and learn its many parts.

In real estate, you must develop skill in financing procedures; you must know various forms used in the course of doing business, the characteristics of buyers and sellers of real property, how to use the telephone, how to qualify a buyer, how to write an offer so the buyer will sign it and the seller will accept it, how to present an offer to a seller, and how to answer objections that are common to the industry.

You must understand yourself and learn how to motivate yourself. You must learn how to motivate clients. You must know how to schedule your time so you make every minute count. You must know how to conduct yourself in your dealings with cooperating salesmen from other offices. You must know how to develop confidence in yourself as a salesman so you can control the many varied situations in which you find yourself.

I DEVELOPED MY SYSTEM During the many years I have been actively engaged in the general brokerage real estate business, I have developed a system of selling which refines these basic elements into a hard-hitting sales technique designed specifically for real estate salesmen.

I have learned the extraordinary ways in which people who want to buy real property conduct themselves in their associations with salesmen. Buyers of real estate often do not react to sales stimuli in a logical, expected manner. You have to know and understand this to be really successful. I have incorporated these discoveries into my system of sales techniques.

My system really works. It works for me. It works for scores of salesmen trained in its techniques. I've seen it turn ordinary salesmen into high income producers in a few short weeks.

AN
EXPERIENCED
MAN HELPED

Some years ago a young man walked into my office and announced he would like to go to work for me as a real estate salesman. He told me he was licensed and had been working for another real estate firm for the past year.

The company he mentioned had an excellent reputation. Its brokers were highly competent. I asked him why he wanted to change offices. He explained he felt he had been wasting his time in real estate. He couldn't seem to get started. He had secured only six listings and made only four sales in the past year.

Once he made a sale his brokers were anxious to help him close the escrow, but they didn't show him how to sell in the first place. He was depending on luck instead of skill. He felt insecure as a salesman. He was uncomfortable dealing with clients. He had a family to support, his funds were running out, and his wife was after him to quit real estate entirely.

He had heard of my training program and my selling system from other salesmen and wanted to talk about it. He asked if I thought he was the right "type" for real estate. I explained there is no real estate "type" and suggested he give real estate one more try before he surrendered to another line of work.

He came to work for me the following day. We both knew his days in real estate were numbered unless he could make some sales right away.

I spent several hours asking him questions about sales procedures, financing, forms, and related subjects. For working a full year in the business, his knowledge was remarkably poor. He knew little more than what he had to learn to pass his state license examination. Unfortunately, most of the material he had committed to memory has little bearing upon the realities of earning a living in real estate.

He had developed some bad habits of telephone technique which, he explained, were copied from observing other salesmen in his former office. He was terrified when he had to discuss financing procedures. He thought that was a province reserved exclusively for brokers or salesmen with years of experience. He had worked in a haphazard fashion, planning nothing in advance.

This poor fellow needed help desperately. He was bright. I knew it wouldn't be hard to get him on the right track.

I began a "crash course" program of instruction for this salesman. I talked and demonstrated. He listened, observed, and remembered.

He saw how easy it was to make sales with just a little more knowledge than he had. As he learned, he realized how close he had been to making sales before, and how his lack of knowledge had allowed him to follow the wrong tack with his clients. He was both happy and sad as he learned my system of increasing sales. He suffered the paradox of being happy to have these sales revelations presented to him, and sad to consider how much money had literally run through his fingers in the past.

This young man developed into one of the highest paid salesmen I know. Certainly my system of real estate sales wasn't the only cause of this. He had many fine qualities such as perseverance, a burning desire to succeed, and an interest in self-improvement, all of which helped my system help him. But without the exposure to these sales procedures, this salesman would surely have failed in real estate.

I have shown my sales system to successful real estate salesmen who have been in the business for years. They have applied it to themselves and seen their sales grow by leaps and bounds.

AN INEXPERIENCED MAN HELPED I have seen it work wonders for the inexperienced salesman. I remember just such a person who came to me for help several months ago. He had been in real estate only a few weeks, working in another office, but already he was a very disillusioned gentleman. He told me a sad, sad story, one I have heard many times before.

His license had been freshly pinned to his broker's wall and he was waiting to be shown how to make money in real estate. What a shock he received!

Instead of good advice and sales suggestions he could follow, the sum total of guidance he received consisted of being given a desk, a telephone, a handful of business cards and the advice to "bring in some business." His training was non-existent. He sputtered through the maze of real estate sales complexities in fits and starts, succeeding only in developing a monumental frustration. His chances of success were slim.

But he was eager. He really wanted to succeed. And he was uncomfortable in his new surroundings, ready to grasp at each tendril of advice directed his way. He was alert, receptive to suggestions.

He was told to go out and knock on doors for a week. So he gave door-to-door cold canvass a try. He didn't receive any preparation for this specialized form of selling. He had no pre-planned sales presentation to help him along. He wasn't sure of his objective. He felt like a lost soul in a sea of disinterested home owners. That can be an extremely lonely feeling.

He told me he thought of terminating his real estate career at that juncture. But he decided to face up to it, so he did as his broker advised. He went out and knocked on doors. And he wasted the entire week. More important, the luster of enthusiasm he had for his new profession quickly tarnished.

He was unhappy with himself. He had given real estate a try not knowing what to expect, and now he was disappointed. All the months of excitement planning his real estate career; the weeks of cheerful study for the license examination; the antici-pation of being part of a fascinating, glamorous, well respected, highly paid profession; all those dreams were crumbling for him.

What a disastrous environment this was for an inexperienced salesman. What a terrible installation into his new profession. He had looked upon the real estate business as a profession. He expected professional treatment, and he deserved it. He wasn't prepared for the unglamorous, non-professional drudgery of door-to-door selling.

When he came into my office he was frightened and de-pressed, receding rapidly into a state of shock. He felt the pro-fession had been misrepresented to him. A knowledge of field-proven sales procedures would give him an entirely dif-ferent picture.

Two weeks after he began learning my system of real estate sales techniques, he made two sales in a single day. He has been going "great guns" ever since.

I have seen my system transform many such persons into

exceptional salesmen. Give my system a chance and it will produce sales you didn't even know existed!

REMEMBER   Pay close attention to the pages that follow so
WHAT YOU   your reading comprehension will be high. Many
READ   people spend valuable time reading page after
                  page of good, sound material but when they
finish they don't know what they've read.

This was brought home to me in dramatic fashion shortly
after publication of my first book on listing procedures (*Real
Estate Listing Magic,* Gael Himmah Publishing Co.) I placed
half a dozen copies of the book in my office library and asked
all my salesmen to read it. Each checked out a copy and some
time later reported back that he had read it. Shortly thereafter,
many salesmen began to show great increases in the number of
listings taken. Average listors became very good listors. I expected this, and was gratified. But a few didn't effect any
change at all. Their listing success was unchanged. This seemed
improbable after they had read my book. I determined to find
out why.

I called a meeting of those salesmen whose listing abilities
hadn't improved and again asked them if they had read my
book. They said they had. They said they understood the
material in the book, remembered it, and used it. But, they
explained, it just didn't work. I quizzed them on the material
they had read and discovered that, in fact, they had a very
poor knowledge of the book.

For example, they knew there were ten questions they should
ask a homeowner when they wanted to get a listing, but none of
them had bothered to remember the questions. They couldn't
expect to use the questions if they didn't know what they were!

They couldn't explain the reason for "points" as regards
Government insured financing. They didn't have a fluid knowledge of methods of pricing a listing, another facet of successful
listing which is of great importance.

I posed the usual homeowner objections to giving a listing as
they are detailed in the book, and asked the salesmen to give me
the suggested answers to each. They could not. Instead of
knowing what to say in advance, they stumbled about in their

answers and tried to think up answers on the spur of the moment—precisely what I advised against in my book.

I could go on and on with such examples. These were salesmen who possessed personal qualities high above the norm. They were salesmen who relied upon their knowledge of real estate listing procedures to earn a living. They had a treasury of valuable information handed to them, information which would increase their incomes many times over, information that was easily understood and readily absorbed. Yet they did not make the effort required to understand what they had read. They didn't take advantage of the golden opportunity presented to them.

It sounds incredible, but it's true. That's human nature in action. Such lack of application has prevented many an ambitious salesman from achieving success.

In this book you are given information of such value that your entire life could be beneficially affected by it. It can make you financially independent. It can even make you rich.

Don't skim casually over the pages and then file their meaning away in some unused cranny of your brain. Think about what you're reading. Think how you can best use the information. Make certain you understand what you read. These pages unfold a series of sales procedures which, if used as I suggest, will bring you outstanding success in real estate.

Lest you feel I am unduly demonstrative in my exultation of real estate as a profession, consider the words of multimillionaire Hetty Green:

> Real estate is an imperishable asset, ever increasing in value.
> It is the most solid security that human ingenuity has devised.
> It is the collateral to be preferred above all others, and the
> safest means of investing money.

Here is what Andrew Carnegie had to say about real estate:

> Ninety percent of all millionaires became so through owning
> real estate. More money has been made in real estate than in
> all industrial investments. The wise young man or wage earner
> invests his money in real estate, and he invests consistently.

Real estate is surely the most valued treasure in a world of riches. Success in this utopian profession is at your fingertips.

POINTS TO KEEP IN MIND

1. *Develop a detailed knowledge of real estate subjects.*
2. *Learn how to motivate yourself.*
3. *Understand buyers' characteristics.*
4. *Rely on skill, not luck.*
5. *Plan your activities in advance.*
6. *Make sure you understand the meaning of what you read.*
7. *Remember what you read, so you can put it to use.*

HOW MY "SYSTEM" WORKS

2

My system for increasing sales requires you to develop knowledge of four key subjects: sales procedures, organized sales talks, general information relative to real estate sales, and sales forms. To facilitate learning the system, these four major subjects are divided into 12 chapters and three appendices.

It is essential that you become thoroughly familiar with all of them. Used together, these subjects become an irresistable sales tool. If you find you are weak in any of the component parts of the system, make an extra effort to develop your knowledge of that part. A thorough knowledge of each subject is necessary for the proper functioning of the entire system.

SALES PROCEDURES Sales procedures are detailed in four chapters; 8, 9, 10, and 11. In these chapters you will learn how to conduct yourself while you show property to a client, how to counter client objections to purchase, how to write the sales contract, and finally, how to present the offer to a home owner.

Many real estate salesmen who realize only moderate success have been handicapped by a faulty "showing" technique. Yet an understanding of the art of showing a home to a client, so easily mastered, could lift these salesmen far above their present level of income production. The fact is, most salesmen don't show a home properly. Nor do they adequately prepare themselves or their clients for a tour of homes. As a result, they lose scores of sales. Property "showing" procedures are detailed in Chapter 8.

Once a client inspects a property that interests him, he will normally pose objections to you. The skill with which you answer these objections has a direct relationship to your income. The most common objections, and their corresponding answers, are discussed in Chapter 9.

If you don't write an offer, you won't make any sales. This is so obvious it seems unnecessary that I mention it. But I have seen many potentially good salesmen stumble badly when the time for writing the offer was at hand.

Sometimes, friendly buyers turn into ferocious anti-social demons when a bumbling salesman produces a deposit receipt and makes gestures indicating they should sign that document and give him a check as a deposit. In the company of a properly trained salesman who is well versed in the psychology of "closing" a sale, these same clients would remain friendly as they happily signed the deposit receipt and handed over their check. Chapter 10 explains how this is done.

Once the offer is written, you must get it accepted by the sellers before you have earned your commission. This is no simple task. Unless your offer is at the full listed price, with terms precisely as specified by the seller, you will have to do some more selling when you present your contract to the sellers. You will be asking them to take less money, and/or poorer financial terms than they had intended. This makes them defensive, somewhat suspicious, and definitely in need of a highly professional sales presentation. Whether the emotional climate is happy or hostile, the act of handing your contract to the sellers becomes your moment of truth. Chapter 11 shows you how to do it properly and get your offer accepted.

ORGANIZED   Sales managers in all industries of American
SALES   business recognize the benefits of a "prepared"
TALKS   sales presentation. In direct selling fields, such
            as educational materials, books, cosmetics, and
light appliances, it has been estimated that 80 per cent of the

gross sales volume results from pre-planned sales presentations. In route sales such as food products, beverages, chemicals, and drugs, 65 per cent of gross sales volume results from prepared sales presentations.

In real estate as well, knowing what you are going to say before you say it separates the good salesmen from the ordinary ones.

It is well known that certain positive statements of fact motivate clients favorably. I have organized a number of these motivating statements into sales talks that have proved successful. It behooves you to adopt these talks yourself. They are illustrated in Chapter 5.

Real estate is a business of paradoxes. You must have experience to function in it successfully, or, as a substitute for experience, you must profit by the experience of others. In many facets of real estate, common sense and logic will lead eventually to failure. Experience proves this. You can't rely on logic alone.

For example, common sense suggests that the best method of locating clients to buy a specific house is to advertise that home in the newspaper. Experience proves that this would be wrong. In most cases, advertising is effective only when the house advertised has sufficient emotional features to make an ad appealing. Advertising some other property with more reader appeal will bring you clients whom you can then "switch" to the property you want to sell.

Understanding what motivates clients to buy a home or call a real estate office in response to a newspaper advertisement is essential information. You will find more of these paradoxes, more unexpected twists, when you read Chapter 5, which gives you valuable insight into the characteristics of buyers of real property. You are shown prepared sales talks which have proved effective in dealing with an unknown client.

Speaking on the telephone so your personality is projected to the caller requires special skill. Speaking to an unknown person who has phoned your office in response to a newspaper advertisement takes even more skill. In Chapter 6, sales talks for use over the telephone are explained in detail.

Once the buyer is in your office, you must determine what he wishes to buy and what he can afford to buy. You must "qualify" this client as to his needs and ability to pay before you decide what properties to show him. Qualifying clients is an essential skill which requires careful attention to basic rules of procedure. This information, molded into an organized sales talk, is given in Chapter 7.

GENERAL   In addition to having a detailed knowledge
INFORMATION   of sales procedures and organized sales talks,
                   the professional real estate salesman must be aware of a fund of general information absolutely essential to success.

One of the outstanding benefits of a career in real estate is the privilege every salesman has to sell from a large inventory of property without the necessity of having to pay for the inventory. The more properties you inspect, the greater your inventory. An ability to remember the different characteristics of many properties will reward you financially. Chapter 3 explains the proper way to inspect property so you will remember it and be able to show it to a client to its best advantage.

After you have shown a piece of property to a buyer and he expresses a desire to purchase, you must know how to finance it so you can complete the sale. Financing is a serious problem to many licensees, but it shouldn't be. Chapter 4 provides you a short but effective course in real estate financing procedures.

I often hear good, experienced salesmen complain they are not working as efficiently as they should. They're wasting time and energy on non-productive activities. This problem is easily remedied by time scheduling. Chapter 12 discusses this important subject. Also included in Chapter 12 is a form I have found to be invaluable for brand new real estate salesmen. I call it the Schedule of Activities For New Salesmen. Every salesman new to the office is handed a copy of this form which lists everything he must do to get going quickly in his new profession. It gives him perspective. It lets him see just where he is in his training every minute and what he still has to do. It removes the uncertainty so familiar to beginners in any industry.

Another complaint common to real estate salesmen is a lack of confidence in themselves. They feel they don't have enough knowledge to perform as professionals. Hence, they don't want to talk to clients. This is a fatal deficiency. In Chapter 13, I show you how to develop confidence.

In the concluding chapter, I describe the events that occur in a typical day in the life of a real estate salesman. In it you can picture the normal environment in which you must function. It's fast, it's furious, it's demanding, and it's fun! Besides, in real estate you are paid very, very well for your time.

THE   There are three appendices in this book.
APPENDICES   Appendix A contains a reproduction of the
             Policy Book used in my own real estate firm.
(See pages 139–165.)

The value of a Policy Book is obvious. It tells you what your broker expects of you and what you may expect of him. Serving to define standard operating procedures of the company, a thorough, detailed Policy Book will save you hours of precious time learning organizational details. After all, you must become well oriented within your own office before you can deal effectively with the public.

Commission disputes between salesmen are eliminated by use of a Policy Book. You can refer to the Policy Book for the solution to many of the problems which arise in a normal brokerage company.

Every real estate office should have a comprehensive Policy Book. It saves countless misunderstandings and welds the office staff into a cohesive unit.

Appendix B presents a Reference Book containing the forms and documents normally used in a general brokerage real estate office. (See Exhibits B1-B50, pages 169–227.) Many of the forms are completed with sample sales information. Detailed instruction is given for filling out the forms. The Rereference Book shown in this appendix helps you learn to use the "tools of the trade."

Appendix C illustrates a visual listing presentation book which many salesmen use to advantage for in-home listing presentations. I include this in a book on sales techniques since nothing will improve your sales ability more than developing listing skills. They are such closely related activities that the truly professional real estate salesman will become proficient in both. While my two books on listing techniques offer a detailed study of listing, the visual listing presentation book in Appendix C is a simple method of securing listings. Use it while you are learning the more advanced techniques described in REAL ESTATE LISTING MAGIC and THE LISTING MASTER.

The chapters in this book are arranged so they correspond to the normal development of your real estate career. Initially you learn some general background information. Then you learn about buyers. Then you speak to clients on the telephone. Next the buyer comes into your office and you qualify him. After that you show him some property, answer his objections, write an offer and present it to a seller.

Then you are given additional information of a general nature. Finally, the appendices complete the "system."

When you have learned this information and know how to use it, you will be assured of success.

POINTS TO KEEP IN MIND

1. *Develop knowledge of sales procedures, sales talks, financing, time scheduling, and sales forms.*
2. *Make certain you learn each part of the "system" thoroughly.*
3. *Don't underestimate the power of a prepared sales presentation.*
4. *Don't rely on logic and common sense decisions. Profit by the experience of successful Realtors.*
5. *Developing listing skills will improve your sales techniques.*

HOW TO INSPECT
PROPERTY

3

"KNOW" YOUR PROPERTY   Your stock-in-trade is the inventory of property you have to sell. Just having a catalog of listings isn't nearly enough. You must "know" the property, from personal inspection. Only by a personal, on-the-spot appraisal can you compare any given property to competing offerings.

Consider the burden of salesmen from time immemorial. Regardless of the product they had to sell, no matter what the size, vitality or location of their market, they all bore the common denominator of product knowledge. "You've got to know your territory. You've got to know your merchandise." Both are axioms of successful salesmanship.

I doubt if you would buy an automobile from a salesman who couldn't answer your questions about the car you were interested in. You wouldn't have confidence in his advice if you felt he didn't know much about the product he was selling. A good auto salesman will make certain he knows all about the different cars he has to sell before he steps onto the floor to greet a customer. He will make it his business to know as much as possible about his competitors' products so he can answer your questions fairly, with accuracy and authority.

Would you buy a major appliance, or an expensive insurance

policy, or a sailboat, or a diesel locomotive from a salesman who didn't exhibit firsthand knowledge of his product? Of course not. The expense involved in such a purchase is too great, the function too important, the decision too large.

Keep in mind that a home is the most expensive material possession the average family ever buys. You're not selling an ordinary, inexpensive product; you're selling a house! You're asking a man to commit himself and his family to a mortgage loan of thousands upon thousands of dollars, a loan which will obligate him for 25 or 30 years into the future.

Think about that. You are the professional advisor to people who are about to make the most important financial decision of their lives.

Are you qualified? Are you competent to give such advice? Certainly you have to know a great deal more than a stockbroker. You're not selling shares in a company. You're selling shelter. A place to live, to raise a family. You are going to advise this family that they can invest 25 per cent of their total income in their home purchase. That's real money.

Do you know your product? Do you know the homes you have to sell? Are you planning to see these homes for the first time with your clients? Many salesmen make up a list of homes to show by consulting their catalog of listings. If the price, geographical location, and number of bedrooms come close to the client's requirements, "put 'em on the list!"

"I might get lucky," the salesman says to himself. "They might see one they like."

Other equally ineffective salesmen rely upon the advice and suggestion of fellow salesmen in their office.

"Know any good three-bedroom ranchers in Oakwood Gardens?" the salesman asks.

Sometimes he gets a few addresses this way. In many instances he gets no information, or the suggestions he receives do not include the exceptionally good buys the other hardworking salesmen have found through their own efforts.

INSPECT   The few really "hot" properties that come for
IT NOW   sale on the market are sold rapidly by those who
                 have taken the trouble to ferret out these gems.
They work on a strict schedule, usually alloting so many hours

each day to the function of inspecting new listings. They learn to spot a potentially good listing from the information card describing it, but they don't stop there. They inspect it personally. Immediately! That is what separates the men from the boys in this business: a sense of urgency to get it done now, not tomorrow, or after a coffee break. Now. Do it now!

SCHEDULE   I mentioned a scheduled approach to inspecting
YOUR TIME   new listings. I believe you should have a scheduled
             approach to all your real estate activities. (See Figures 12-2 and 12-3, pages 113–114.) Your working time each day should be regulated by pre-scheduling your activities. There should be a time, each day, for securing new listings, inspecting property, and showing property to clients. If you're not trying to find property to show to clients, you should be listing. That is not to be interpreted conversely to mean if you're inspecting property to show to clients you can neglect your listing activity.

Listing is the one function that stands head and shoulders above all others in this business as a source of income. Never let up on your listing efforts. Always bring in new listings. And plan your listing time on a scheduled basis.

For example, plan to spend three hours each morning listing. From nine to ten you might telephone For-Sale-By-Owner ads in the newspaper to obtain the addresses of the properties for sale. (See *Real Estate Listing Magic* by Gael Himmah.) From ten to eleven you should drive to each of the addresses you have obtained the day before and ask the ten listing questions detailed in my listing book. From eleven until noon you should conduct a door-to-door canvass of a neighborhood where listings are at a premium.

The same type of scheduling must be applied to the inspection of new properties that come for sale in your marketing area. Perhaps the early afternoon is a good time to inspect listings. I prefer the morning for this as the new Mart listings are distributed in the morning and I don't want to delay checking them out personally.

The number of new listings published through my Real Estate Board's multiple listing service is so great that it would be physically impossible to inspect all the properties that are offered for sale. The geographical area serviced by my Board is tremendous, making it almost impossible to know all the proprety in the entire area. Hence, it is mandatory that you stake out for yourself a price range of properties and a geographical area of properties wherein you will devote your primary efforts.

It is far better to be an expert in one area or price range or type of property, and be recognized as such, than to be the proverbial "Jack-of-all-trades and master of none." The expert earns as an expert. The Jack-of-all-trades earns only mediocrity of performance, professionalism, and pay. Don't let that happen to you.

It is a good idea to have a bulletin board or blackboard in the office where information on good, new listings can be shared. Set aside time during regularly scheduled sales meetings to describe sought-after properties. Encourage suggestions about properties that might meet your requirements.

Learn what merchandise you have to put on the shelf. Learn what you have to offer for sale. Learn your stock. Inspect your listings—in person!

YOUR   You are in a wonderfully unique position as
FREE   concerns inventory. In all other industries the
INVENTORY   businessman has to spend his own hard earned
                  money in order to purchase an inventory which he can then offer for sale. If it doesn't sell, he's stuck with it. He can readily lose a great deal of money this way.

In the real estate business you don't have to put a dime "up front" for inventory acquisition. You can keep your money in the bank and use it to buy good investment properties as they present themselves. You can have all the inventory you need just for the asking.

Anyone who belongs to the multiple listing service in my Board area has, at any one time, over 3,000 properties to show clients, to sell, and to collect commissions on. He doesn't have to put up a dime. The gross dollar value of such an inventory would be fantastic. And it's there, waiting to be moved off the shelves.

CLIENTS   When a client walks into your office unan-
WANT A   nounced, a "walk-in," and you are the floor man,
CHOICE   the end result of your "client qualifying" process
                will be focused on your knowledge of the market.
It is unusual that a client answering a newspaper advertisement
will buy the house that motivated him to call. Clients buy homes
as the result of an emotional reaction to the physical inspection
of a property.

The English language is so complex that the precise interpretation of 50 words of advertising copy will differ with every
reader. A room which is large to one reader will be considered
a small room by another. A lot which seems small to one man
might look like a football field to another. The interpretation
of the meaning of adjectives is predicated upon the sum total
of the reader's past experiences.

The purpose of a newspaper advertisement is to cause a
prospective buyer to phone in or, preferably, walk into your
office. Once he's in the office, it is the responsibility of the salesman to "qualify" the buyer, to find out what he wants to buy
and what he is financially able to buy.

My own experience as a salesman has shown me that the
walk-in client is seldom interested in the property that caused
him to respond. Either he needs more bedrooms, or the location
isn't right, or the yard is too big, or the financing too difficult. I
usually spend my time showing him properties that were not
advertised at all.

To do this you have to know the market. To know the market
you have to inspect it.

GO ALONE   When you leave the office to inspect some new
                listings (let's say you have selected six homes),
it is preferable that you go alone. You should devote your full
attention to where you are going and what you are seeing. If
you're in a group, soon you're chatting away about everything
but real estate. Your mind is not on your work.

If you drive yourself to each home, you will learn how to get
there! When someone else drives you, your mind isn't alert to
the problems of direction. All of us have experienced the odd

sensation of being driven to some unfamiliar location and then, when we later tried to retrace our journey, we found we couldn't do it. Many salesmen get lost trying to drive clients to a property, or they make a wrong turn and fumble around getting to the home. This makes a very poor impression on clients.

Suppose you were able to watch a surgeon remove your appendix while you were under a local anesthetic. If he missed the appendix and probed around until he located the pancreas, said, "Oops, that's not it," and retraced his steps, corrected his aim and finally found the appendix, you would probably faint from fright. The analogy is clear. By driving yourself, you're forced to learn your way around the anatomy of your city's street system.

When I began in real estate I did most things wrong. I used to look forward to the days we inspected property. They were fun days. We would get five or six people in half a dozen cars and drive all over town looking at the new listings. We had some natural born comedians in the office and as luck would have it one would ride in each car telling jokes as we drove. We laughed and looked at homes and laughed some more. It was thoroughly enjoyable, but after a few months I realized I knew a lot of jokes but I didn't know my merchandise as well as I should. I immediately began inspecting property by myself. My knowledge increased along with my confidence. The sales followed close behind.

Real estate is a business for loners, just as a professional doing his job well does his job alone. Only those who work alone make real money in real estate. Go alone on your inspection tours. You'll benefit from it in many ways.

FIND THE EMOTIONAL APPEAL   Once at the home, before you ring the doorbell, look about, try to get the feeling of the home, the emotional feeling. Remember, you're going to be selling emotion to your clients.

A large sycamore in the front yard, or a well landscaped block of houses, or a rose covered split-rail fence, or a unique architectural style, any or all of these things might catch your eye before you step inside the house.

I have a little trick I play on myself whenever I inspect a

property. I have written ads describing real estate every week for more years than I care to count. I am keenly aware of the difficult task of writing newspaper copy with emotional appeal and am therefore constantly on the lookout for items of emotional impact, no matter how small.

Whenever you inspect a property, as you step out of your car and get ready to make your tour, pretend you are going to have to write a newspaper ad on the property after you get back to the office. Be alert for anything unusual about the home. Every home has bedrooms and a bath or two and a yard. Those features are of clinical interest to a client but they don't make sales.

Look for a Dutch door, or a wooden mantel over a raised hearth fireplace, or a wallpapered kitchen ceiling, or a sunken bathtub, or a private, enclosed sun patio off the master bedroom.

By going alone on my inspection tours of property, I have an opportunity to take a little longer in each home. After I have inspected a house, I enter into a conversation with the housewife. I explain that emotion is the dominant motivating factor in home sales. "People buy homes because of their emotional reaction to them," I say, "and I wouldn't be so presumptuous to walk into your home as a real estate agent and in a few moments expect to assess all the emotional qualities of your home. It would be impossible." I explain that no one would know more about the emotional qualities of her home than she herself. After all, she has lived there for years. She has raised her family there. "Mrs. Housewife," I ask, "what do you like best about your home? What features mean the most to you?"

I receive the most provocative answers. I hear features of homes I would never have imagined. Emotional features—to be sure. That's what I'm looking for. They're the most important because they're the ones that sell houses!

Later on, when I am showing these homes, my sole sales talk consists of pointing out to my buying clients the emotional features of each home *according to the homeowners*—NOT according to myself.

Using this sales technique, I have had clients tell me I am the most innovative salesman they have ever met. They tell me they have worked with many different salesmen, but once a salesman shows them a few houses, each falls into a pattern. Each has his own techniques and procedures from which he never varies. But I am, in their opinion, a thoroughly original salesman. The irony is that I merely repeat to my clients the emotional characteristics of each home as the different home-owners described them to me. I benefit from the accumulated subjective thinking of hundreds of homeowners about their own homes. And I end up with the most powerful selling tool a real estate salesman ever stumbled upon—a knowledge of the emotional features of homes according to homeowners.

It is foolhardy to rely upon your own powers of observation when you inspect property. You simply cannot "read" a house in depth during a five minute inspection. Let the homeowners do this job for you. They've had years to think about it.

Many times I have inspected property during rainstorms when the homes showed poorly. It would be impossible for me to recognize many important emotional features of these homes which would be apparent only on bright, sunny days. By asking the homeowners what they like best about their homes, I overcome this problem and come up with many unexpected sales gems. You will often be surprised at the features homeowners point out to you, but don't take them lightly. I have sold homes for reasons I never dreamed would interest my clients.

Once, after an inspection of a home, I began talking with the housewife. I mentioned how important emotional features were to me in selling and asked her what she liked best about her home.

"Come into the kitchen," she said to me. "I want to show you something."

I followed her into the kitchen where she pointed to a break-fast nook which I had passed without a second thought a few minutes earlier.

"You're going to think I'm crazy," she began, "but this is one of the nicest things about our home."

I looked at the breakfast nook, but still had no idea what she was referring to. It looked like a thousand other breakfast nooks to me. Outside, it was raining. A totally gloomy day.

"See that bay window?" she asked. I nodded. "In the springtime, and in the summer, the sun shines right through that window in the morning and shines on the breakfast table. My husband says it actually lights his glass of orange juice. He loves to sit with his back to the window when he's having his breakfast, the sun warming his spine, his orange juice lit up by the sunlight. It's a wonderful way to start the day." She looked at me with a little grin. "When we're off on a vacation and think about our home, that's the first thing he always says when he's getting ready to come home. 'Let's get some sunshine in my orange juice.'"

She asked me if I thought she was silly and I assured her I did not. I dutifully wrote on the back of my listing card, "SUNSHINE ON ORANGE JUICE". I knew I had a powerful sales point when I showed that house.

I actually did sell that house because of the orange juice story, a story I would never have imagined if I had not taken the time to talk with the housewife and ask her to describe the emotional qualities of her home.

I know the orange juice story sold the house for I make it a practice, after I have sold a property, to go back to my clients within a month of the close of escrow. I explain that I have a clinical interest in what motivates people to buy homes and then ask if there was any one thing which triggered their interest in owning the house they had purchased from me. In this case, they told me the sunlight on the orange juice had kindled such cozy feelings that the other properties they were looking at had paled in comparison. That is a classic example of the power of emotion in selling.

I remember another case very well. A listing came out on multiple listing on a house which was located in an unpopular part of town. I knew all the houses in that area were run down and unattractive but it was the only property in that price range so I decided to inspect it and add it to my inventory on the chance that I might get a client for just that kind of property.

I inspected the house and found it was just as I feared it would be. It was a disaster. I nearly walked out the front door after a brief "walk through" but something reminded me of my policy of chatting with the housewife after an inspection.

I found her and explained the important role emotional features would play in the sale of her home. I told her I wouldn't presume to be able to identify all the features of her property on such a short inspection and asked her what she liked best about it. I expected her to say, "The thought of moving!" But she fooled me.

"Come into the kitchen," she said and led the way back into her cluttered kitchen. "See through the window?" she asked and gestured for me to look.

I leaned over the sink, looked out, and saw only the side of their garage across a small back yard. "That's some garage," I said. I didn't know what else to say and I certainly didn't know what she had in mind. Again, it was a wintry day. A blustery wind swooped in from the ocean and howled around the house.

"Not the garage," she said, "the planting bed in front of it."

I looked more closely and saw weeds two feet tall growing along the side of the garage. "Nice," I said out of courtesy. I was more mystified than ever.

And then she told me. "In the springtime I plant sweet peas in that bed. There's something in the soil, and the temperature against the side of the garage, we're not sure what causes it, but the sweet peas grow all over the side of the garage and onto the roof and they're the biggest sweet peas anyone has ever seen. People come from all over to look at our sweet peas."

And there I had it. Another valuable emotional feature I would never have known if I hadn't asked. I wrote "SWEET PEAS" on the back of my listing card and knew I had something to say if I ever had a client for that house.

And again my "emotional features" explorations paid off. I sold that house to a couple several weeks later. The husband was a grouchy sort which made my job even more difficult, but I made the sale. Later, when I stopped by to discuss their new home with them and ask my "What motivated you to buy" question, I wasn't prepared for the answer.

"Do you know what you've done to me?" he asked, his voice seething with menace.

"I just wondered how you like your new home?" I countered.

He wasn't having any. "Do you know what you've done to me?" he repeated.

"Not really," I said. It was a totally honest statement. I didn't have the slightest idea what he was talking about. Buyers can get strange.

"You and you're damn sweet peas," he exploded. "That's all my wife could talk about after you showed us this house. Those damn sweet peas. When she was a little girl in New Jersey, she and her mother used to plant sweet peas and Iceland poppies every year. They took care of them together. She hasn't seen sweet peas since we moved to California ten years ago.

"This spring," he went on, fire in his eyes, "I'm going to have to send an airline ticket to my mother-in-law in New Jersey and she's flying out here and she and my wife are going to plant those damn sweet peas and she's going to stay all summer with us to watch them grow." By this time he was breathless, the thought of his mother-in-law's prolonged visit working him into a rage.

I smiled feebly, waved at his wife through the window and beat a hasty retreat to my car, fortified in my confidence of the power of selling emotion.

When you get back to your car, immediately, before you touch the starter, jot down some distinguishing features about the house.

"Carved front door, two fireplaces, sunken family room with double handled sword on wall, looked like Prince Valiant lived there."

Make notations to yourself that will set this home apart from the others so it will jump back into sharp focus when you bring it out of your mental storehouse.

As an example of the power of emotion in selling, study the following newspaper advertisement which we ran some time ago. We sold scores of homes from this ad. When it first appeared in the Sunday paper, buyers jammed into our office like sardines, all wanting to see this property.

The ad is obviously packed with emotional punch. Buyers react immediately to a well written ad which has emotional impact. This ad demonstrates your advertising doesn't have to be misleading. We were absolutely honest in this ad. The home was literally a dump. So we titled our ad, EL DUMPO. Incidentally, the sellers were so tickled by the ad they made a little

EL DUMPO sign and hung it on the hedge next to their home. They knew their home would have given Mr. Clean a coronary!

When people came to our office and demanded to be shown EL DUMPO, we told them they wouldn't like the property as it was in a terrible state of disrepair. But they would prevail and when we showed it to them, they agreed they wouldn't be interested. We would then sell them another house.

The newspaper ad did its job. It produced buyers for us. It made our firm interesting to them. They stopped by our office to see what this ad was all about. EMOTION had made them react!

EL DUMPO

It's low down and dirty. Looks like the home where the buffalo roamed! A handyman's paradise. Paint 'n profit. A long, winding country lane, shaded beneath an umbrella of giant trees leads to this rustic hideaway. Big wooden rancher with family room PLUS a separate 5 room guest cottage. The setting is magnificient. Huge lot completely secluded. Trees too numerous to count. Soap and water needed desperately. Shovel 'em out, paint 'em up, and you've got yourself an estate. Priced dirt cheap—which seems only right! Just $26,950 in a $50,000 neighborhood.

We described the property accurately in the advertising copy. It was secluded, it had two run down houses, and it needed cleaning and repair badly. And we were careful to point out to all our buyers that there wasn't a factory in the neighborhood worth less than $50,000! (See REAL ESTATE LISTING MAGIC for a complete discussion of how to advertise your listings.)

POINTS TO KEEP IN MIND

1. *You must inspect property personally before you add it to your inventory.*
2. *Learn as much as you can about each property.*
3. *Schedule the time you will devote to inspecting new listings.*
4. *Build up as large an inventory as possible. Your clients want to choose from a numer of properties.*
5. *Specialize in a geographical area and price range.*

6. *Inspect property by yourself.*
7. *Find the emotional features of each house according to the homeowners.*
8. *Write these emotional features on the back of the listing cards. They will become your "sales talk" for each house.*

FINANCING

4

Financing home purchases is one of the major obstacles to success in real estate sales. It's a mysterious, misunderstood, constantly changing subject. It frustrates and confounds. Financing information is usually skirted by brokers, thus leaving the salesman to his own devices and the sporadic process of assimilation over an extended period of time.

This is a sorry kettle of fish. Financing knowledge is one of the unavoidable essentials in real estate sales. After a house in the desired location and price range has been found, and after all other hurdles have been cleared, the sale will depend upon terms of financing.

"How much down and how much a month?" are classic questions in this business of real estate. If the salesman is skilled in financing and if he is well acquainted with the mortgage money currently available, he can tailor a method of financing the purchase which will meet the buyer's needs. The sale will be completed and the salesman will earn a commission.

Financing is really not very complicated. There are two major types of mortgage loans available to finance home purchases; government insured loans and conventional loans. Some states have their own financing plans. If your state has such a program, check into it. Government insured and conventional loans comprise over 90 per cent of our business, the state programs being used much less frequently.

35

STATE   It would be well to discuss a typical state pro-
LOANS   gram now, so that we can move on to the other
               more important areas of financing.

In California, Cal Vet loans are made by the California Department of Veterans' Affairs directly to eligible war veterans
who were bona fide residents of California at the time they
entered military service.

Briefly, the maximum loan amount is $25,000 for a term of
approximately 23 years, with interest that can escalate from
2½ to 5 per cent. The exact interest rate varies, depending
upon the current rate the state must pay for bonds it sells to
finance the program. At this writing, the interest rate on a Cal
Vet loan is 4¼ per cent. The state actually purchases the home
for the Cal Vet buyer, holds title in the name of the state, and
then sells it back to him on the installment plan.

The Cal Vet purchaser enters into a contract of sale with the
state. He makes his monthly payments to the state, but he does
not take title to the property until the entire loan balance is paid
off. Then the state deeds the property over to the Cal Vet purchaser.

This is an excellent program because of the unusually low
interest rate charged the purchaser, but its benefits decrease
rapidly as the purchase price of the property increases. Since
the maximum loan is $25,000, the difference between the sales
price of the home and the $25,000 loan must be paid in cash.
If a Cal Vet buyer wants to purchase a $38,000 home, he could
get a $25,000 loan and would have to have an additional $13,000
in cash for his down payment. This is the primary reason why
more eligible persons do not use their Cal Vet privilege.

GOVERNMENT   There are two kinds of government insured
INSURED   loans; FHA (Federal Housing Administration),
LOANS   and G.I. (Veteran's Administration).

               I am not going to discuss the statutory re-
quirements for eligibility to receive a government insured loan.
Suffice it to know that your buyers will usually know if they are
eligible for a G.I. loan. They have to have had a certain period
of active military service within specified time periods. There
are no statutory requirements for eligibility for an FHA loan.

For both the G.I. and FHA loan programs, the buyer must be able to make the monthly payments and the property must be appraised for value by a government appraiser.

A family which can afford only a small down payment and can make only small monthly payments will probably need a government insured loan. On G.I. and FHA loans the period of loan repayment is very long, up to 30 years, which reduces the size of the monthly payment. On conventional loans the down payment required is greater and the period of loan repayment shorter.

A home buyer can get a G.I. loan for the entire amount of the purchase. This is the famous "No Down Payment" loan. For example, if the purchase price of a house is $25,000, the veteran purchaser could apply for a $25,000 G.I. loan for a term of 30 years. The current interest rate on a G.I. loan is 9½ per cent. Of course, the buyer and property would have to qualify for the loan; i.e., the home would have to be worth $25,000 in the professional opinion of the G.I. appraiser who will physically inspect the property. The buyer must give documentary evidence that he is financially capable of paying off a $25,000 loan. The appraisal and the formal buyer qualification documents will be handled by the mortgage lender to whom we assign the loan after we make the sale.

Every real estate salesman should bear in mind that he is just that, a REAL ESTATE SALESMAN. He is not a lawyer. He shouldn't give legal advice. He isn't an accountant. He shouldn't give tax advice. And he isn't a money lender. He should leave that to the professional institutional lenders and loan correspondents. Surely a real estate salesman must have a certain knowledge of law, accounting and financing as it applies to the sale of real estate, but he must use his limited knowledge judiciously, reserving the details for the qualified specialists.

As a real estate salesman you must know the status of mortgage funds available so you can advise your buyers, but once the sale is made, you should immediately turn the details of the financing over to the lender of your choice and he will take it from there.

THE GI   Back to the G.I. buyer. He doesn't have to
BUYER   purchase on a no-down-payment basis. He can
                   put as much cash down as he wishes. The more
money he uses as a cash down payment, the smaller the amount
of his mortgage loan. This will reduce his monthly payments. As
a rule of thumb, monthly payments for principal and interest
will be reduced approximately $7.72 for each $1,000 that the
loan is reduced. If a buyer wants to lower his monthly payments
$15.00 per month after you have computed them for him, he
would have to increase his down payment by approximately
$2,000 which would reduce the balance of his mortgage loan
by a corresponding $2,000. Of course his equity increases pro-
portionately as his down payment increases.

There is not statutory limit to the amount of a G.I. loan for
home purchase, but currently the maximum loan available is
$62,500. I have seen a few $70,000 G.I. loans. The money for
both G.I. and FHA loans is advanced by private lending institutions such as banks. Their lending policies change continually
with the fluctuating money market.

THE FHA   If a buyer is not eligible for a G.I. loan but has
BUYER   limited funds available for a down payment, he
                   should consider purchasing on an FHA basis. A
down payment is required on all FHA loans (other than one
type of Section 221.d2 loan) but the down payment is much
less than that required for a conventional loan. The maximum
FHA term is 30 years and the current interest rate is 9½ per
cent plus ½ per cent for mortgage insurance.

Following is a schedule of down payments required for FHA
home purchase loans:

> 3 per cent of the first $25,000 of appraised value.
> 10 per cent of the next $10,000 of appraised value.
> 20 per cent of the balance of appraised value.
> The maximum FHA single family home loan is $45,000.

To express this another way, the FHA home purchaser is able
to secure an FHA loan in the amount computed as follows:

> 97 per cent of the first $25,000 of appraised value.
> 90 per cent of the next $10,000 of appraised value.

80 per cent of the balance of appraised value to a maximum
loan of $45,000.

If the home to be purchased appraised for $20,000, the FHA
buyer could secure an FHA loan of $19,000 with a minimum
required down payment of $1,000. (FHA loans are computed
to the nearest $100.)

The buyer can request a 30-year term on his FHA loan. If
the home is quite old, the FHA appraiser will probably recommend a shorter term loan. If the home is in need of improvements of a serious nature (peeling paint, and so forth), they
may be required before the loan will be approved.

One of my salesmen recently sold a home on an FHA basis.
When the appraisal returned from the regional FHA office there
was a notation that the west exterior wall of the garage had to
be repainted (the paint was peeling off this wall in ringlets)
and the door between the house and the garage had to be fire-
proofed with sheet metal.

CONVENTIONAL   Conventional loans are so named because
LOANS   they are made available by the "conventional"
                    money lenders, such as banks, savings and
loan associations, and insurance companies. They all have different statutory limitations regarding the maximum terms of their
respective mortgage loans and their loan-to-appraised-value
ratios.

Figure 4-1 is a sample schedule of typical conventional loans
available.

Keep a similar schedule in your sales kit and amend it faithfully as changes occur.

As you can see from this schedule, the minimum down payment required for a conventional loan, without a second mortgage, is 5 per cent of the appraised value of the home. The
interest rate usually increases as the term of the loan increases.
Banks and insurance companies require a larger down payment
than savings and loan associations but their interest rates and
loan fees are lower.

Savings and loan associations permit buyers to purchase a
home with only a 10 per cent down payment and a 10%
"second." In this instance, the seller of the home would carry

	DOWN PAYMENT	1ST LOAN	2ND LOAN	INTEREST RATE	TERM (YEARS)	MORTGAGE LOAN FEE
SAVINGS & LOAN	20%	80%		9½%	30	1% + $50
SAVINGS & LOAN	20%	80%		9¼%	25	1% + $50
SAVINGS & LOAN	10%	80%	10%	9¾%	30	1½% + $50
SAVINGS & LOAN	10%	90%		10%	30	2% + $50
SAVINGS & LOAN	5%	95%		10½%	30	3% + $50
INSURANCE COMPANY	25%	75%		9¼%	30	1%
BANK	10%	90%		10%	30	2% + $50

Figure 4-1
Conventional Loans Available

back a note secured by a second deed of trust on his home in the amount of 10 per cent of the sales price. The terms of the second would be a matter of negotiation between buyer and seller. The most common seconds are written at 7 per cent to 10 per cent interest, paying off at 1 per cent of the face amount per month with a due date of three to five years.

For example—a buyer wants to purchase a $30,000 home on a conventional basis. He doesn't have the 20 per cent cash down payment, $6,000, to qualify for a "normal" savings and loan association loan. But he does have $3,000 plus normal closing costs. (Closing costs are detailed in the Reference Book. (See Exhibit B-41, p. 216.) You could write the terms of the deposit receipt as follows:

1. Buyer to make a cash down payment of $3,000.
2. Buyer and property to qualify for a new conventional loan in the amount of $24,000 with interest not to exceed 9¾ per cent for a term of 30 years.
3. Buyer to give and seller to take back a note secured by a second deed of trust in the amount of $3,000 with monthly payments of $30.00 or more, including 10 per cent interest, all due and payable three years from date of making.

ADVANTAGES OF CONVENTIONAL LOANS   Aside from the more obvious differences of down payment, term, and interest rates between Government insured and conventional loans, there are more subtle differences between these two types of loans.

Because lenders must accept lower interest rates on the G.I. and FHA loans they make, they charge a loan premium fee to the seller at the time the loan is made. This fee is known in the trade as "points." (See "The Story of Points" in *Real Estate Listing Magic* by Gael Himmah.) Federal law specifies that only a seller may pay points. As the interest rate on conventional loans increases and the percentage spread between conventional and government insured interest rates grows greater, the institutional lenders will increase the number of points the sellers must pay.

The government insured money market, at the time of this writing, is three to four points, depending upon the credit stability of the buyer and the size of his down payment. For example, if a buyer wishes to purchase a $20,000 home on a no-down-payment G.I. loan basis, the seller would have to be willing to pay four points if he were to accept the buyer's offer. A point is 1 per cent of the loan requested. One point on this $20,000 loan would be $200. Four points would amount to $800. Many sellers are not willing to write off that much money so a buyer may secure a government insured loan. If the seller refuses to pay these points, the buyer's only alternative is to seek conventional financing.

Another disadvantage of government insured financing is the extended period of time required to process a loan application and close a sale. The average conventional loan can be closed within ten days of the date of sale. The average G.I. or FHA loan will not close for 45 to 60 days. Often they require 80 to 90 days. Cal Vet loans are often processing four months after the sale was made.

When you speak to a buyer about real estate financing, you must not only determine the amount of money he has for a down payment and his ability to repay a mortgage loan, but you must determine how urgent is his need for the sale to close.

So here you have an outline of real estate financing of home purchases. It isn't complicated. It should no longer be a mystery. Don't be intimidated by it. Every lender in town is anxious to help you with your questions. They will help you in any way they can. They dont' make money if they don't make loans, so rely upon them to support your efforts. Get to know several lenders' representatives. They will keep you posted on current changes in the money market.

POINTS TO KEEP IN MIND

1. There are two major types of mortgage loans; Government insured loans and conventional loans.
2. Some states have their own special financing plans.
3. The maximum Cal Vet loan is $25,000.
4. GI loans require no down payment.
5. FHA loans require a small down payment.
6. Government insured loans usually have a longer term than con-

ventional loans, hence, their monthly amortized payments are lower.

7. Conventional loans require larger down payments than Government insured loans.

8. An escrow will "close" more rapidly if the purchase is financed through conventional lenders.

INTRODUCTION TO
THE BUYER

5

Let's make real estate selling simple. Just as you must know your merchandise, so you must also know your buyers. There are two basic methods of gaining introductions to prospective buyers; by telephone contact or direct, personal meeting in your office.

These two crucial sales conditions you must master: 1) handling the telephone inquiry, and 2) the first in-person meeting with the client. If these two challenges are properly met, all other procedures in selling will develop easily and naturally.

Before probing the mechanics of selling, we should consider the physical arrangement of a well-organized general brokerage real estate office.

There should be a floor man who sits at a neat, well-located desk. Answering client telephone and walk-in inquiries is his primary responsibility. There should be at least one private conference room (the term "closing room" is not professional) furnished with a desk and three or four chairs. A supply of forms necessary for listing and/or selling a home should be maintained in the conference room.

KEEP YOUR   A real estate office does not have to be pre-
OFFICE NEAT   tentious in its physical appearance but it is
                   mandatory that it be neat. The floors, if they
are wood or tile, should be cleaned, waxed and polished. Carpet-
ing should be vacuumed clean and free of stains and worn areas.
The windows should be crystal clean, free of decals and stickers.
Walls, ceilings and light fixtures should be sparkling clean.
Desks must be neat and free from litter.

You expect clients to contract for the purchase of an expensive commodity—property. Surely these clients are entitled to
do business in a neat, clean, attractive, professional environment. You deserve the same pleasant working environment.

Soap and water, paint, and a broom can transform a dingy
office into a bright, cheerful, professional place of business.
Hang a few paintings on the wall. Repaint the sign on your
building. Fix up your office as you'd fix up a run-down house
for resale.

A spruced-up office improves performance. That's a fact!

FIND THE   You sell homes to people who want to own
MOTIVE   their own home. The reason an individual de-
                   sires to own a home is most important. Learn
the individual's motive for buying a home and you will discover
how to sell it to him. The best way to find what motivates a
buyer is simply to ask him.

"Why are you in the market for a home?"

His answer will give you a valuable clue to your sales tack.
It will point you in the right direction.

A home buyer's methods of finding a home are limited. These
also are of great importance to the real estate salesman. An individual wishing to purchase a home might begin following real
estate ads in newspapers. He does this to develop a feeling for
relative prices in various areas.

He next might spend a few hours driving through different
sections of the city to discover some neighborhoods he finds
attractive. He can then take his chances with the for-sale-by-
owners or select a Realtor to assist him. The prudent home
purchaser who understands the investment nature of home
ownership and recognizes the risks involved in dealing directly

with a home owner dismisses the for-sale-by-owners as necessary evils within the industry. He begins his search for a Realtor.

There are two primary tacks the home seeker can follow: a Realtor's FOR SALE sign in front of an appealing property, or a Realtor's advertisements in the newspaper.

At this juncture, you must be made aware of a real estate paradox.

When a prospective home purchaser inquires at a real estate office about a property brought to his attention by a FOR SALE sign on the premises, that buyer wants the property to be the one he has been looking for. He wants to hear a favorable description of the property from the salesman. He doesn't necessarily expect a favorable report, but he's hoping.

However, when a home buyer calls a real estate office in response to a newspaper advertisement, he wants to strike that property off his list of homes he must inspect in person. Many ads looked inviting to him. He doesn't have time to see them all. He has to eliminate some. He actually wants to hear an unfavorable description of the property. If you make one unfavorable comment about such a property to a telephone call-in client, he will hang up and you will be out a prospective buyer.

FOUR BASIC   Be prepared to handle four basic client in-
SITUATIONS   quiry situations; a walk-in on a FOR SALE sign, a walk-in on a newspaper advertisement, a telephone inquiry on a FOR SALE sign, and a telephone inquiry on a newspaper advertisement.

A walk-in is defined as a prospective client who physically walks into the office seeking your assistance.

WALK-IN   When a prospective purchaser walks into the
ON SIGN   office and announces he has seen one of your signs in front of an attractive property, you must be prepared to take charge immediately. The customer intends to give you only a moment of his time, just long enough to learn the price and vital statistics of the home he has seen. One wrong answer and the customer will be out the door like a shot. A good prospect will be lost forever.

Homes are purchased because of an emotional reaction to

the property. Remember that. I repeat it time and again because it is of primary importance. If, in your client relationship, you can properly develop the emotional appeal of a home, the price and terms will be of secondary importance. Begin conditioning you new, walk-in client as soon as he enters the door.

Stand up promptly, walk across the office to meet him, and smile.

"Good morning," you welcome him. "May I help you?"

"I saw one of your signs on a house that looked pretty good to me."

"Where was that?" you ask.

"Over on Oak, by Cleveland Road."

You now have an opportunity to be a real salesman. Look directly into his eyes, smile warmly and advise him, "You picked a good one. Let's sit down in here (gesture to a private conference room) and I'll give you the details."

You've made him feel good, as though he made a wise decision. He's more than happy to follow you into the conference room.

"You picked a good one," are five words of pure magic!

It is of utmost importance that you have a private room or area in your office wherein you can interview clients. You must receive honest answers from a client if you expect to sell him a home. A client is hesitant to mention such personal items as outstanding debts, salary level, take-home pay, prior bankruptcies, divorces, and so forth, all vital information of financial qualification for a new loan, if other salesmen and clients can overhear his conversation.

Quickly usher a walk-in client into a private room and begin your interview. Dont' hesitate in this.

Don't stand in the middle of the office and discuss the property with a client. Get him into the conference room.

Dont' reply to a walk-in client, as soon as you have learned which property interests him, "Let's take a look at it." Don't be so anxious to get a client out of the office and into a home that you forget all about qualifying him. This is fatal!

I'll never forget a real estate salesman who had floor duty on a Sunday afternoon. The newspaper ads were especially effective that day. This salesman, by actual count, had twenty-three walk-in clients who responded to various ads and signs. In each case the salesman learned which ad or sign prompted the client to come to the office. As soon as he had the answer, he whisked them out the door to see that very property. He gave nary a thought to qualifying the buyer. Each client said he wanted to see a certain property and the salesman obliged.

When each client was shown the property, each would express a lack of interest. The salesman would dutifully return each client to his car and hurry back to the office to meet another. At the end of the day, the salesman announced to the astounded sales force that not one client was any good.

Needless to say, that salesman didn't last long in the real estate business. He didn't bother to qualify a single buyer. He didn't find out what the client wanted to buy. He didn't know the market. He didn't have a list of properties comparable to the advertised properties to show a client. In short, he was badly prepared to meet a client.

Interview your clients before you react to their requests.

Once in the conference room, bring out the Client Interview Sheet (see Exhibit B-2, page 170) and begin asking the questions shown on it. When you ask questions, you are in control of the conversation.

It is unlikely the walk-in client will buy the home that motivated him to come into the office, so don't expect it. If he happens to buy the house, all well and good. But you should "process" all walk-in clients the same way, regardless of what prompted the client to come to the office. He should be greeted warmly, reassured as to his wise choice of properties ("you picked a good one"), escorted into a private conference room, and then asked the questions on the Client Interview Sheet.

The client who comes to the office in response to a FOR SALE sign might comment that all he wants is information on the house he saw. He says he doesn't want to talk about anything else or any other houses.

You shouldn't falter. This is the normal, expected client approach. Proceed with your questions. Explain that you need some preliminary information to determine if the house would suit his needs.

If the price seems to be the issue and you feel you will lose him if you don't disclose the price, go ahead and give him the information. However, if you sense the listed price will disillusion the client, you might advise him you are uncertain about the price as the listing agent has mentioned a price adjustment. Listing agents should always be concerned with the prices of their unsold properties, so this statement is accurate. With the price issue out of the way, you can continue with the questions on the Client Interview Sheet.

WALK-IN   When a prospective buyer walks into the
ON AD   office in response to a newspaper advertisement,
                 you should conduct yourself in the same fashion
as a walk-in on a sign. Greet him with a firm handshake (women as well as men should shake hands with the new client), re- · assure him on his choice of properties ("you picked a good one"), escort him into a conference room, and begin asking the questions on the Client Interview Sheet.

If, when the client walks in with an ad in his hand, he says, "I want some information on this property," you should reply, "I'd be happy to give you all the details. Let's step into this conference room and I'll get my listing book."

Don't wait for the client to lead the way into the conference room. You lead the way. Walk to the door, hold it open and motion the client inside. Offer him a seat and take your chair behind the desk. Without further ado, take a Client Interview Sheet from the desk and begin asking the questions and filling in the answers.

Any questions the client might raise about the necessity of this should be countered as explained previously.

TELEPHONE   The telephone call-in on a FOR SALE sign is
CALL-IN   more difficult to handle. It requires a skillful
ON SIGN   salesman to turn the caller into a good buying
                 prospect. Your primary goal is to cause the
caller to come to the office to meet with you personally.

YOU CAN'T GET A CONTRACT SIGNED OVER THE TELEPHONE!

As is the case with the client who walks in on a sign, the

customer who calls in on a FOR SALE sign is looking for one or two answers (i.e., price, number of bedrooms, and so on) and can be lost instantly with an improper reply.

Get his name and telephone number. Ask him to come by the office so you can give him the details. Explain to him that our exclusive listing contract with the owner of the property forbids us to give out any information on the telephone. For all we know, it might be the owner himself calling, checking on us. With tact and a careful explanation, the caller will understand and, if he is a sincere buyer, make an appointment to meet you at the office.

Do not give information to a client over the telephone. It cannot possibly earn you a commission. As a professional, give information only in your office. If the caller refuses to come to the office and will not identify himself, let him hang up. He wasnt' a buyer anyway. You've saved yourself time and trouble.

Once the client comes into the office, conduct him into the conference room and proceed as with any walk-in client.

If a client calls in on a sign and wants to meet you at the property, go, and make the best of it.

TELEPHONE   In an active real estate office that advertises
CALL-IN   consistently, the majority of client inquiries will
ON AD   come from newspaper advertisements. These
                   sales calls should be handled in the same pre-
cise manner.

When you answer the telephone and a buyer is inquiring about one of your ads, ask these ten questions (see Exhibit B-1, page 169):

1. ARE YOU A BROKER?
2. ARE YOU CALLING LONG DISTANCE?
3. ARE YOU FAMILIAR WITH OUR AREA?
4. WAS IT THE (for example, seclusion) ASPECT OF THE AD THAT ATTRACTED YOUR ATTENTION?
5. HOW SOON DO YOU NEED A HOME?
6. DO YOU OWN YOUR OWN HOME NOW?
7. HAVE YOU HAD AN OPPORTUNITY TO LOOK AT ANY PROPERTY IN THIS AREA?

8. WOULD YOU LIKE AN UNUSUAL HOME?
9. WHAT PORTION OF YOUR SAVINGS WILL YOU USE AS A DOWN PAYMENT?
10. WOULD *(day and time)* BE CONVENIENT FOR YOU TO INSPECT THIS PROPERTY?

These questions can also be used very effectively in an initial interview with a walk-in client although you should eliminate questions 1 and 2.

POINTS TO KEEP IN MIND

1. Keep your office neat and clean.
2. Have a conference room in your office where you can interview clients privately.
3. Learn your client's motive for buying a home.
4. Homes are purchased as the result of an emotional reaction to the property.
5. Remember to reassure a walk-in client by using the phrase, "You picked a good one."
6. Qualify your client before you show him property.
7. Make a list of the 10 questions you should ask a telephone call-in client. Keep this list handy when you're the floor man in your office.

6

TELEPHONE TECHNIQUE

When a client sees an appealing ad in the paper and decides to call the real estate office for more information, he has several questions in mind. He has pre-planned his pattern of inquiry. He's wary of the unknown voice who will answer the telephone. That's you! Many times such a caller has conjured up an unflattering mental picture of the salesman. Keep this in mind when you answer the telephone and make every effort to project a warm, pleasing personality to the caller.

BE CHEERFUL   Many people blessed with naturally friendly personalities become awesome creatures of dull wit and curt conversations when they pick up a telephone. Be cheerful on the telephone. Let the caller know you're smiling while you're talking to him. Let him know you're pleased he called you.

The client who calls a real estate office on a newspaper ad seldom buys the property he calls on. Every reader will picture an advertised house differently.

A survey conducted among real estate offices demonstrated that it required over 200 sales calls into a real estate office before someone calling would buy the house advertised. We place ads in the newspaper to secure buying prospects, not to sell specific homes. The exception to this rule is the unique property for which an ádvertisement would necessarily produce a buyer because the ,unusual features can be accurately described in the copy of the ad.

When you are the floor man, consider the sales call as being a person who wants to buy a house, but not necessarily the property advertised. You have to get him into the office. That's your job.

An ad on a home specifying a down payment of $3,000, for example, is not intended to sell that particular home. It is intended to provide you with a house buying client who has $3,000, or perhaps $30,000, to spend.

Everyone is looking for a bargain. Many times I have taken sales calls on ads listing several thousand dollars down payment only to discover that the callers wouldn't think of living in such a modest home, had $15,000 or $20,000 for a down payment, and were merely calling on the ads out of curiosity.

The ad does its job in finding the client. Finding the specific house is your job.

DON'T GIVE Often a caller will ask the address or details
PROPERTY of an advertised property. "I see you've got an
ADDRESS ad in the paper for a secluded rancher," he begins, "how many bedrooms does it have?"

You must resist the impulse to blurt out the information. Successful salesmen don't answer questions over the telephone. The telephone is to be used only to cause the client to come into the office. Remember, people call on the telephone hoping the ad they're calling on is NOT a house they want to buy. They probably marked fifteen or twenty ads in the paper that looked interesting to them. They know they can't go to twenty different real estate offices so they make some telephone calls and ask their questions hoping to eliminate as many offices as they can.

When they call you, they're hoping to mark you off their list, so don't answer their questions. After all, how could you expect to know the answers they want to hear? Do they want a large yard or a small yard? You dont' know. How many bedrooms do they want? How can you know? If they ask how many bedrooms your advertised house has, how do you know the number of bedrooms they want? Perhaps they want a low maintenance yard. What does that mean to that particular caller? To some people a low maintenance yard means a small yard with some landscaping. To others it means a large yard covered with concrete.

Don't paint yourself into a corner by answering caller's questions. There are many different ways to handle such an inquiry. When someone asks, "What's this ad you have in the paper?" you can reply, "When we wrote that ad we had three different properties in mind. What interested you most about it?" In this manner you're getting the caller to reveal his desires in a house.

Another method of answering a caller's questions is to say, "Just a minute and I'll look at the listing card." Then put the telephone receiver down on your desk while you compose your thoughts. In a moment pick up the telephone and say, "I see we had several different properties in mind when we wrote this ad. What interested you most about it?"

Often callers insist on getting an address so they can drive by. Under no circumstances should you ever give out a property address over the telephone. If you do, one of two things will happen, neither of which will result in a sale for you.

If the caller drives by the property and doesn't like it, he will keep right on going and you certainly won't hear from him again. If he drives by and likes the property from the outside, he won't call you to see the inside. Instead, he'll call his brother-in-law or some friend (everyone has a friend with a real estate license) and get him to show it to him. If the likes the house, he'll buy it from him. In addition, I've sold many homes to people who didnt' like the outside appearance of the homes. But because I was with them, they had to accompany me on an interior inspection. Once inside the houses, they became very enthusiastic about the properties and bought them from me. Many homes have an uninspired front elevation yet are magnificent inside.

If you let telephone callers lead you around, and you give them property addresses, you are cutting yourself off from all of these sales. In one year I earned over eleven thousand dollars in commissions from the sale of properties to clients who didn't like them when they first saw them from the outside. That's a lot of money some salesmen are washing down the drain when they give out addresses over the telephone.

There are many methods of countering a demand that you give out an address. When you answer a telephone inquiry and the caller asks for the property address, you can say, "I'm sorry, we're not permitted to give out addresses." Sometimes that satisfies them.

"Come on," they often persist, "give me the address. I want to drive by."

In this case, where the caller is getting insistent, you can say, "Just a minute, let me find the listing card." Again, you put the telephone receiver down on your desk and rustle a few papers. The caller will be thinking to himself, "Here's another stupid real estate salesman, just like the other ones I've talked to this morning. They all gave me addresses and he's going to also."

But you're going to surprise him. When you come back on the phone, say, "I see on the listing card that when we took the listing the home owner specifically asked that we don't give the address out to anyone. We assured him we wouldn't. We even wrote it in our contract with him. We're certainly going to honor our contract with him. We'd do the same if we represented you. For all I know, you're the seller checking up on us." Often this suffices.

But this time the caller is adamant. "I'm not the seller," he insists. "Give me the address."

In this case, you have to be even more subtle. I've learned a sure fire technique to regain control of a telephone conversation when it seems to be getting away from me. I don't change the subject of the conversation. I merely begin to whisper. It works like magic. The caller becomes instantly attentive, abandons his abrasive tone, and begins to whisper himself!

"I'm not supposed to give out addresses," I whisper to my insistent caller.

"It's all right," he whispers back.

"There's a salesman sitting at the desk right behind me and I don't want him to hear me," I confide.

"It's alright," the caller whispers, now joining in a conspiratorial tone.

"You have to have an address?" I whisper into the telephone.

"Yeah," he whispers back. He thinks he has me going along with him.

"Have you got a piece of paper?"

"Yeah."

"Got a pencil?" I whisper.

"Yeah," comes the whisper back.

"You ready?"

"Yeah."

"Thirty six seventy eight Mount Diablo Boulevard," I whisper.

"Thanks a lot," he shouts triumphantly and slams down the receiver, satisfied he has outfoxed another real estate salesman.

What he doesn't know is that I gave him the address of my office. He insisted I give him an address, so I did!

Again, one of two things will happen. When he arrives at the address I gave him and he sees it's my office, if he roars off in his car in a fit of anger, I figure he wasn't a buyer anyway. Most often he will shake his head and come walking in with a grin on his face.

"You got me that time," he might say.

"Not at all," I reply. "The property is close to the office and I wanted an opportunity to point out some of its features before we inspected it. Then we can use my car. Burn my gasoline. Only thinking of you."

Again, be reminded—don't let your callers lead you. You must take the initiative. Your clients want it that way.

USING
THE 10
QUESTIONS
The most professional method of handling a telephone sales call is to use the 10 Sales Questions. When the telephone rings, pick it up before it rings a second time.

"Good morning, Granada Realty," you welcome the caller.

"I see an ad in the paper. Looks interesting."

"Which ad are you referring to?" you ask. "Is it in the *Tribune* or the *Times*?"

"*Tribune*," the voice replies. "Says it's an 'Old Farm.'"

"Oh, yes, I know the property," you answer. "Are you a broker?"

Think for a moment how this question upsets the caller's planned pattern of questions. This is an unusual question. He wasn't expecting it. If the caller is a broker seeking information, you can quickly comply and ready yourself for a sales call. As a courtesy, whenever a licensee calls a cooperating real estate office for information on their listings, he should immediately identify himself and his office and ask the cooperation of the listing office.

"This is John Bellon from Ajax Realty. I see your 'Old Farm' ad in the *Tribune*. Are you cooperating on this?"

In my office we cooperate on all listed properties with all members of Real Estate Boards.

Now let's assume the caller in question is a prospective home buyer. You have asked him if he is a broker and he has assured you he is not.

"I asked if you were a broker," you explain to the caller, "because that particular property is so appealing many real estate brokers have been calling for information on it."

Consider the effect of this first question if your caller was the proverbial "Little Old Lady." You ask her if she's a broker and she's stumped.

"Why no, young man," I've had them say to me, "Do I have to be? I just wanted to find out about the 'Old Farm' house you have in the paper."

Your explanation of the interest other brokers have in that particular property will serve to deepen the curiosity of the caller.

Question #1, *"Are you a broker?"* will get you off to a good start.

GET THE   Sometimes I ask a caller his name and tele-
NAME AND   phone number immediately, before I begin
PHONE NUMBER   asking the questions. Sometimes I wait until
                   the telephone interview is nearly over. I
can't give a positive time for securing this information during a
telephone conversation. You will have to sense it yourself.
Sometimes a caller is antagonized if you commence your conversation with a request for his name and phone number.

We use Question #1 to short circuit the plans of the caller. Question #2 serves two purposes.

"Are you calling long distance?" you ask.

This question further leads the caller from his planned approach. Also, if the customer is calling long distance, you can offer to get his number and call him right back so you will incur the telephone charges. He will like this. It is considerate. And it lets you get his telephone number.

"Are you familiar with our area?" you then ask. "Do you know where Wildwood Acres Number Two is located?"

Of course, no one knows the subdivision names of all the neighborhoods in an area.

"I'm not sure where that is," the caller replies.

"It's in the southwest part of Walnut Creek," you might answer.

Be vague in your description. Don't pinpoint the location of the property. The caller might not be interested in certain areas.

"Was it the seclusion aspect of the ad that interested you?"

Every ad should have several features of reader interest such as price, number of bedrooms, location, size of lot, seclusion, unusual terms, unique style, and so on. It is important to find out just what piqued the curiosity of this caller. You can use this information to great advantage in selecting properties to show him.

"How soon do you need a home?" establishes the urgency of the caller to purchase.

"Do you own your own home now?" tips us off to the "contingent buyer," the prospect who has to sell his current home before he can buy a new house. In such an instance, you should immediately consider the caller to be a good listing prospect. Offer to give the caller a free appraisal of his home. I don't mean a long, involved, detailed square footage appraisal. You should make an appointment to inspect the home when both husband and wife are at home (both signatures are required on a listing contract), and then proceed on your listing tack. (See *Real Estate Listing Magic* by Gael Himmah for a detailed discussion of this.)

"Have you had an opportunity to look at property in this area?"

The answer to this question tells us if the caller has been inspecting homes for a year or if he has just begun. The average home purchase is made after the buyer has been shown two and two-thirds homes. Of course there are exceptions, but if the caller has been looking at homes for months, the chances of you making the sale are slim. Spend your time with him accordingly.

"Would you like an unusual home?" is a question designed to give the caller an opportunity to rhapsodize, to dream about his future home. It instantly kindles the curiosity of the caller. Everyone would like to see a unique property. In this day and age, every home that is not in a subdivision is unusual. You won't have trouble finding homes to show him, but if you handle this question correctly, you will have trouble keeping him away from the office.

"What portion of your savings will you use as a down payment?"

Don't ask him, "How much money have you got for a down payment?" It lacks tact. The client will feel better if you suggest he has a savings account and the sum required for the down payment will only be a portion of that account. We know that most buyers will use every dime they have to purchase a home they like, but why make it obvious?

"Would three o'clock this afternoon be convenient for you to inspect this property?"

You name the time for the appointment. Don't wait for the client to suggest it.

Finally, after you have asked the ten questions, if you have not yet done so, secure the caller's name and telephone number.

"My name is Gael Himmah. May I have your name please? Your telephone number? Thank you so much for calling, Mr. Wilson. I'll see you this afternoon at three."

When Mr. Wilson enters the office, greet him warmly, escort him into a conference room and ask the questions on the Client Interview Sheet.

Question number seven, "Have you had an opportunity to look at property in this area?" is the most important of all the 10

Sales Questions. If only I had known this question when I started my real estate career, I would have saved myself many months of frustration and wasted effort.

Every salesman remembers his first client. Mine was a lovely lady named Mrs. Aguar. I had been in the business only a week or so when the broker came to me one morning and told me he was leaving for the rest of the day and I was in charge of the office. I experienced instant panic. I was totally unprepared to handle any business but I sat at my desk, alone, frightened, praying the telephone wouldn't ring.

Five minutes later it rang. Nervously I answered it. A very pleasant lady was on the phone. "I see you're advertising a house in the Sunset district," she said sweetly.

It was news to me, but I was happy to hear we were advertising. (That gives you an idea of how ill prepared I was.) "Why yes we are," I said, faking it as best I could.

"Could you tell me something about it?" she asked.

"Hold on just a minute," I said. I put the phone on my desk and searched frantically for the advertising book. Presently I found it, located the ad she was calling on, picked up the phone and read her the details of the house.

"I'd like to see it if I may," she said.

"Fine," I said in my most professional voice, hoping my tone wouldn't betray my ignorance of real estate matters. I was a stranger to San Francisco and still had trouble finding my way around. She asked me to pick her up at her home which was just around the corner from my office. We made an appointment for thirty minutes later.

I picked her up right on time and with her help found the advertised property. She raved about it as I showed her through. "Look at the huge living room," she gushed. "Oh, my, the bedrooms are gorgeous. And what a lovely yard." She practically swooned over the kitchen. Then she stumped me. "What's the financing on this house?" she asked brightly.

I didn't know anything about financing. I looked dumbly at the listing card which I was holding in my hand, couldn't decifer the strange notations in the financing section, and, as a last resort, shoved the card toward her. Mrs. Aguar took it from me, glanced at it, then told me what the financing was.

"The financing is terrific," she bubbled.

Sensing a sale, I moved in for the close. "Would you like to buy it?" I asked.

"No thank you," she said sweetly.

Oh well, I figured that's the way the real estate business was. On the drive back to her house I told her I now knew what type of property she was interested in and asked if she would like me to call her whenever I found something I thought she might be interested in. She said that would be wonderful and would be waiting to hear from me.

I thought I had myself a blue chip client. I didn't know that I had, on that drive back to her home, asked a question that most salesmen ask in similar situations when they have shown property to a client but didn't make a sale. I couldn't know at that early stage in my real estate career that the question was a complete waste of time, but then I had an excuse. I was brand new in the business. It's sad to realize that many real estate salesmen continue in this non professional, non productive vein throughout their real estate careers. You should never get yourself into the position where you have to ask such a valueless question.

If you become a skilled salesman as I will demonstrate in these pages, every time you take a client out of your office to inspect property you will end the day getting a purchase contract signed. Every time! It can be done. I'm going to show you how. But you have to abandon your old habit of taxiing clients around, showing property day after day to the same customers until they finally find a house they decide to buy, or one day they don't come back at all.

Mrs. Aguar was my first "buyer" and I was excited. I hurried back to the office, went to the files, and pulled every listing within five thousand dollars of the price home I had just showed her. There were nearly two hundred listings, but I didn't have anything else to do. My broker hadn't given me a hint of a training program and absolutely no guidance, so I elected to inspect all two hundred listings hoping to find a home Mrs. Aguar would want to buy.

In the next three weeks I burned out a set of brakes on my car driving up and down the hills of San Francisco inspecting property. Each time I found a house I thought Mrs. Aguar would like I called her and asked her to inspect it.

She was always happy to hear from me. Always she would find time to inspect my latest find. Always she gushed enthusiastically as she toured the houses. And always she concluded each inspection tour by saying she didn't want to buy the house. I began to wonder how anyone made a sale in this business.

It was about this time I attended my first real estate board multiple listing breakfast meeting. Those are meetings where everyone sits around and tells each other how well they're doing. I was talking to two salesmen I had just met. We were engaged in one of salesmen's favorite pastimes, exaggerating our successes.

"I've got a super client," the fellow sitting across the table from me said.

"I think my client is the best one I've ever had," the fellow sitting next to me said, all the while maintaining just the proper expression of boredom to evidence sophistication.

I wasn't about to be outdone. "Well I've got a client who makes yours look silly," I said shamelessly.

The fellow sitting across from me wasn't impressed. "My client is always ready to look at properties," he said between sips of coffee.

The one next to me said, "Financing isn't a problem with mine."

I countered with, "My client likes everything I show her."

The fellow next to me had about enough. "I don't care what you say, Mrs. Aguar is the best client I've ever had," he announced.

The fellow across the table coughed violently and sputtered, "Mrs. Aguar?" He was incredulous.

"Mrs. Aguar?" I cried.

At once, the three biggest braggars in the room sat looking dumbly at each other as awareness began to take hold.

If only I had known question number seven, "Have you had an opportunity to look at property in this area?" I would have asked Mrs. Aguar that question during our first telephone conversation. She would have answered, "Why yes, I have. I've been looking at property since nineteen thirty nine!"

It happened that Mrs. Aguar, unknown to the three of us for we were all new in the business, was what is known in the industry as a professional looker. Looking at houses was her hobby. She inspected real estate as some people watch television.

And Mrs. Aguar, because of her years of accumulated real estate knowledge, knew as much about single family real estate in the Sunset and Parkside districts of San Francisco as the most experienced broker. Salesmen used to call her when they got a new listing and ask her what she thought it would sell for. Sometimes they even stopped by her home and took her on a tour of property with them just so she wouldn't be alone all day.

Clients such as Mrs. Aguar are pleasant to be around but they won't make you a dime. Don't make the mistake of agreeing to invest your time showing property to clients until you first determine their urgency and motivation to buy.

RULES OF TELEPHONE COURTESY   In addition to knowing how to use the ten questions, you should be aware of these basic rules of telephone courtesy.

1. Speak directly into the mouthpiece in a normal tone of voice.
2. If you must leave the phone, explain that you have to step away, then set the phone down gently.
3. When you return to the phone, thank the caller for waiting.
4. Frequently address the caller by name.
5. If you tell someone you will call back, make sure you keep your promise as soon as possible.
6. Listen attentively without interrupting.
7. At the close of the conversation thank the person for calling.
8. Wait for the other person to hang up first.

POINTS TO KEEP IN MIND

1. *When you use the telephone, speak in a friendly, cheerful tone. Do your best to project a pleasing personality.*
2. *A call-in client seldom buys the home he called on.*
3. *Your primary job, upon answering a telephone "sales call" ad inquiry, is to get the client to come into the office.*
4. *Always get the caller's name and phone number.*

5. *Don't answer questions on the telephone.*
6. *Never give an address over the telephone.*
7. *Practice using the 10 telephone questions.*
8. *Observe the rules of telephone courtesy.*

7

QUALIFYING
THE BUYER

Qualifying a buyer consists of two functions, finding what the client wants, and what he can afford.

CLIENT   The Client Interview Sheet (see Exhibit B-2,
INTERVIEW   page 170) gives you this information. Its use is
SHEET   self-explanatory. Consider going to a doctor for
                  a physical examination. It is your first visit to
the doctor. Before he so much as takes your temperature he sits down at his desk, takes out a medical history form, and begins asking questions. It is precisely the same function you will perform upon your first meeting with a client.

Before you can find the house he wants, you have to diagnose his desires, his price limitations, his likes and dislikes. Everyone expects to answer questions when they visit a doctor. If you have a professional demeanor, your clients will consider the client interview questions as the normal function of an unusually efficient real estate salesman.

You may explain that you will have a much clearer picture of his housing desires, and both of you will be saved a good deal of time, if the client will bear with you for a few moments while you make a few notes.

Some of the questions on the Client Interview Sheet have a value not readily apparent. If I get an affirmative response to the question, "Have you seen anything you like?", I make a point to get the address of the house. Often such a client will tell me he found a house he liked several weeks earlier but it was sold before he could act on it. That's valuable information. If I don't sell him a house that day, later in the evening I'll drive by the house he liked and see first hand what type of property motivated him to want to buy. I've made many sales as a result of asking just such a question.

If you don't use a Client Interview Sheet, you can easily overlook the most important questions. One Sunday afternoon I was sitting in the back of one of my offices observing my salesmen. The floor man was a young man who had been in the business about six months.

I saw a shiny new Cadillac pull up and a handsome couple step out and walk into the office. My salesman rose to meet them at the door. The husband spoke in a booming voice.

"I want to see this house," he announced, pointing to a circled newspaper ad. It was an eighty thousand dollar listing. "I don't care about financing," he bellowed with a grand gesture of his manicured hand, "we're cash buyers."

Forgetting the myriad incantations of my managers to qualify walk-ins before showing them property, my salesman was out the door with them like a shot. He jumped into the gleaming Cadillac and the three of them disappeared around the corner.

Forty five minutes later my salesman burst into the office and ran down the aisle toward me leaving the front door open. He was grinning from ear to ear.

"You see those clients?" he called as he slid to a stop beside me. I nodded. "Best buyers I ever had." He wiped his forehead with his handkerchief. "They're going to buy the Wolferman house. All cash," he announced to the office. "They've gone to get their check book."

I'd heard that story so many times before. "What's their name?" I asked.

He looked at me strangely, but didn't speak.

"Where do they live?"

Again, that strange look, but no reply.

"What's their telephone number?" I asked.

He began to grin sheepishly.

"Do you know if they even have a bank account? Where does he work?"

"That was a brand new Cadillac," my salesman said feebly.

"Do they own it, or does the bank just let them drive it?" I asked.

"Well, they'll be back," he said defensively and lowered himself onto a chair.

Of course he never saw them again. They were two more house lookers who make a big show and waste salesmen's time but don't buy anything. The use of the Client Interview Sheet and a short pre-showing interview would have saved my salesman the disappointment he had to suffer. Top dollar producing salesmen show homes to less than half the people who walk into their offices with ads in their hands. This means over half the walk-ins you will meet aren't buyers at all. If you react to every walk-in by immediately showing him property without first qualifying him, you will be reducing your potential for income production over fifty percent. Using the Client Interview Sheet helps you identify the buyers to whom you can profitably devote your time and attention.

QUALIFY THE BUYER FINANCIALLY   Once you have asked the questions on the Client Interview Sheet, you can qualify the buyer financially. You want to determine the highest price he can pay for a home so you won't waste your time and his showing properties priced so high he couldn't possibly afford them.

Sometimes a client will announce that he wants to buy a $40,000 house. You accept his word at face value, and show him only $40,000 homes. After much time and effort have been devoted to the $40,000 home market, you discover the buyer cannot possibly qualify financially for a home priced higher than $25,000. If you permit this to happen, you have wasted a good deal of time. Qualify your clients carefully!

RULES   As a rule of thumb, a family can afford a home
OF   priced at two and a half (2½) times their
THUMB   annual income. Thus, a family with an annual
                  income of $10,000 can afford a home priced up
to $25,000 but they would be straining their resources to pur-
chase a home for $30,000.

Another rule of thumb says that a home buyer's *net* monthly
income (after tax deductions) should be at least four (4)
times greater than the monthly payments including principal,
interest, taxes and insurance.

AN EXAMPLE   "What portion of your savings will you use
OF QUALIFYING   as a down payment?" you asked on the
A BUYER   Client Interview Sheet conversation.
                     "Ten thousand dollars," the client an-
swered.

"Must this include the closing costs or do you have additional
resources for that?"

"How much are closing costs?" the client asked.

"About 3 per cent of the purchase price of a home if we use
conventional loan sources, about 4 per cent if we use FHA or
G.I. financing. If you buy a home for $30,000 and we finance it
through a savings and loan association, your closing costs will
be about $900 to $1,000. If you decide to buy on an FHA or
G.I. basis, closing costs will be about $1,200, but you will have
45 to 90 days to get this money together because it takes that
long for the escrow to close. Closing costs are payable at the
close of an escrow."

"I can pay the closing costs in addition to the $10,000," your
client replies. (A detailed breakdown of buyer's and seller's
closing costs is given in the Reference Book in Appendix B,
Exhibit B-41, page 216.)

You have determined "how much down." Next, find out
"how much a month."

On the Client Interview Sheet you see that the client advised
you he could spend $400 monthly.

"Does this include payments for taxes and insurance or only
principal and interest?" you ask.

You explain that the basic monthly financing charges for

home ownership are principal and interest on the loan and the sums required for the payment of taxes and insurance.

"How much are taxes?" the client asks.

Taxes vary according to the value of the home purchased. As a rule of thumb, in my marketing area on San Francisco Bay, a $30,000 home will have taxes of about $600; a $40,000 home will have taxes of about $800. This varies with geographical area. You should be prepared to answer this question for your marketing area.

The ratio of taxes-to-value can be reduced to a simple formula which can be modified for your specific area.

$$\text{Taxes} \times 50 = \textit{Valuation}$$
$$\$600 \times 50 = \$30,000$$
$$\$800 \times 50 = \$40,000$$

By using a variation of this formula, you can get a rough estimate of a home's taxes by first determining its value.

$$\text{Taxes} = \frac{\text{Valuation}}{50}$$

$$\text{Taxes} = \frac{\$40,000}{50} = \$800$$

Your client says he can spend $400 a month on his real estate investment. (Always refer to monthly payments on a home as a monthly investment in real estate.)

In order to qualify for a loan, there are certain payment-to-earnings ratios lenders require. Even though the client says he can spend $400 monthly, you must make certain his income will support this payment. The three basic qualifying ratios are for purchase of a home under FHA, G.I., or conventional financing. Here are the rules of thumb payment-to-earnings ratios for each:

FHA: Buyer's *gross* monthly income must be five times the monthly payment, including taxes and insurance.

G.I.: Buyer's *net* monthly income must be four and a half times the monthly payment, including taxes and insurance.

CONVENTIONAL: Buyer's *net* monthly income must be four times the monthly payment for principal and interest only.

Our Client Interview Sheet indicates the buyer's gross monthly income to be $1700 which would qualify him for payments of $400 under any of these types of financing, since he did not have any outstanding debts or installment payments to make.

This $400 will have to cover the monthly charges for principal, interest, taxes and insurance. Since you want to determine the maximum loan for which he can qualify, it will be best to consider these charges in inverse order.

INSURANCE: Your client can purchase all the fire insurance he needs for $10.00 monthly. This does not include an elaborate homeowner's policy. Fire insurance is all we must consider for loan qualifications.

TAXES: Considering a $10,000 down payment and $400 monthly payments, experience tells us that the home this client can purchase is in the $40,000 to $60,000 price range. Taxes on a $50,000 house will be about $1,000 yearly. That is equal to approximately $84.00 monthly.

Totaling the monthly payment for insurance ($10.00) and taxes ($84.00), we see the sum to be $94.00. Subtract this sum from the total monthly payment the buyer is willing to make ($400.00):

$$\begin{array}{r} \$400.00 \\ -94.00 \\ \hline \$306.00 \end{array}$$

So, $306.00 of the original $400 remains to provide for principal and interest payments.

Since the average conventional real estate loan is funded at 9½ per cent for a 30 year term, and 60 per cent of homes sold or financed on an FHA or G.I. basis which bear a 30 year term, use a 9½ per cent, 30 year term loan as the guide to finding the principal amount of the loan your client can afford.

In your loan amortization book you find the 9½ per cent section and the 30 year term column. Move along the column until you find a principal sum that is amortized with payments of approximately $306.00. A $36,000 loan, 9½ per cent interest for a term of 30 years will amortize with monthly payments of $302.80.

Hence, your client can afford, and qualify for, a loan of approximately $36,000. Add to this the amount of his down payment ($10,000) and you see the total purchase price of a home for our client should approximate $46,000.

He can't afford more, so don't bother to show him $70,000 properties. Many buyers will miraculously produce more money for a down payment for a home they really want, so don't make the mistake of limiting the properties you show your client to *precisely* the amount determined by this loan qualification procedure. If a client could readily qualify for a $50,000 property, I would not hesitate to show him properties priced to $60,000.

Once you have qualified your buyer, select several properties to show him from your inventory and proceed immediately to show these properties. Here is where your attention to the mechanics of inspecting listings really pays off.

If you have looked at many listings on a regular, scheduled basis, you will be well prepared. You will know where the good buys are. You will know which homes your client will be interested in. You won't waste his time and you won't waste your own time.

Again, it pays to know your merchandise.

POINTS TO KEEP IN MIND

1. *You must determine what a buyer wants and what he can afford.*
2. *Answers to the questions of the Client Interview Sheet give you all the information necessary to qualify your buyer.*
3. *Study the questions on the Client Interview Sheet. A copy of this form is shown in Appendix B, Exhibit B-2, page 170.*
4. *Qualify your clients—carefully!*
5. *Find the maximum purchase price he can afford by using the down payment, monthly income, and lender qualifying ratios shown in the example.*
6. *Once you have qualified your buyer, show him property immediately.*

HOW TO SHOW PROPERTY
TO A CLIENT

SHOW HOMES Before you can show property to a client,
THAT ARE   you have to decide which properties to in-
GOOD BUYS   clude on a tour. Selecting the proper homes
to show takes special skill. Just because a
buyer says he wants a rancher with three bedrooms, two baths,
and a family room doesn't mean you must show him only three
bedroom, two bath ranchers. Highly successful real estate salesmen show homes which are good buys but don't necessarily
have the specific amenities requested by their clients. They have
discovered a little known secret of real estate;

PEOPLE BUY HOMES THAT ARE GOOD BUYS.

By a good buy, I don't mean a property priced below fair
market value. There are many things other than price which
cause a property to be a good buy. The most compelling are
emotional factors such as an idyllic setting on a stream, or under
a canopy of spreading trees, or a property secluded in a clearing
in the woods, or atop a knoll overlooking the valley. These are
all emotional pluses which make their respective properties
stand apart from all the others.

I feel all homes have bedrooms and bathrooms and living

rooms and yards. But it's the emotional characteristics which make them unique. And an awareness of these emotional features will make you a success in this business if you make a point to discover them when you inspect property and talk about them when you're showing it.

There is a valley in the area where I do business which was one of the first inhabited areas of the county. It still has many of the original homesteads complete with little two bedroom, one bath cottages. I've made an extraordinary amount of money selling these tiny, functionally obsolete houses to clients who told me they wanted at least four bedrooms, two or three baths, family rooms, formal dining rooms, swimming pools, and on and on, ending always with the advice that price was no problem if they found what they wanted.

I don't remember ever meeting one of these clients who hadn't already been looking with half the real estate salesmen in the county. But I made the sales because I knew these people would buy if I showed them property that was a good buy.

I knew many of them could easily spend one hundred thousand dollars on a house. I also knew other salesmen had already shown them all the luxury homes on the market in that price range and they were still looking. Obviously, a buyer with that kind of money is awfully choosy. He can have a home custom built if he doesn't find what he wants.

Knowing all this, I would take one of these buyers out to the little valley and pull up in front of a tiny, old, run down farm house. "What's this?" they would always ask. They were used to driving onto manicured grounds and inspecting elegant homes.

"I want to show you something interesting," was all I would say as I began to show them the property. I would point out the house was situated on nearly two acres of ground and all the homes around were valued at eighty thousand to two hundred thousand dollars.

"But this is a shack," they would say.

I agreed, but pointed out that it could be either remodeled or torn down and a new house built on the site. Usually they made the decision to remodel after I described how the old fashioned bathtub with curly legs could be built into a new bathroom with modern facilities. The tiny basement could be made into an elegant wine cellar. I showed them pictures I had accumulated of other similar properties that had been remodeled combining antique fixtures with modern ones.

I explained how I had worked for years with several remodeling contractors and offered to drive them to their offices to see some examples of their work. But most important, I pointed out the emotional values of the property which made it a good buy. That it was the type of neighborhood in which they were interested was certainly a necessary ingredient of the sale, but because I showed them a property that was a good buy, I made the sale.

SHOW YOUR   After I have selected several properties and
URGENCY   before I leave the office, I always ask one im-
TO SELL   portant question. "Mr. and Mrs. Buyer, if I
                show you a house today which you like, will
you buy it today?"

The purpose of the question is to establish urgency—my urgency in wanting to make a sale. Too many salesmen spend all their time trying to determine if their clients have urgency to buy and never think of making it clear to their clients that they have an urgency to sell. After all, you're not in this business to taxi people around.

If the buyers say they don't think so, I tell them I would like to suggest several other real estate offices down the street who would be happy to drive them around as long as they like but I have located several properties which are such good buys I am certain I can sell one of them and perhaps both of them in the next few days. I am careful to explain that I don't want to rush them in any way and want them to feel comfortable looking at property but they can surely understand my position. I am successful because I can locate exceptional properties better than most salesmen and I must show them to clients who are ready to buy before all the other salesmen find out about them.

With such an explanation, your clients will understand your position and go along with it. You will also have piqued their curiosity to see these exceptional buys. Of course, if the buyers are new in town, I would be willing to give them a tour of the different residential areas and work with them for several days or even a week. But the average buyer lives in the same town in which he is looking. Establishing your urgency to sell is a vital sales procedure you shouldn't overlook.

Showing property is an art in itself. Don't consider it a routine function of salesmanship. Your actions, comments and methods should be well conceived and calculated to move the client to his emotional peak of buyer's interest.

As soon as you have concluded the client interview and qualified the buyer financially, scan your memory, your knowledge of the market, and select three or four houses to show him. Don't make the mistake of selecting ten or fifteen homes for his inspection. This is a common error in real estate sales. Don't subject your client to an endurance test. Three or four houses will suffice if, and it's a big "if," you know your property —if you know which properties have the greatest emotional appeal in each price range, architectural style, and geographical area.

DON'T LET
YOUR CLIENT
LEAD YOU
When selecting the homes to show your client, be careful not to fall into a convenient trap. A client will often walk into a real estate office professing his desire to own a contemporary, or a colonial style house, or a Cape Cod or a California stucco. He presently owns a ranch style home. When he eventually makes his decision to buy, he will probably buy another ranch style home.

As happens so often, someone in the market for a new home experiences the excitement of anticipating a complete change of style. Perhaps he, or she, has recently seen a motion picture wherein a contemporary or colonial style home was featured in a flattering environment. Perhaps a magazine feature or a visit to a friend's home prompted the impulsive desire for a home styled differently than the one presently owned. Most buyers, when their house hunting gets to the stage of writing out deposit checks, will purchase a home styled the same as their current home. They feel comfortable in a familiarly styled house. As in most everything, we're creatures of habit. Don't overlook the possibility of the client buying a different style home. Just be aware of this paradox.

If, in the client interview, the client tells you his present home is ranch style but he now wants to look at colonials, you should show him one or two houses of each style.

ARRANGE YOUR TOUR CAREFULLY   Let's assume you have selected four properties to show your client. They are in the price range he can afford, in neighborhoods which should please him, and all have most of the amenities he wants. No property will meet every demand of a particular client.

If you feel one house in particular will motivate your client to buy, you may choose to save that property for the end of your inspection tour. The other homes you show him will serve to persuade him to buy the last house. Perhaps it is priced more attractively than the other homes, offers more features, is in better repair, or has more charm.

However, if you feel that all the properties you are going to show your client have appeal, arrange your tour to get him back to the office in the shortest possible time.

Before you leave the office to begin the tour of properties, you should advise your client that you have selected the outstanding properties in the entire area and a decision to purchase should be made from one of them. Repeat this several times during the tour.

Don't make imprudent remarks like, "This first house isn't really a good buy but I want to show it to you so you'll see what a bargain the second one is." It might happen that the client will like the first house better than the second but he will be hesitant to commit himself to purchase it because of your remark. Don't anticipate *vocally* what a buyer will or will not like. It's awfully easy to talk yourself out of a sale before you've shown a single house.

I remember most vividly making just such a mistake a few years ago. I was working with a young couple who had recently been transferred to California from England. They were very well educated. The husband was an executive with an international beverage firm. His wife was born and raised in Rhodesia, the daughter of an English government official. They had met while the husband was on a business trip to Rhodesia. I enjoyed talking to them about their experiences living in

Africa and England. It gave me an excellent opportunity to boast a bit about the merits of California living.

I had prepared a tour of four lovely homes for this charming couple. They were all in the $40,000 to $50,000 price range. The first home I planned to show them was a fine property but it had one disadvantage. It was backed up against an elementary school playground.

I showed the home to my clients. They were visibly impressed and as we drove on to the next home they enthused about it. I agreed with them and then mentioned how sad it was, being located next to a schoolyard.

"If it wasn't for that,"I told them, "it would be an excellent buy."

We completed our tour of homes. They were politely enthusiastic about the other homes but they liked the first one best of all.

"We would have bought it," they told me just as they were leaving my office, "except for your remark about the schoolyard. You see, in Rhodesia, a house located next to a schoolyard is in the most desirable location of all!"

I had talked myself out of a sale. That's a terribly painful error for anyone to make.

PLAN
YOUR
ROUTE
When you leave the office to begin your inspection tour, drive your client to the homes by the route which offers the most appealing views along the way. If you have a choice of neighborhoods on your route, purposefully take the best. Don't drive past a factory if you can drive through a park just as well. Good real estate men plan their routes in advance of their "showings" with the care of a military commander.

SHOWING
THE
PROPERTY
When showing a property, a minimum of conversation from the real estate agent is mandatory. You're not going to talk a client into buying a house he doesn't want. False enthusiasm and a steady stream of chatter will only serve to alienate a buyer.

If you keep your client relationship on a positive note by conditioning him to say, "Yes," you won't have to worry about the close. This can be as easy as exclaiming, "It's a wonderful day, isn't it?" Then continue in this vein. Construct your sales talk with questions that require a "yes" answer. This is easily accomplished by turning positive statements into questions.

For example, instead of saying, "This is an excellent investment," you should say, "Don't you agree this is an excellent investment?" "This is a wonderful neighborhood," can more effectively be phrased, "This is a wonderful neighborhood, isn't it?" Help your client to answer affirmatively by smiling and nodding your head slightly as you ask the question.

Remember, when you ask questions you are in control of the conversation. Each "yes" response puts you that much closer to a sale. The "yes" system has an irresistible psychological effect on clients. It sets the stage for a smooth, professional close.

As you show a home you must point out any important features which might otherwise go unnoticed, and describe any articles of personal property which are to be included in the sales price, but limit your conversation to that. If your client wants to know something, he will ask you.

You can help your clients make a decision to purchase with leading questions which make them think of the property as if they already owned it. One such question used frequently is:

"How would you arrange your furniture in this (the living) room?"

Then you stand back and let the happy couple visualize their own furniture in the house. It is very effective, most of the time. As in all sales techniques, you have to be careful in their application. An effective sales tool is often a double edged sword.

One of my salesmen was showing a home to a couple who were obviously pleased with their inspection of the property. When they came to the living room she decided to apply the perfect close.

"And how would you arrange your furniture in this room?" she asked merrily.

As the couple began to ponder her question she stepped back to witness the impending transformation from interested clients to excited buyers and owners.

But instead, a disaster occurred! It seems the husband and

wife could never agree on furniture arranging and they were both highly volatile on the subject. They began arguing. Quietly, at first, with hushed disagreements. Then louder, with less restraint. Finally they were shouting, actually screaming at each other over their furniture. The end result was no sale, two steamed-up clients, and a real estate salesman who felt like taping her mouth shut.

Another seemingly innocuous question on a later day felled another of my salesmen.

An elderly, gruff, uncommunicative couple arrived at my office in response to a newspaper ad. After an interview, they departed with my salesman for an inspection tour. As they cruised along a country lane my salesman, valiantly trying to establish rapport with this introverted couple, asked,

"What made you decide to look for homes in this area?"

They had, during the interview, mentioned that they were presently living in San Francisco.

My salesman's question somehow triggered a latent emotional fuse in the wife's psyche.

"As a matter of fact," she rasped, "I think this country is lousy!"

She turned to her spouse. "Orville," she bellowed, "let's get out of here."

The moral of these little vignettes is plain: be thrifty with your conversation when you are showing property.

When you escort the client into a home, ask him to inspect it himself, explaining that you will be happy to answer any questions he might have. If the homeowner is at home, don't introduce the buyers by name. It is sufficient to introduce yourself and advise the homeowner the client will inspect the home by himself.

Point out any features or conditions that would not be readily apparent to your clients such as the property lines, the taxes, what schools the children would go to, etc. Then let them inspect the property by themselves. Buyers are perfectly capable of identifying the living room, kitchen, bedrooms and bathrooms without help from you. I don't believe in following clients around like "the little shadow who goes in and out with me".

In know that many real estate salesmen prefer to escort their clients through a home. If you do this and you're successful selling real estate, there's no reason to change. But I have learned that buyers like to get the feel of a home they are considering buying. It has to do with the emotional condition of buying. They aren't going to feel inclined to discuss many personal, emotional things which are important to them with a real estate salesman breathing down their neck.

I prefer to let them inspect the home themselves. As they leave on their inspection tour I tell them I'll be waiting for them in the living room or under the oak tree on the back patio to answer any questions they might have. And off they go. While they are touring the property I review the comments I have written on the back of the listing card, the emotional features of the home according to the homeowners, the comments I wrote the day I inspected the home by myself and took the time to discuss it with the homeowners.

If your client comments on deficiencies in the house, agree with his criticism. I have read entire books devoted to the one subject of how to counter clients' objections. I could have saved myself the trouble for I have learned this is a mistake.

As an example, these books advise when a client comments that the bedrooms are small, you are to reply, "But look how large the living room is. When you invest in a home you should spend your money on the living areas of the house, where you spend the most time, not the sleeping areas."

That sounds fine, but it doesn't motivate clients to buy houses. Instead, it alienates them. It makes them feel you aren't on their side. They begin to think that you consider all the objections they raise to be insignificant. Soon they don't want to talk to you at all.

I have discovered a sales tool that is so powerful it can turn you into a super salesman in a flash. And it's simple to learn;

AGREE WITH YOUR CLIENTS' CRITICISM

When I'm showing a house and the client says, "Look at those cracks in the wall," I don't try to parry his criticism. Just the opposite. I say, "My goodness, those are large cracks." That's all. I don't go on and on about the cracks. I merely agree with his criticism.

We inspect the bathroom and my client says, "Look at that. All the grout is out of the tile."

I say, "Hang on to your son, he might fall through the floor."

Of course he can tell I'm being facetious. But I am also agreeing with him.

We inspect the back yard and he says, "Those weeds must be six feet tall."

I say, "Don't walk out there, might be something hiding in the bushes."

Again, I'm agreeing with him, agreeing that the weeds are taking over the yard. By making light of it, it doesn't seem to be such a serious problem. I certainly don't express concern at the condition of the yard.

If you employ this technique of agreeing with your clients' criticism, you will find a strange thing happening as you show houses. If your client likes the property at all, he will begin to sell it to himself. He will say, "I guess we can cut the weeds in the yard." You reassure him. "No problem at all. We can hire a kid down the block and rent a rototiller and get the whole job done for about five dollars."

Now your client is getting enthused. He knows you're on his side. He feels it. He can tell, because you agree with everything he's said. You haven't made the mistake most real estate salesmen make and challenged him. You've shown him that you are allies instead of opponents. Most salesmen adopt the adversary technique and this costs them their careers. Don't you do it. Agree with your clients.

Your client says, "I guess it wouldn't be too hard to fix the grout in the tile," and you say, "Just get one of those tubes of grout at the hardware store for a dollar, squeeze it in, wipe it off, and the job's done in twenty minutes."

He says, "I think I can fix the cracks in the wall." You tell him, "A can of spackle and a putty knife is all it takes."

"I think I can do it," he says.

"I know you can," you answer, and you've made a sale.

You can't force people to buy a house they don't like, but you can force them to dislike you—by challenging their comments, by disagreeing with their criticism. Don't make that mistake. Give this "agree with your client" sales technique a try. It will amaze you!

ASK IF   As soon as the client has completed his inspec-
HE WANTS   tion, go on to the next property unless he has
TO BUY   evidenced interest in the home. If he seems
                       interested, ask for the order. "Would you like to buy this home?"

Many times a client will want to buy the first home you show him, but he won't tell you so unless you ask. If he answers in the affirmative, write a deposit receipt on the spot, in the house, if the owners are not home, in your car if they are. Don't wait to return to the office if your client has made his decision to buy.

And don't let your client get together with the home owners. In an effort to be helpful, a homeowner can easily make a remark which will kill the sale.

I recall a time when one of my salesmen was showing a home to his clients. The homeowners were away for the day. The clients were new to the San Francisco Bay area. They expressed a desire to buy, so my salesman, being alert to a sale, promptly escorted the clients to the dining room table and began writing out a deposit receipt. The only question in the client's mind was the difficulty of commuting from Lafayette to Oakland, a distance of sixteen miles. My salesman truthfully advised the buyer that it wasn't a difficult chore although the traffic didn't move rapidly during rush hours.

My salesman was proceeding with the writing of the deposit receipt when the homeowners returned. They were thrilled to see that someone was interested in buying their home. They immediately became chummy.

"We know you'll love it here," Mrs. Homeowner gushed to our clients. "We hate selling our home but John hates commuting and the trip from here to Oakland is simply horrible."

My salesman almost fell through the floor. And the homeowners were practically knocked to the ground by the slipstream caused when our clients streaked out the door like rockets. Naturally, the sale was lost.

Homeowners are not professional salesmen. One ill-conceived comment can destroy a client's desires to purchase a home. Keep them apart!

START   If, after you have shown several homes to
A   your clients, they haven't expressed an interest
CONTRACT   in buying any of them, don't drive them back to
                the office with the idea of sending them on their
way. That's what the average real estate salesman would do. But you're going to become a money maker. You're going to do something different. You're going to start a contract.

As you pull up in front of your office, tell your clients you want to discuss a few details with them before they leave. Once they are seated in your office, take out the listing cards of the homes you have just shown them and hold them up in front of you.

"All of these homes are good buys," you begin. "They're priced right, located well, and have most of the features you want in a house." Then, still holding the cards above your desk, you ask, "Which of these houses did you like the best?"

Usually your clients will tell you they didn't like any of them enough to buy. Expect this. "I understand that," you say, "but you must have liked one better than the rest. It will help me to know."

"Well," the husband says, "the yellow one was pretty nice but the yard was too large. I don't want to spend all my spare time being a gardener."

Now you're getting somewhere. You've just focused your clients' attention on a specific house. Lay the rest of the cards aside and glance at the card describing the yellow house.

"They're asking forty thousand for that house," you say. "That's a good price."

"Not to me, it isn't," your client says.

I've already mentioned the importance of emotion in selling. Stress emotional features whenever you can. But today you've shown several homes to your clients and none of them elicited the emotional reaction necessary to cause them to want to buy. Therefore you can assume nothing you can say now will

suddenly cause your clients to change their minds about any
of the houses. If emotion fails you, as in this case, switch
immediately to price, to the financial or economic aspects of
real estate.

"I understand the yard is larger than you wish," you begin,
"but there must be some price at which you would be happy
to own this property."

This thought is so foreign to most buyers that they usually
just shrug and say they would rather look at other properties.
Understand you can't force anyone to buy anything they don't
want to buy. That's not the idea. What you're going to do is
give your clients a new idea—the idea of purchasing a piece of
property that fits most of their needs at an exceptionally good
price. The only price at which I am certain I can deliver a
piece of property is the listed price, but in circumstances such
as I am describing, your clients haven't seen anything they
want to take away from you. Rather than lose them, you should
cause them to sign a contract to purchase one of the homes at
some price lower than the listed price.

"I don't like the yellow house enough to buy it," your client
repeats.

Now you must suggest prices to your clients. "If you could
buy this property for thirty seven five," you begin "that would
be an excellent buy." Carefully note their reaction.

"No," they say, "we don't like it that much."

Try a lower figure. It's a fact that most people would be
willing to purchase any property in the country at a given
price. Your job is to find that specific price for these buyers and
the yellow house.

"Thirty six thousand sound more like it?" you ask.

You see a glimmer of interest flash across the husband's face,
then disappear as he says, "No, I dont' think so."

"If you could buy that house for thirty five thousand dollars,
you would have the buy of the year."

The husband looks at his wife. Her eyes widen as she looks
back at him. He looks at you and says, "You think they would
take thirty five thousand?"

"I don't know," you answer honestly. "The only price I am

sure of is the listed price but if the house isn't worth that to you, and thirty five thousand is, I'll try it for you. You'll have made a sensational buy if it goes through."

With that you take out a purchase contract and complete it. Now you're being a creative salesman. You have started a contract where ninety nine out of one hundred salesmen would have been wondering where their next clients were coming from. The amount of money you make in real estate depends upon the number of contracts you write. Starting a contract, even for a price much lower than the listing price, is better than no contract at all. And more often than you would imagine, you'll get your contracts accepted. (I'll discuss presenting the offer in Chapter 11.) As soon as you leave your clients to present the low offer, they will begin thinking more seriously of the property. It will occur to them that you just might get their offer accepted since you got them to agree to buy the house and they didn't even like it! If you return with a counter offer, they will usually be prepared to amend their original offer.

Some salesmen have wondered if this policy of starting a contract at any price possible might be dangerous in that if the offer doesn't go through, the next time you find these buyers a property they like, they might want to make another low offer. This won't be a problem. Just point out to your clients that the last time they made a low offer, they didn't get the house. Since they like this house and want to own it, only by agreeing to pay the listed price can they insure the success of their offer.

Every time you leave your office to show property, you must have a positive attitude. You must be determined to sell one of the houses to your clients that day. If you don't show them anything they want to buy for the usual emotional reasons, you can cause them to buy for economic (price) reasons. Start a contract if all else fails, but get your clients to sign some kind of a purchase agreement before you leave them.

That is how sales are made.

POINTS TO KEEP IN MIND

1. *Show homes that are good buys.*
2. *Establish your urgency to sell.*
3. *Show only three or four homes at a time to a client.*

4. *Arrange your tour carefully, saving the most impressive property for last.*

5. *Plan the route you follow to get to the properties so that you pass through the most appealing neighborhoods.*

6. *Don't criticize any of the properties you show a client. If he doesn't like them he will do that himself.*

7. *Hold your conversation to a minimum while the client is inspecting a property.*

8. *Condition your client to say, "Yes."*

9. *When your client has completed his inspection of a property, ask him if he wants to buy it.*

10. *"Start" a sale, even if the offering price seems ridiculously low.*

ANSWERING OBJECTIONS

THE
"BE-BACK"
CLIENT

As any successful real estate man will tell you, you have to write deposit receipts to make money. You have to write them, if at all possible, on your first meeting with the buyers. Don't be put off. Don't be the victim of a "be back," the buyer who expresses an interest in buying and assures the salesman he will be back. He usually won't.

There is a much revered expression among real estate people:

"Buyers are liars."

It's harsh, but true. Those buyers who bought through you are, naturally, excepted. They're wonderful. The expression refers to potential buyers who, for one reason or another, did not buy through you.

Buyers don't usually know what type of home they will buy. They don't know how much they will spend for a home, or on a down payment. They don't know when they will buy a house. They don't know where they will buy a home. They don't know most of the details of motivation of home ownership. They have general, vague notions about these subjects, but nothing more definite than that.

Most buyers react to impulse. You ask them a question and they think they have to answer, so they do, usually with anything that comes to mind. Don't accept their answers as being definitive.

A buyer may say, "I don't want to live in Concord. I want a house in Walnut Creek or Lafayette."

If you believe this and elect not to show the client Concord homes, you will lose money over the course of the year. Many such clients will buy a home in Concord when they are shown a beautiful, spacious home in a lovely neighborhood at a price much lower than a similar Walnut Creek or Lafayette home.

The buyer who responds to an $18,500 newspaper ad will often buy a $40,000 home.

Use your common sense and don't take anything at face value when interviewing a client.

You must write the deposit receipt immediately after you have shown your client a property he likes. Don't take "no" for an answer. Don't let the client put you off. Don't be the victim of a "be back."

COMMON OBJECTIONS   If your cilents won't sign the deposit receipt you have prepared, they must have an objection you have not successfully countered. As in most responses from balky clients, you have to take their explanations with a grain of salt. Usually they want only a plausible answer, nothing more complex than that. Vague, hesitant answers won't do.

Here are some of the most common objections and suggested answers.

"We want to sleep on it."

"Mr. and Mrs. Buyer, you know more about this property now than you will half an hour from now, or tomorrow. Certainly the decision to buy a home is important. You should make that decision when I am here to answer your questions and the details of the home are fresh in your mind. Precisely what is causing you concern?

"I'm not sure I can afford it."

"Is this your first home? How much are you paying now for rent?"

Compute the payments your client will have to meet upon the purchase of the new home and equate this figure to his current payments for shelter.

"You will only be spending $25 a month more than you are paying right now. I'm sure you will agree it's worth that to put an end to sharing laundry facilities, the garage, and the back-yard with other tenants in your apartment house. It's certainly worth more than that for an investment in real estate, which is exactly what you are doing when you purchase a home. Your monthly payments are truly monthly investments. In addition, you can deduct your payments for taxes and interest from your federal income tax returns. As you know, Mr. and Mrs. Buyer, on an amortized mortgage loan, the greatest portion of each monthly payment is spent on interest. You should also be aware of the old real estate axiom, "You pay for the property you live in." It is far more prudent to be buying the home for yourself than paying for an apartment building for someone else."

"I'm not sure I can raise the money for the closing costs."

"Mr. and Mrs. Buyer, you don't have to have the money for closing costs until the escrow is ready to close. Since you're purchasing on an FHA basis, you'll have nearly two months. I'm certain you can raise the money in that time."

"I want to show the house to a contractor friend before I buy."

It is always frustrating to have to sell a house not only to the buyers themselves but to the buyers' friends, relatives and advisors.

"Why put your friend on the spot? This house was built under county building codes, which are very rigid. If you purchase under Government insured financing, the federal appraisers inspect the property. If you purchase under conventional financing, the appraiser for the institutional lender inspects the property. They won't lend the money if they're not satisfied the home is a good value."

If this doesn't satisfy your client, write the deposit receipt with a contingency clause in it, as follows:

"This offer subject to the approval of Joseph Welsh, Welsh Construction on his inspection of said property within 24 hours of sellers' acceptance."

"The price is too high."

Yesterday's overpriced homes are today's bargains! Don't be intimidated by a buyer and don't feel you have to defend a listed price. That's the wrong attitude.

What the buyer who poses such an objection wants to hear is an intelligent, businesslike discussion of real estate values. He actually wants a short course in appraising from you. You have to be on his side or he won't sign his name to a deposit receipt.

When you hear this objection, counter it by giving a discussion of "comparative analysis" appraising.

"Mr. Buyer, similar homes in this neighborhood have sold recently. Here is a list of the sales prices."

And you go on to discuss the sales, the physical condition of the various properties at the time of their sales, and any other information you have about these comparable sales which you feel would be of interest to your buyer.

Of course, if the listed price is too high, you will have to suggest the buyer make an offer at a price he feels to be reasonable.

A FEW "CLOSING" STORIES   One tack you might try with balky clients is something I have used with great success over the years. Instead of getting into a discussion of specific objections, I instead tell my clients a trilogy of stories of the strange experiences I have had with buyers. This puts my clients at ease for they can see other buyers have the same qualms about purchasing they are feeling. By describing them with humor, it takes the sting out of it.

"Once," I begin, a smile on my face, "I had a young couple who said they wanted to bring their father through a house they were considering buying. They said they would feel better if Dad gave it his okay. The next day I watched in amazement as dear old Dad walked through the house opening and closing every cabinet in the kitchen. That's the only room in the house he bothered to inspect. When he was through, I asked him what he was doing. He advised me that if the cabinet doors opened and closed easily, that meant the house hadn't settled, so it probably had been built well. With this extraordinary logic leading to Dad's approval, the couple made the decision to buy the house. It shows what a non professional job non professionals are capable of doing."

I look at my clients and go on to the next story. "I once had a couple bring their father to inspect a house for them. He wasn't a cabinet opener. He was more peculiar than that. He walked through the house tapping every light bulb with his finger. He explained that if the lights didn't flicker, the wiring was installed properly and that signified to him the house was sound. I imagined he was a reincarnated moth!"

My clients always laugh at that. I finish with the third vignette. "I was trying to sell a brand new house to a young attorney who decided he should first show it to his father who was also an attorney, which could explain his odd performance!

"When we entered the house, the father stationed his son at the kitchen sink and explained that he was going to go into the bathroom, flush the toilet, and while the toilet was flushing he would yell down the bathtub drain. The son was to listen at the kitchen sink. If he could hear his father calling through the drain, the plumbing must be hooked up correctly and since plumbing was the most important component of a house in his opinion, the son could feel certain he was making a wise purchase.

"While the father and son got ready for their toilet flushing routine, I decided not to take any chances. I walked out the front door, then dashed around the side of the house, into the garage, and put my ear against the common wall dividing the garage from the kitchen. When I heard the toilet flushing I hollered, 'Hello,' through the wall. 'I can hear it, Dad,' the young lawyer called to his father. And the sale was made!"

Clients love this story. It's absolutely true and demonstrates house inspections should be left to the experts, such as real estate salesmen, mortgage lenders, institutional appraisers, government appraisers, and the like.

BE   If a client presents an objection for which you
PERSISTENT   don't have a pat answer ready and waiting,
                 pause a moment before speaking and THINK!
What does the client want to hear?

He wants to hear a reason or two why he should buy *now*.
He's in the mood to buy. Just give him a few good reasons and
you're in business.

Once you have answered an objection, ask your client to sign
the deposit receipt. If he still refuses, he must have another
objection. Find out what it is. Ask him what's causing him to be
hesitant. When you discover this, answer the objection and
again ask him to sign.

Be persistent. Keep after the buyer. Continue to give answers
to his objections and ask for his signature until he signs his
name to the contract. Don't give up. Show some courage.
Everyone, even a balky client, admires a strong salesman.

It's not difficult to counter most objections. Whatever you do,
make sure you write a deposit receipt and get it signed by the
buyers before they leave the office on that first day of your
meeting. Even if you have to write an offer at a price you
consider unreasonable, if it's the only way you can get your
buyer to sign his name, go ahead and write it.

POINTS TO KEEP IN MIND

1. Don't let a client put you off when you try to "close" him. Don't
   be the victim of a "be back."
2. You must write the deposit receipt immediately after you have
   shown the client a property he likes.
3. Think a moment before answering a client objection. Try to
   imagine what's really bothering him. Imagine what he wants to
   hear. Then tell him just that.
4. Be persistent. Answer objections and ask for his signature until
   your client signs the deposit receipt.

WRITING THE OFFER

The success you will realize in selling real estate is directly related to the number of deposit receipts you write. If you write enough offers, you will make sufficient sales to provide an exceptional income.

PRACTICE
WRITING
CONTRACTS
The key to writing offers lies in developing a knowledge of the types of financing available, a knowledge of the properties available for sale, and learning how to motivate clients to sign their names to deposit receipts. You must be familiar with the various documents and forms used in preparing an offer. You must feel comfortable discussing financing with your clients, using the loan amortization book and FHA slide rule. Practice is an excellent teacher, so practice. Practice writing all kinds of offers on hypothetical properties. Practice using different kinds of financing methods. Ask someone to check your work.

The biggest obstacle you will face when writing an offer is getting the client's cooperation while you prepare it. It is natural for a client to put you off, to stall you, to do practically anything to keep you from "writing up" an offer. Unless he is one of those much admired but rare breed of cats who can make a decision and act upon it, your client will probably be uncertain of his next move. That's your cue, your key to success.

Lead him. Get him in the habit of following your direction. Get a deposit receipt filled out and signed or you won't have an offer to present. No offer equals no commisison.

GET YOUR CLIENT INTO THE OFFICE When you return to the office with clients after inspecting property, don't sit in your car and discuss real estate. Get them into the office. As soon as you set the brake on your car, open your door and get out.

"Let's go into the office," you suggest, "it's more comfortable," or, "I can write some information down on paper for you."

Then walk into the office, holding the door open for your clients. They will follow you.

As soon as you are all seated in a private conference room, take out a deposit receipt form and begin completing it. (See Exhibits B-14-B-26, pages 182–199.) If your client questions you, explain that you want to show him what a deposit receipt would look like should he decide to purchase a home.

Don't feel that the sight of a deposit receipt will enrage a client. It won't. If you're selling properly, you have long since established "sales leadership" over your client. He is conditioned to follow your lead. Delay in producing the deposit receipt and you make the future moment awkward when you finally decide to bring it out.

As soon as the deposit receipt form is on your desk, quickly write in the date. Then ask the buyers,

"How do you spell your name?"

Wait with poised pen while they give you their answer.

"Your first name?" you ask. "Your middle initial? Your wife's first name? Does she use an initial?"

This rapidly establishes the mood of the moment—that of filling out a deposit receipt.

DON'T BARGAIN WITH CLIENT Write in the full listed price of the property and the down payment suggested from the client interview. Don't make an issue over purchase price. If your client has expressed a desire to purchase a certain home, don't ask him what price he wants to offer. Write the deposit receipt at the full listed price. Don't set yourself up as an expert on bargaining procedures. The buyer should be advised to make his highest and best offer first. It is unwise to make a calculated low offer initially with an intent of accepting a reasonable counter offer from the seller.

Often a buyer will ask the salesman what he thinks the seller will take for a property.

"What do you think I should offer?" is a question you must consider with extreme caution.

Let's say a home is offered for sale for $25,000. You've shown your clients some properties and they're enthusiastic about this one house. They're ready to make an offer. You have developed a friendly relationship with them. They treat you like a professional, with courtesy and respect. You recognize this, appreciate it, and therefore feel like going out of your way to do a good job for them.

As you sit at your desk and begin to fill in the deposit receipt, they suddenly ask you, "How much should we offer?"

A natural inclination in such an atmosphere is to suggest offering something less than the asking price. You know many homes are sold for prices less than listed price. You have a feeling the sellers would take a reasonable offer. And you would like to shave a few hundred dollars off the price for these nice people.

If you advise your clients to make a lower offer, they might be able to buy the house at that figure. And they might not! Don't try to be a hero. You've done your job when you found a house they wanted and could afford. Don't set yourself up as a Yankee trader.

You must next determine the method of financing most advantageous to your client.

WHAT   The size of down payment available to the
TYPE OF   buyer is the primary consideration in determin-
FINANCING?   ing the type of financing for home purchase. If
              the maximum loan and the minimum cash out-
lay is desired, the no-down-payment G.I. loan offers the greatest purchasing leverage to the buyer.

Next advantageous, from the standpoint of low down payment, is the FHA purchase wherein the down payment averages 4 per cent of the purchase price on a graduated loan-to-value ratio.

If interest rates are of great concern to the buyer, the G.I. loan offers the lowest rate at a current 9½ per cent. FHA represents its interest rate as being 9½ per cent plus ½ per cent for mutual mortgage insurance. Actually, the effective rate of interest an FHA purchaser pays is approximately 10.165 per cent. This is determined as follows:

	per cent
Basic, statutory FHA rate	9.500
Actual mutual mortgage insurance rate	.415
1 per cent loan fee charged purchaser	.125
Closing costs 1 per cent greater than conventional loan	.125
	10.165

By way of explanation of the above breakdown of FHA interest rates, it has been calculated that every percentile (1 per cent) of purchass price a buyer spends in cash at the time of purchase raises the effective rate of interest on the loan by one eighth of one percent (0.125 per cent). Thus, the 1 per cent FHA loan fee and additional closing costs increase the effective rate of interest by one quarter of 1 per cent.

If a buyer has 20 per cent of the purchase price as a down payment, he can secure a loan with an interest rate (9½ per cent) lower than that offered by FHA and a term as long as the FHA maximum (30 years). FHA is of great benefit only to the lower down payment buyers.

The lowest interest rates of all conventional lenders are offered by insurance companies which require a down payment of at least 25 per cent of appraisal.

Sales financed by conventional loans normally close escrow much more rapidly than sales financed by government insured loans. If the buyer is anxious to purchase a home in the most timely fashion, use conventional financing.

There are less common methods of financing home purchases which are very attractive to buyers. Such methods are the FHA or G.I. repossessions wherein the buyer has to pay only a nominal down payment, usually limited to $300 or $400. Before the government puts these repossession properties on the market for sale, they completely refurbish them, so, in many cases, they are better than new.

GET A   If the buyer hasn't a personal check for a de-
DEPOSIT   posit, offer him a counter check. As a last resort
CHECK   use a promissory note "to be redeemed in cash
                   within five days of sellers' acceptance" of the
contract. (See Exhibit B-4, page 172.)

A deposit of at least 2 per cent of the purchase price should be taken at the time the buyer signs the deposit receipt. This demonstrates to the seller the good faith of the buyer. If you must take a deposit of less than 2 per cent of the purchase price, include, as a condition in the deposit receipt, that a sum equal to 2 per cent of the purchase price will be deposited by the buyer immediately upon acceptance of the offer by the seller.

Don't ask your client how much of a deposit he can make. Fill in the amount of the deposit (based on the 2 per cent minimum) on your own initiative. Your clients expect you to take the lead.

Make certain you prepare all necessary forms for the buyers' signatures, such as termite forms (see Exhibit B-36, page 211), personal property transfer forms, (see Exhibit B-31, page 204), FHA amendment forms, (see Exhibit B-28, page 201) and so on.

Once the contract is prepared, show the forms to the buyers, explain the entries to them, hand a pen to each and indicate where they are to sign.

POINTS TO KEEP IN MIND

1. Practice writing sales contracts until it becomes second nature.
2. When you return from showing properties, get your client out of your car and into the office.
3. Once in your office, immediately bring out a deposit receipt form and begin filling it in.
4. Write the contract at the full listed price if at all possible. Don't suggest offering a lower price.

5. *Write out the method of financing most advantageous to the buyer.*

6. *Get a check for a deposit. Take a note only as a last resort.*

11

PRESENTING
THE OFFER

Once you have a deposit receipt signed by the buyers, it remains for you to secure the sellers' acceptance. Without this, your efforts will have added up to a lot of good practice. No money—just practice. Since money is our goal, you've got to get the sellers' signatures.

Let's assume the property on which you have just written a contract is listed by some other cooperating real estate office. Phone the listing salesman immediately, even if it's ten o'clock at night, tell him you have a deposit on his listing, and ask him to set up an appointment with the sellers so you can present the offer to them. It would be to your advantage, psychologically, if the sellers would agree to come to your office to read the contract. The listing agent's office is the next best place. Presenting a contract in the sellers' home is the poorest location of all, for, surrounded by all the connotations of family, security, and so forth, the sellers will be more reticent to accept or negotiate a contract that offers them less than they had agreed to on the listing contract.

KEEP
TERMS
SECRET
If the listing salesman asks you what the offer is, don't tell him. It's none of his business. As a licensed real estate agent, his sole function at this time is to review a contract for technical

errors and answer his clients' (the sellers) questions, if any. He will have ample opportunity to examine the contract when the sellers are present. Never forget that this listing agent is also a competing salesman. Perhaps he has a party interested in making an offer on the same property. If he finds out what your offer is, he can telephone his people, advise them of the terms of your offer, and thus use this information in an attempt to push his clients into making an offer of their own. Of course, their offer would be just a little better than yours. This is done every day in the business. It is unethical, but that's what you have to be alert to.

Salesmen in your own office are in business for themselves, just as you are. When you have written an offer, never discuss it with your fellow salesmen. Don't tell them what property you have the offer on and don't tell them the price or terms offered. Your broker or manager, of course, should know, because he is responsible for your actions under your license, but keep it a secret from everyone else.

Even if your fellow office salesmen would never think of intentionally using any such information to your disadvantage, they are still in business to make money. If any of them had been working with an interested party on the same property but hadn't been able to get them to write an offer, the knowledge of your offer might be enough to push their client into action.

Only bitterness and lost commissions result from talking about an offer before it is accepted by the seller and the property taken off the market.

DON'T BE FRIVOLOUS Once you have an appointment with the sellers and their agent, be on time. Be businesslike in your manner throughout your association with these people. No seller ever signed his name to a deposit receipt merely because he thought the selling salesman was an entertaining fellow. Make certain your conversation remains focused on the contract.

In most cases, it will be necessary for you to assert yourself when you present an offer. If you wait for the listing salesman to jump on the bandwagon and give an enthusiastic presentation of your offer, you'll die of old age.

Introduce yourself to the sellers. Give each of them one of your business cards so they can look at your name during the course of the evening's discussion. As soon as you are seated, give the contract to the listing salesman so he can review it before he passes it on to the home owners.

There is no need for you to say anything at this time. Sit quietly while the listing agent reads. He might suddenly launch into a magnificient presentation of your contract and get the seller's signature on the deposit receipt before you know what happened. This has happened to me. I like to sit back and see what develops before I begin a lengthy discussion.

SELL YOUR CONTRACT YOURSELF   It is the selling salesman's position, and his job, to sell his contract to the home owners. This is not the listing agent's responsibility, although, when the roles are reversed and someone has an offer on one of my listings, I do my very best to get all reasonable contracts accepted. Since it is your job to sell your contract, be ready to do just that.

After the listing agent has looked over your contract he should hand a copy to the sellers and let them read it. Laymen are not familiar with the forms we use. It takes them a little longer to understand the terms of the offer.

The listing agent should briefly explain the offer to the sellers as soon as they have finished their inspection of it. But if he doesn't do this, don't wait for him. Take the initiative and explain the offer yourself.

Don't ever run down a home to the home owners as the reason for a low offer. A home owner is usually proud of his house, and if he's not proud of it, then he's sensitive about its defects, and certainly won't welcome any critical remarks by a real estate agent.

Don't ever apologize for an offer. I've heard selling salesmen begin their contract presentations to home owners by saying, "I'm sorry about the price but it's the best I could do."

Or, "I know the price is awfully low but my buyers expect a counter offer."

Or worse yet, "You're not going to like this offer. I don't either, but it's as high as the buyer would go."

In some of these instances I know the sellers would have

accepted the offers if the negative remark had not been made by the salesman. After such a remark, the seller would consider himself a dunce if he accepted it without a counter offer.

BE   Be proud of your offers. I always am. I feel
ENTHUSIASTIC   fine whenever someone thinks enough of a
                  property I have shown him to give me a sub-
stantial deposit and sign his name to a deposit receipt. That's a real buyer! His offer deserves consideration. And it deserves an enthusiastic sales effort by you when you present it to the home owners.

Explain the terms of your contract with enthusiasm in your voice. You know how infectious that is.

It is always best not to take a counter offer but if you just cannot overcome the sellers' objections to some of the terms, get a counter offer. Don't you dare leave the sellers' house without getting their signature on that deposit receipt, no matter how drastically it has to be modified.

It's the same principle you followed when you took an offer at the best terms you could get. In that case you had to learn precisely what a buyer would offer. Now, by insisting on a written, signed counter offer, you are learning precisely what a seller will accept. Once you know that, you will be able to bring them to a meeting of the minds.

If a seller objects to price, explain that the true sales price of any home is what a buyer is willing to pay for it and that the offer represents what the home is worth to this particular buyer. The seller may feel confident another buyer will soon come along who will offer more money. Explain that it's the old story of the bird in the hand being worth two in the bush. You have a buyer with money who has expressed an interest in buying the home now. No one can foretell when another buyer might come along. If there are currently more homes for sale than there are buyers (a buyer's market), tell him. Point out the competition he faces.

If your sellers are indignant at a low offer, don't be cowed. Keep a positive attitude throughout your presentation and continue to compliment them on their home. No one can remain angry with you amid a tide of persistent, sincere praise.

Explain that your buyers are so excited about their home they are willing to spend every penny they could muster in hopes of owning it. "If my buyers had more money," you might tell them, "they would be happy to increase their offering price. They just don't have any more." This will successfully counter the sellers' feeling the buyers are trying to "steal" their home from them and cause them to think twice about making a counter offer. Continue to compliment the sellers' home in this vein and they will be inclined to accept your offer as written.

If they seem insistent upon making a counter offer, use my "Las Vegas analogy".

"Mr. and Mrs. Homeowner," you begin, "I want you to be aware of something which may make you think twice about making a counter offer. You're asking forty five thousand dollars for your home. My buyers offered thirty eight thousand dollars. You suggest a counter offer of forty two thousand dollars. By making a counter offer of forty two thousand dollars, you obviously are willing to sell your home for that amount. You and the buyers are four thousand dollars apart.

"By suggesting we make a counter offer to my buyers, you are risking the entire thirty eight thousand dollars my buyers are offering you in hopes of making four thousand dollars. Many times a counter offer scares a buyer away. It's as if you were a gambler in Las Vegas who puts thirty eight thousand dollars on a gambling table hoping to make four thousand dollars. That's a very poor bet. The percentages are all against you. However, doing just the opposite would be a reasonable risk. If you placed four thousand dollars on a gambling table hoping to make thirty eight thousand dollars, you would be making a reasonable bet. But risking thirty eight thousand dollars in an attempt to make four thousand dollars is a highly speculative gamble at best. I suggest you accept the offer as written. Then your home will be sold for a certainty, and you can begin planning your move into your new home."

This brief analogy has persuaded many homeowners to accept an offer as written rather than risk losing a buyer by making a counter offer.

If some of the terms are unacceptable, explain why they were included as they are. Modify them only as a last resort.

Remember, once you have amended the price or terms of a deposit receipt, you have to start all over and sell the buyer again.

POINTS TO KEEP IN MIND

1. Don't discuss the terms of your contract with anyone before you present it to the seller.
2. Be prompt in your appointment with the seller.
3. Be businesslike in your presentation. Don't be frivolous.
4. "Sell" your contract to the sellers. Don't expect help from the listing agent.
5. Don't criticize the sellers' property as an excuse for a low offer.
6. Be enthusiastic about your contract.
7. Don't leave the sellers without getting their signatures, even if you have to take a counter offer.

12

DAILY SCHEDULE
FOR SALESMEN

A SCHEDULE
INCREASES
EARNINGS All real estate salesmen would increase their earnings if they scheduled their time. However, just making a schedule and following it isn't enough. You must constantly assess your results as you work your schedule. You will see changes to be made.

Perhaps you are spending too much time inspecting property and not enough time listing. Perhaps you are not working with enough clients, or you might have too many. Every salesman has a different capacity and aptitude. You might not be devoting enough hours a day to real estate activities in general. Many salesmen suffer from the reciprocal of this. They spend too many hours a week in real estate and don't allow for time off. They become stale on the job. I like my salesmen to take at least one day off each week and three days in succession once a month.

As a real estate salesman, there are three primary activities to which you should devote your time: listing, inspecting property, and showing property to clients.

The keystone of a successful real estate career is listing prowess. Certainly there are exceptions. I have seen salesmen who earn large incomes solely from sales activity. They don't secure three listings a year. And I have seen similarly successful salesmen who devote their time exclusively to listing. They make a sale only if they're forced into it. They don't bother to inspect properties as they come on the market. They don't suffer the frustrations so readily identified with dealing with capricious clients. They spend every working moment listing and presenting offers on their listings. They make a great deal of money. You can be sure of that.

But these highly specialized salesmen are in a class by themselves. Most successful real estate salesmen "work both sides of the stream." Real estate is a sporadic business. Some weeks buyers flock into offices in droves, house hunting with the intensity of locusts going through a wheat field. Other weeks, you couldn't shake a buyer out of a tree to save your soul. It's the same with listing. Some weeks seem more fruitful than others. It goes in cycles. The hard working salesman will always prosper. No matter what phase of the business cycle he happens to be in, he will be able to list and he will be able to sell.

SCHEDULE   Because of the cyclical nature of real estate,
YOUR   there is a great tendency to rely upon one's in-
ACTIVITIES   stinct to decide when the time is right for listing
                  and when more attention should be spent on
selling. This is wrong. That's why a schedule is so important. Your instinct can be wrong as much as it is right, but a schedule won't allow you to get off the track. Yet a good schedule allows for the cyclical peaks we've been discussing.

For example, let's say your schedule calls for intensive listing activity for the next three days. When you arrive at the office in the morning the telephones are ringing off the hooks with clients calling in on an especially appealing newspaper advertisement. The floor man has long since departed with a walk-in client and is out in the field showing him property. The "back up" floor man is also out with a client. No other salesmen are around. The secretary is frantically taking names and phone numbers of clients which she will give to salesmen as they return to the office. Here is an excellent opportunity to pick up a good buyer and make a sale. You should defer your listing plans and leap into the din of sales activity. Schedules are made to be broken. Just make certain you break them only to better your chances of making money.

Figure 12-1 shows a schedule form. You can fill it in as you see fit.

When you make up a schedule for yourself, begin by charting all the time already committed, such as sales meetings, floor time and days off. Then, when you can see just how few working hours are actually left in the week, carefully plot your week's activities.

Figure 12-2 shows a salesman's typical weekly schedule.

Although I don't like to burden salesmen with paperwork, I believe a great benefit will be gained by any sales force if they will check their overall sales performance every so often. I use a form we call a Weekly Sales Report. (See Figure 12-3).

Every two or three months I pass out these forms and have the salesmen use them for several weeks. They are filled out in duplicate. My manager gets the original. It is a very revealing tool, to say the least. This form shows precisely why a salesman is not doing well or how he can improve his performance. Study this form and ask yourself if a similar form might help you.

Figure 12-4 shows an example of this form as it was completed by one of my own salesmen.

As you can see, this form is set up with a measured standard of performance which will net the salesman at least $1,000 per month. The normal activities are listed in separate columns. (D-T-D = door to door; FSBO = for sale by owners; MLS = multiple listing service.) Across the bottom of the form the minimum standards are listed for each activity.

This salesman has to work to meet the minimum standards shown on this form, but he earns $1,000 or more per month.

If you haven't been scheduling your real estate activities, give it a try. Stick to your schedule for two or three months and you'll be amazed at the results.

SCHEDULE OF ACTIVITIES FOR NEW SALESMEN

The Schedule Of Activities For New Salesmen form (Figure 12-5) is possibly the most important training aid of all. It has proved invaluable in speeding new licensees along the road to sales success. Salesmen new to an office are necessarily ill at ease when they report for work in a strange environment. Every office has procedures and routines which differ from those of other offices. It is this uniqueness which

TIME OF DAY

	9-10	10-11	11-12	12-1	1-2	2-3	3-4	4-5	5-6	6-7	7-8	8-9
MONDAY												
TUESDAY												
WEDNESDAY												
THURSDAY												
FRIDAY												
SATURDAY												
SUNDAY												

Figure 12-1
Daily Schedule (Blank)

	9-10	10-11	11-12	12-1	1-2	2-3	3-4	4-5	5-6	6-7	7-8	8-9
MONDAY	←—— Floor Time ——→			Lunch	←—— Inspect Property ——→				←——————— List ———————→			
TUESDAY	←— Inspect Property —→		Phone FSBO / ←— Lunch				List			←——— Show Property ———→		
WEDNESDAY	←——————————— Day Off ———————————→											
THURSDAY	←—— List ——→			←— Lunch	←— Inspect Property —→		←— Open —→		←—— Floor Time ——→			
FRIDAY	←——— Sales Meeting ———→				Lunch	←—— Show Property ——→				←— List —→		
SATURDAY	←—— List ——→			←—— List ——→		Lunch	←— Show Property —→			✕	✕	✕
SUNDAY	✕		←——— List ———→			←—— Hold Home Open ——→				✕	✕	✕

Figure 12-2

Example of Salesman's Schedule

113

WEEKLY SALES REPORT   For week ending _____   Salesman _____

Grade for week's activity [ ]

	Listings inspected	New prospects interviewed	Calls to develop new buyers	Prospects obtained	Prospects worked with	Listings shown	Closing efforts; Sales	Homes held open	Cold canvass phone calls	Cold canvass D-T-D calls	FSBO "ad" calls	FSBO "sign" calls	Expired MLS calls	Closing efforts; Listing	Hours worked	Sales	Listings	Listings sold	Commission earned
MON																			
TUE																			
WED																			
THU																			
FRI																			
SAT																			
SUN																			
Totals																			
Standard	30	10	20	5	5	20	4	1	25	10	10	5	10	10	55		2		$250
Rating																			

Sales 65 activities — Listing 70 activities

A – Excellent   B – Good   C – Fair   D – Poor

Figure 12-3
Weekly Sales Report (Blank)

114

WEEKLY SALES REPORT — For week ending Nov. 15th — Gestor Salesman

Grade for week's activity: (A)

Day	Listings inspected	New prospects interviewed	Calls to develop new buyers	Prospects obtained	Prospects worked with	Listings shown	Closing efforts; Sales	Homes held open	Cold canvass phone calls	Cold canvass D-T-D calls	FSBO "ad" calls	FSBO "sign" calls	Expired MLS calls	Closing efforts; Listing	Hours worked	Sales	Listings	Listings sold	Commission earned
MON	2	1	3				1	1	10	7	4	3	1	2	10				
TUE	4	5		1	1	7	1		5		3	1	4	3	12		1		
WED	← Day Off →														→				
THU	5	2	7	3					5					1	7				
FRI	10	2	4	2	1	6	1		5		4				8				
SAT	4	2	7	1	3	11	1				5		3	2	9	1	1	1	$500
SUN	1	3	7		2	4	2				2				7				
Totals	26	13	21	7	7	28	5	1	25	7	18	4	8	8	53	1	1	1	$500
Standard	30	10	20	5	5	20	4	1	25	10	10	5	10	10	55		2		$250
Rating	B	A	A	A	A	A	A	A	A	B	A	B	B	B	B				

Sales 65 activities — Listing 70 activities

A – Excellent   B – Good   C – Fair   D – Poor

Figure 12-4
Weekly Sales Report (Completed)

GRANADA REALTY

SCHEDULE OF ACTIVITIES FOR NEW SALESMEN

ITEM #	SALESMAN'S NAME:		DATE ITEM COMPLETED	VERIFIED BY
1	Read, sign and return Salesman's Contract and Policy Book.		/////	////
2	Office orientation:		/////	////
	(a) Forms cabinet, files, phones, sign storage	(a)		
	(b) House listing book - Ad book	(b)		
	(c) Procedure for opening and closing office	(c)		
	(d) Use of conference rooms	(d)		
	(e) Sales meeting schedule - Punctuality Pot	(e)		
3	Receive GRANADA REALTY office keys			
4	Receive temporary business cards			
5	Receive GRANADA REALTY Reference Book			
6	Receive FHA sliderule			
7	Receive loan amortization book			
8	Compile blank listing and sales forms			
9	Real Estate Board Functions:		/////	////
	(a) Join Real Estate Board	(a)		
	(b) Purchase Lokbox key from Board office	(b)		
	(c) Secure listing book from Board office	(c)		
	(d) Attend 6 Mart breakfast meetings	(d)		
	(e) Attend Real Estate Board orientation class	(e)		
10	Receive listing computer review from sales manager			
11	Purchase listing binder and listing file box			
12	Purchase 100' tape, claw hammer, 3 lb. sledge hammer			
13	Compile your file of GRANADA REALTY listing information cards.		/////	////
14	Read REAL ESTATE LISTING MAGIC by Gael Himmah			
15	Read REAL ESTATE SELLING MAGIC by Gael Himmah			
16	Read THE LISTING MASTER by Gael Himmah			
17	Inspect all GRANADA REALTY listings			
18	Write 3 sample ads on GRANADA REALTY listings			
19	Inspect new Multiple Listings			
20	Learn to list:		/////	////
	(a) Locate 5 For-Sale-By-Owner listings	(a)		
	(b) Estimate their value from office files	(b)		
	(c) Secure 1st listing	(c)		
	(d) Secure 2nd listing	(d)		
	(e) Secure 3rd listing	(e)		
21	Hold home open 3 Sundays as scheduled			
22	Observe experienced salesmen handling floor time			
23	Get "checked out" on your telephone technique by sales manager		/////	////
24	Be assigned floor time			
25	Attend GRANADA REALTY special training classes for 6 months		/////	////
26	Review your activities semi-monthly with sales manager, as scheduled		/////	////

Figure 12-5
Schedule of Activities For New Salesmen

gives real estate offices their different identities and at the same time causes such uncertainty in the hearts of new associates.

By having a form such as the Schedule Of Activities For New Salesmen and handing it to a new man as soon as he reports for work in your office, he can immediately see what is expected of him. The form I show has 26 different activities the new salesman must complete before he will be considered a full fledged member of the firm. The speed with which he completes the assignments is entirely up to him. He may proceed at his own speed and continue on as quickly as he wishes.

Most of the form is self explanatory. The Salesman's Contract and Policy Book I refer to in Item 1 is shown in its entirety in Appendix A (pages 139–165). Every office should have a written employment contract with each salesman and a Policy Book stating in writing the policies of the broker.

The office orientation in Item 2 refers to a physical tour of the office facilities given the new salesman by the sales manager. So often this is left for the new man to discover by himself.

Items 3, 4, and 5, giving the new man keys to the office, temporary business cards while regular cards are being printed, and handing him a reference book of intra-office forms and how they are to be used again are often overlooked in many offices. See Appendix B (pages 167–227) for the complete GRANADA REALTY Reference Book.

The FHA sliderule referred to in Item 6 is an inexpensive cardboard sliderule-type tool upon which the current FHA loan amortization schedules are printed. They are made available to salesmen by various mortgage lenders as a complimentary service.

The new salesman should immediately compile an inventory of all the blank listing and sales forms he will be using and put them in his briefcase so they will be readily available.

If joining the local real estate board is a requirement in your office, you should advise the new salesman immediately upon his association with you and list each specific step he must take to complete this requirement.

Item 10 refers to a review of the use of the office listing computer. The listing binder and listing file box referred to in Item 11 are methods of storing listings. All offices have their own recommended methods of filing listings.

Item 12 always receives a lot of comment. Salesmen ask why they should purchase a tape measure, a claw hammer and a sledge hammer. The tape is to measure houses, determine property lines, etc. The new salesman is always surprised to find so many uses for his tape measure once he owns one. The claw hammer is for nailing real estate signs to posts. The 3 pound sledge hammer is for driving 2 × 2 sign posts into the front lawns of your new listings. These are all little, easily overlooked items the new man is going to need in short order.

The office secretary will usually help the new associate compile a list of the office listings. These are filed in the listing binder book.

I recommend the new salesman read all three of my real estate books, the two on listing techniques and one on sales procedures. (Real Estate Listing Magic, The Listing Master, Real Estate Selling Magic.) They will give him a head start of several years over the man who isn't exposed to this information. I have in my files hundreds of letters from salesmen all over the country who were kind enough to write to tell me my books made them successful in real estate. Many report they would have dropped out of the industry if it hadn't been for the help they found in the pages of my books. Merely reading the pages won't guarantee your success. You have to learn the material and then apply it.

Next on the Schedule Of Activities is Item 17 wherein the new salesman must leave the office and personally inspect all the office listings. This has a manifold purpose; it not only lets him see what properties the office has for sale, but it teaches him the geography of his new marketing area, gives him an introduction to the relative prices of properties, and gives him a sense of becoming directly involved in the business.

After the new man inspects the office listings, he is instructed in Item 18 to write 3 sample ads on the properties he has just seen. This makes him put into words his impressions of the houses he has inspected. This causes him to think about the listings. There's no substitute for thinking!

Inspecting the new multiple listings is usually done in an office tour on the days when the listings are published. The sales manager normally advises the new man on that.

Item 20 directs the new salesman to learn to list and outlines 5 steps he must follow. This is discussed in more detail in Chapter 13, page 121.

Items 21, 22, and 23 are self explanatory and continue the salesman's training. Finally, by the time the new man gets to Item 24, he is assigned floor time. He is NEVER assigned floor time until he has completed the previous 23 items and has secured three listings. This is extremely important. If a new salesman is assigned floor time immediately upon his association with the office, he will certainly not know what he is doing, but more significantly, he will usually develop in the classic non productive pattern of becoming a selling salesman, forever neglecting listing. Listing requires more "learning" than selling. If the new salesman is allowed to begin selling without first being required to put in the effort necessary to learn to list, he will probably never be worth a hill of beans as a listor. The complete salesman both lists and sells. But listing should come first.

The final two items refer to a continuing training program successful offices offer their salesmen, combined with regularly scheduled reviews of each man's performance.

Close adherence to a similar schedule, which can easily be modified to your own office's particular needs, will improve the performance of your present salesmen, markedly help the new salesmen, and lower your salesman turnover rate drastically. Give it a try!

POINTS TO KEEP IN MIND

1. *Constantly amend your schedule to keep it current.*
2. *Scheduling your activities keeps you in the mainstream of sales activities. You don't have to rely on your instinct of market conditions.*

13

HOW TO DEVELOP CONFIDENCE IN YOURSELF

Webster defines confidence as "assurance of one's own ability." Any highly skilled person cannot be considered a professional until he gains that elusive element—confidence. A real estate man without self-confidence is certainly not a professional. He can't hope to compete with his well-trained, highly educated, self-confident colleagues.

Confidence, then, is the measure of a man who not only has learned the techniques of his profession but has gained that comfortable feeling of knowing what he's doing. He knows his job well, and it shows. The confident real estate man radiates self-assurance and success.

It's all well and good to talk about confidence. Many beginning salesmen feel they will never gain the confidence they need to become successful. They worry so much about the mechanics of financing and the mysteries of the many documents that self-confidence seems as remote as success itself.

Whenever I think of what confidence means I remember an incident that happened in my office many years ago.

I had hired a new salesman who had been on the job about three weeks. He was very bright, very personable, and very energetic, a combination that spelled success. His first weeks

in the business were spent in the normal pursuits of tyro salesmen. He spent time in the office arranging his listings, and time
away from the office. He asked the right questions and demonstrated proper spirit. This young man was on his way.

And then, like an unexpected revelation, I realized he wasn't
producing. For all his hustle and bustle and drive, he hadn't
secured a single listing nor made a sale. I had to find out why.

I stopped by his desk as he sat there filing multiple listing
cards.

"How's it going?" I asked.

"Great," was the earnest reply. "As soon as I finish filing these
cards I'm going out to get a listing that was promised to me."

I was greatly relieved.

Several days later I realized this salesman had not yet produced a listing. Again I stopped by his desk for a chat. This
time he was busily snipping For-Sale-By-Owner ads from the
newspaper.

"How's it going?" I asked again.

"Great," he replied. "See all the listing leads I have? As soon
as I finish getting the ads out of the paper I'm off to get a
listing."

"What happened to the listing you were going to get a few
days ago?" I asked.

"They had already listed with someone else. I just can't
understand it."

I didn't want him to get discouraged.

"That's all right," I said in my most comforting tone. "That
happens to all of us. You just can't trust home owners when
they make proimses to salesmen. Don't get discouraged. You're
going to do just fine."

Several more days passed. Still no listing. He had several
opportunities to take walk-in clients and in each case he dutifully asked all the questions on the Client Interview Sheet
before he showed them property. In fact, he was so methodical
in his qualification questioning that he spent over an hour on
this one activity with each client, and he never got around to
showing any property at all.

I asked him about this, mentioning that he seemed to be
spending too much time qualifying his buyers. He replied that

he wasn't about to waste his time showing property to people who were "lookers." And sure enough, he asked so many questions for so long a time that all his clients succeeded in convincing him they were only lookers.

The time had come for us to have a long, broker-to-salesman talk. After much conversation he finally confessed his lack of self-confidence. He was unsure of his knowledge and ability as a sophisticated real estate salesman. He was a perfectionist by nature. It was important to him that people respect him for his professionalism and he knew they would rapidly discover his shortcomings when they talked to him.

He said he needed more time to study, more time to familiarize himself with the mechanics of the business before he opened himself up to the critical eye of the public. He confessed he hadn't been making as many calls as he led me to believe. His listing appointments were figments of his imagination.

For weeks thereafter this salesman studied, made charts of his activities, filed listing cards, answered the phone, and kept himself busy. But he wouldn't go out and talk to people. He was afraid of people! I knew this was true. For all his superior intelligence and personable demeanor, he was afraid of being refused. He was scared to death someone would say "no" to him.

DON'T FEAR REJECTION   This fear of being refused is a serious problem to salesmen. It makes them rationalize their failures. It keeps them from calling on their clients and literally drives some to drink.

The only cure for this malady is confidence in one's ability. The only way to achieve confidence is to practice your new found skills until they become second nature to you.

I tell new salesmen in my office, after they have assimilated all the intra-office detail, "Go out and talk to sellers. Try to get a listing. Knock on some doors. Get yourself insulted!"

You will never feel at ease talking to buyers or sellers until you have done it so many times that you realize you can master any situation. It doesn't take as long as you might expect before you find you know the answers your clients ask. You get a good feeling when they begin asking you questions and taking your advice. In short, clients begin to treat you as a professional because, with a little practice on the "firing line," you have finally gained that wondrous facet of true professionalism—confidence.

Some men enter real estate with great self-confidence and no knowledge. They usually have an easier time of it. They follow their broker's advice to the letter and, not having a fear of their clients, they go out and make sales and secure listings while they're still as green as peas.

One of my salesmen came to me while he was a carpenter. He was sure of his ability but admitted he knew nothing of real estate. He tore into my training program like a man possessed, learned my system to the letter, let me help him prepare a time schedule, followed my advice, and worked like a demon. I paid him over $10,000 in commissions in his first five months in the business.

Another salesman I hired was an 18-year old girl. She looked younger than her years and spoke so softly you could scarcely hear her. I had serious reservations about hiring her but something about her demeanor overcame my first impulse and I decided to give her an opportunity to prove herself.

She was an instant success. Much to the chagrin of some of the other salesmen who were older, wiser, and lazier, she became a bearcat as soon as I pinned her license to my wall. She called clients on the phone, all hours of the night, and insisted they inspect several homes she had found "just for them." She wouldn't take "no" for an answer. She chased listing leads down like an Indian scout. Clients were often amused at her apparent youth when they first met her. And they were rapidly impressed.

She began to sell very expensive property. Her reputation grew by leaps and bounds. People called in for her, insisting on doing business only with her.

After several years of outstanding success and thrifty attention to her money, she purchased a huge piece of real estate in the center of town. This was an investment. It is going to make her rich.

This girl succeeded so dramatically because she had confidence in herself. She wasn't afraid of people. She wouldn't be refused. She learned the details of the business by practice. Together, knowledge and confidence make a formidable sales tool. At the ripe old age of twenty-one she retired from active business life. She married and is now raising a family.

That is a sterling example of what confidence can do for you. Don't hide behind the protective screen of "lack of knowledge." You can have confidence and not know a thing! Although such a condition can have its liabilities, people of this ilk rely on confidence to get them by until their knowledge catches up.

The easiest way is to develop confidence and knowledge at the same time. If you don't have confidence in your ability, don't sit there and brood about it. Get out of the protective cloister of your office and talk to people. Talk about real estate. Knock on some doors. Get a listing. If someone says, "No" to you, say "So what" to yourself and go on to the next house. It'll be easier next time.

Don't expect your broker to impart confidence to you like some miraculous angel. Get it for yourself, by working with clients! That's the only way, and it's really quite painless.

BUILDING CONFIDENCE IN 3 DAYS   One of the most crucial periods for a real estate salesman pursuant to motivation and the development of self confidence is the first few weeks of the new man's tenure in his new profession. I have developed a method of instilling a prodigious amount of self confidence in new salesmen by carefully scheduling their first three days in the business. Give me a new man for this first three days and I can make him a winner!

A bold statement, but true. Let me describe this procedure for you. Imagine it is your first day in real estate and I am your sales manager. I take you into my office and we have a talk.

"I'm going to tell you everything I want you to do in the next three days," I begin. "I don't want you to do anything other than what I tell you to do. Each day, when you have completed the tasks I have assigned you, I want you to go home, or go shopping, or play a round of golf. Just don't do anything else in real estate for the day.

"Today, as soon as we finish talking, I want you to get into your car and drive around the residential neighborhoods in this part of town. Just drive around. I don't want you getting out of your car and talking to people. At this stage of your career you don't know how to talk intelligently about real estate.

"Just drive around and look for For-Sale-By-Owner signs in the front lawns of homes. Whenever you see a For-Sale-By-Owner sign, jot the address down on a piece of paper. And do one more thing. Slow down when you see a For-Sale-By-Owner sign and take an extra look at the house. As you drive away, try to imagine what the house might sell for. I know you don't know the prices of properties, but I want you to make a guess. I don't care if you're one hundred thousand dollars off. I want you to guess. Then write that figure on your note pad next to the address of the house.

"When you have five addresses and five estimates of value, come back here to the office. We have complete files of the sales prices of all properties sold in the city, filed alphabetically, according to street name. (If your office does not maintain such files, your real estate board probably does. Use their files.) Look in our files and see how close your guesses were to the sales prices of properties selling on that street or in the same area. Often you will find sales for the very homes you have noted on your paper. Can you do that?" I ask. You tell me you can, and you're on your way.

The second day I again outline your day's activity. "Today I want you to drive back to two of the five For-Sale-By-Owner houses you located yesterday. But this time I want you to stop your car at each of the two, go to the front door, ring the bell, introduce yourself, and then compliment the homeowner on some aspect of his home. You can always find something nice to say about a property if you take the trouble to look and think while you're walking up to the front door.

"Perhaps there is a nice lawn, or a pretty garden, or lovely trees, or the house has a new coat of paint. If you can't find anything about the house that strikes your fancy, you can always say, 'This is one of the nicest neighborhoods we sell houses in.' No one is going to be angry with you for complimenting them."

I don't leave anything to a new salesman's imagination. I tell them every word to say. "When the housewife answers the door, hand her your business card. She will probably tell you she's not going to list her house with the real estate people. You tell her you aren't there to get a listing. Say, 'I was just driving down the street on my way to an appointment and I happened to see your sign in the front lawn. You have such a beautiful front yard, it's so well cared for, that I had to stop and tell you. This is a lovely home. You should be able to sell it. I wish you luck.' With that, you walk back to your car, get in, and drive away. That's all I want you to do. You won't get rejected because you aren't going to ask for anything. No one is going to be mad at you because you aren't going to put anyone on the defensive. You're only going to compliment the two people you talk to. Just a compliment, and you're on your way. Do you think you can do that?" Again, you assure me you can.

On the third day I say, "Today I want you to drive back to the other three homes you found two days ago. This time I want you to do just what you did yesterday. Compliment the housewife when she answers the door. Tell her something nice about her house. And then ask her three questions. Say to her, 'You have a lovely home. How much are you asking? Have you had any offers? How long has your home been on the market?' "

I explain to you that these are the first of what I call my Ten Magic Questions, the basis for my listing technique. (See REAL ESTATE LISTING MAGIC and THE LISTING MASTER by Gael Himmah for full discussions of the Ten Magic Questions and a detailed description of listing procedures.) Again, you assure me you can complete this assignment. And you will do it.

That's all there is to it! The first three days of a spanking new salesman's career seem simple enough, but upon closer inspection these apparently simple tasks have a profound influence upon the course of the salesman's entire career. The first day the new salesman not only learned how to prospect for listings by driving around residential neighborhoods looking for For-Sale-By-Owner signs, but he took his first steps in overcoming one of the most intimidating conditions facing the inexperienced real estate salesman—learning to appraise property. He learned how to go back to the office and check out the addresses in the office files, and he came up with the sales prices of comparable properties. And he did this by himself! He thought appraising was a mysterious gift reserved for the chosen few who had long tenure in the industry. And now, his first day in the business, he's already learned to do it himself. What a confidence booster!

The second day, by having a new man talk to homeowners by himself, he discovers that he doesn't need a sales manager or a broker or two or three other salesmen to hold his hand. He discovers that people are pretty nice when given the opportunity.

The third day he has begun to learn the basic listing technique described in my listing books. But far more important, each of the three days just passed have found the new salesman successfully completing every task assigned to him. Unknown to him, he has subconsciously begun to develop a habit pattern of successful performance. I was careful to assign the new salesman only tasks which I knew he could perform successfully. I believe in the power of psycho cybernetics—the programming of one's self for successful performance. (See THE LISTING MASTER by Gael Himmah for a discussion of this.)

This is precisely where the training programs in many offices fail dismally. They assign new salesmen goals that are difficult, if not impossible to achieve. For example, a new salesman might be told to go out and get a listing. That's all he's told. It's his work assignment. And for the next ninety days he flails around trying to get a listing when he hasn't been shown the necessary steps to go through to secure a listing. Every day, for the first three months of his real estate career, this man returns to the office a failure. He has established a habit pattern of failure whether he recognizes it or not. Soon failure becomes a habit he can't break and real estate has lost another potentially good salesman.

I believe in the simple task approach to confidence building. I have seen many new men return to the office, their eyes gleaming with excitement, for they have completed another assignment successfully. They know they're getting someplace. And I know they are too!

THE MYTH   Confidence building is closely related to sales-
OF GOAL   man motivation. I disagree with most of the so-
SETTING   called motivation experts. I have found their
most cherished theories don't work. The com-
mon denominator of every motivational expert I have ever
heard or read is this; Set a goal for yourself. They travel around
the country preaching this goal-setting gospel as if they were
divine oracles descended upon the earth with a message of
infinite wisdom.

It sounds good, I must agree. But it doesn't work for the new
man in real estate. Assume you are a brand new salesman and
I am your sales manager and I tell you I'm going to set a goal
for you. I tell you to go out and get ten listings. That's certainly
a goal. But you don't have the slightest idea of how to achieve
your goal. Hence, the failing of the goal setting dictum.

I remember many years ago, before I had entered real estate,
a gentleman came to San Francisco who was billed as the
greatest motivation expert of his day. I decided I should hear
him speak. I went to the Fairmont Hotel where three dollars
was charged at the door as an admission fee.

For the next two hours I sat in complete boredom as this
pompous, slow witted speaker droned on and on. There was
practically no content to his speech. I couldn't associate him
with his reputation. Finally, he said, "Do you want to get
motivated?"

Ah, he'd struck a responsive nerve. Everyone shook awake
from their reverie. I held my pencil ready. This was what I had
been waiting for.

"This is the secret of motivation," he began. "Set a goal for
yourself."

I wrote that down on my paper. "Set a goal for yourself."

"Take a money goal," he shouted across the room.

I wrote, "a money goal" on my paper.

"Take twenty five thousand dollars," he said.

Now we were getting someplace. Twenty five thousand
dollars was a lot of money. I wrote "$25,000" on my paper.

"Here's how you can assure yourself of earning twenty five
thousand dollars in the next year."

I was getting excited. This was going to be worth every penny of the three dollar admission fee.

"Tonight," he purred into the microphone, "when you get home, go directly into your bathroom and write your goal on the bathroom mirror in shaving soap. Write twenty five thousand dollars on your mirror so that every morning the first thing you will see will be your goal. Then take a piece of paper and write your goal on it and put it in your wallet or your purse so that for the next year every time you reach into your wallet you will see your goal."

He stepped back from the lectern and looked haughtily over the spellbound audience. "Now you have it," he whispered. "My secret of success."

I could hardly wait to get home. I ran into the bathroom, grabbed a bar of soap, and just as I started to write on the mirror a thought flashed across my mind. If it's that easy, I think I'll give myself a raise! I wrote "$30,000" on the mirror. Instead of one piece of paper, I took four pieces of paper and wrote "$30,000" on each of them and put one in each of my pockets.

For the next year I was the biggest litterbug in Northern California. Everywhere I went pieces of paper with "$30,000" written on them kept falling out of my pockets. My goal was firmly fixed in my mind every moment of that year. But when the year ended, I didn't have any more money than the previous year. The only one who had any more money was the motivation speaker who had my three dollar admission fee.

I learned from that to look with a jaundiced eye upon simple methods of success, simple methods of gaining wealth, and simple methods of salesman motivation. They are complicated subjects. (See THE LISTING MASTER by Gael Himmah for a discussion of salesman motivation.)

Salesman motivation as I have presented it in THE LISTING MASTER has many facets but it can be outlined in three basic points; set sub-goals for yourself, work alone, and know what to say. Sub-goals rather than main goals make the difference in motivation and thus in confidence building. The new salesman who hasn't the slightest idea how to get a listing will get right to work when I outline for him the easy steps just described in the first three days in a salesman's career. Hence, you can see the sub-goal theory rather than the main goal theory gets results.

Working alone is as necessary for success in real estate as working in an office with a good training program. Real estate is a business for loners. I say it over and over again. The money makers in my profession rely upon themselves. They work alone.

And finally, knowing what to say is of paramount importance in an industry where the spoken word is your primary means of communication. In my three real estate books you will find the exact words to say in all situations, both selling and listing.

POINTS TO KEEP IN MIND

1. You must be confident of your ability in order to be truly professional.
2. Don't be afraid someone will say, "No."
3. Get out and talk to people.
4. Don't delay gaining confidence until you feel you have developed knowledge of real estate subjects. Develop knowledge and confidence together.
5. Set sub-goals for yourself.
6. Work alone.
7. Learn what to say.

14

A DAY IN THE LIFE
OF A SUCCESSFUL
SALESMAN

"What is the real estate business like?" is a question asked time and again by beginning salesmen. Here follows a typical working day of a successful salesman:

He rises at 7:30 A.M. As he showers, he goes over his day's activities. He has scheduled himself to make cold canvass telephone calls for 15 minutes after he arrives in the office. If any seem promising he'll follow up on them immediately.

After his calls he'll inspect new listings for several hours. He has a client who is going to buy in the next few days. This client is very specific in his desires, so our salesman wants to show him only those properties that seem to meet his requirements. He knows he will have to search out the few homes that will appeal to him.

In the afternoon he will follow some listing leads developed several days ago from For-Sale-By-Owner newspaper ads.

He has a four o'clock appointment to show property to his client who is actually living in a motel until he is able to buy a house. Our salesman will be busy all day.

HE MAKES   He arrives in the office a little before nine
LISTING   o'clock. He checks his message box, finds nothing
CALLS   urgent, and immediately begins calling home
owners to develop listing leads. He uses the "reverse" street-address telephone directory which lists addresses,
names and phone numbers of telephone subscribers alphabetically by street name. He has selected a neighborhood where
listings are at a premium. His calls are short and to the point.
As soon as the party answers the phone he says,

"Hello, this is Bob Turner from Granada Realty. When are
you going to be selling your home?"

That's all he says. The home owner knows he's in the real
estate business and knows what he wants. The direct question
takes them by surprise but they react favorably to the candor of
the salesman. Many times they will ask him how he found out
they had decided to sell. Whenever that happens, he has a
prime listing lead.

On this particular morning he didn't get any good leads from
his telephone canvassing. Now he is going to have to find some
property to show his client this afternoon. A four-bedroom, two
story colonial with separate family and dining rooms and a
swimming pool, priced under $45,000, within walking distance
of schools and shops, yet secluded, is a tough bill to fill. His
client has expressed a desire for a house with character.

He sits back in his chair and thinks about all the homes he
has seen in the last few weeks. He makes note of several.
He checks his catalog of current multiple listings for others. He
quickly scans Realtor ads in the newspaper to see if any homes
sound like what he's looking for. Presently he has compiled a
list of 16 properties which he has not seen personally and which
have the general qualifications demanded by his client.

HE   He signs out of the office until four o'clock
INSPECTS   and begins his inspection tour. It would take all
PROPERTY   day to thoroughly inspect 16 different homes,
but this isn't necessary. He eliminates some
homes as he drives down the street and looks at the property
from his car. He knows that the neighborhood, or the block, or
the house next door, or the home itself just wouldn't suit his
client.

Of the homes he inspects personally, he doesn't spend more than five minutes in each one. He wants to get the "feel" of each house. This he accomplishes as soon as he steps through the front door. He chats briefly with the housewife, asks her what she thinks are the outstanding characteristics of her home, checks the floor plan, inspects the various rooms and the yard and he leaves for the next property. He makes a few notes to himself on the listing information card to remind him of each house and then he is on his way. He actually spends more time traveling from house to house than he does inspecting.

MORE LISTING CALLS   He finishes his tour of homes at 12:30 and stops at a restaurant for lunch. Then he spends the next several hours making calls, in person, on owners who have been advertising their homes for sale in the newspaper. Several days ago he had telephoned each of these advertisers and learned their addresses. (For a detailed discussion of this subject, see *Real Estate Listing Magic* and *The Listing Master* by Gael Himmah.)

Now he calls on each of these home owners and begins his listing technique of asking the "Ten Magic Questions." (See Exhibit B-10, page 178.) By the time his four o'clock appointment is nearing, he has excellent leads on two listings which he will follow up on the first evening or weekend he has free. He must wait until the husband is home from work before he can make his final listing presentation to these home owners.

Returning to his office to wait for his client, he finds a message to call a salesman who works for another real estate firm. He calls him and learns that the other salesman has an offer to present on one of his listings.

He phones his delighted sellers with this information, makes an appointment for 7:30 that evening to present the offer and calls the other salesman back to give him the time. They will meet at the sellers' home to present the offer.

HE SHOWS PROPERTY   His client arrives. He has selected five homes to show him. The client is very enthusiastic about one home but it is not close to schools or shops, one of his basic requirements. The salesman explains that no home will meet all of the client's requirements. This particular home, he points out, has the bedrooms, dining room, family room, swimming pool, floor plan, architectural style and price the client wants. It is in a secluded, woodsy setting and has loads of charm. He further explains that in our country-type area, no one lives next to both schools and shops.

There are no little grocery stores sprinkled about the country-side and there are not a great number of small schools. Instead, there are several large shopping centers and several large schools. The children are bussed to the schools and are conveniently picked up right at the corner by the bus. It is no problem to drive a mile to the supermarket as our country roads are not congested. The large stores offer much better prices and a greater variety of merchandise than the small neighborhood stores the client had in mind.

The client accepts this information, is satisfied by it, and agrees to sign a deposit receipt which had been filled out in the car while it was parked in front of the house. There are still two more homes on the tour which he hasn't shown his cilent. Since the client has already found what he wants and is ready to buy, it would be foolish to continue inspecting homes.

When he arrives back at his office he makes a phone call to the listing agent with news of his contract. An appointment is made to present this offer at 9:30 that evening.

He rushes home for dinner, making certain he will be ready for his two evening appointments.

This might sound as if a real estate salesman works awfully hard. He does! And he gets paid for it. If his listing sells and his offer is accepted for his client, he will have earned nearly $1,000 for his day's work. That's worth working for.

Now it's up to you. Selling real estate is really not difficult. Your initial meeting with the client is the key to your success. You have to take the initiative.

Be a salesman.

Ask the questions.

Show several homes and write a deposit receipt.

POINTS TO KEEP IN MIND

Don't complicate the functions of selling real estate. Don't let your client lead you. He wants your direction, so give it to him.

Your next client will be a sale.
Remember, stand up and greet him warmly.
Remember, "You picked a good one."
Remember, "Which house did you like best?"
Remember, confidence comes from practice.

APPENDIX A

THE POLICY BOOK

The Policy Book used by my real estate company is reproduced in this Appendix. Such a manual is invaluable in the progressive firm. It can easily be tailored to fit your own needs.

INTRODUCTION

Welcome to GRANADA REALTY.

We are active members of the Contra Costa Board of Realtors, Multiple Listing Service, the California Real Estate Association, and the National Association of Real Estate Boards.

GRANADA REALTY is a sole proprietorship owned by GAEL HIMMAH, who is licensed as a Real Estate Broker and Business Opportunity Broker. The Executive Staff consists of the President, Gael Himmah, and a Vice-President.

In making your decision for real estate, you have chosen well. In selecting GRANADA REALTY as your vehicle to success, you have put your trust in our company. That trust must foster a bond of mutual respect if we are to succeed. The careful study of this manual will insure a mutually profitable association.

The purpose of this manual is to stabilize the activities of the members of this company so together we will expand our reputation as an ethical, active, professional real estate company.

Every GRANADA REALTY licensee must conduct himself and his activities with honor, integrity, and high moral principles. GRANADA REALTY is dedicated to the tenets of professional and ethical conduct in our associations with the public and one another.

GENERAL POLICIES

BROKER-SALESMAN RELATIONSHIP

The Broker is responsible for the acts of his salesmen. Salesmen must keep this in mind at all times. Don't perform any act which would prejudice your license or that of the Broker.

GRANADA REALTY salesmen, and brokers associated with GRANADA REALTY as salesmen (hereinafter referred to as 'salesmen'), are required to work under the standard GRANADA REALTY Broker-Salesman Contract. Advice of association and termination must be maintained on record with the Division of Real Estate and is the responsibility of the salesman. All policies and procedures outlined in this manual are applicable to all sales personnel associated with GRANADA REALTY.

Read the Real Estate Law of the State of California. Salesmen of GRANADA REALTY are required to conform to every tenet of the law.

GRANADA REALTY salesmen are required to subscribe to the Code of Ethics of the National Association of Real Estate Boards and the Code of Practices of the California Real Estate Association. These Codes are included herein for ready reference.

CODE OF ETHICS
NATIONAL ASSOCIATION OF REAL ESTATE BOARDS

Preamble

UNDER all is the land. Upon its wise utilization and widely allocated ownership depend the survival and growth of free institutions and of our civilization. The Realtor is the instrumentality through which the land resource of the nation reaches its highest use and through which land ownership attains its widest distribution. He is a creator of homes, a builder of cities, a developer of industries and productive farms.

Such functions impose obligations beyond those of ordinary commerce. They impose grave social responsibility and a patriotic duty to which the Realtor should dedicate himself, and for which he should be diligent in preparing himself. The Realtor, therefore, is zealous to maintain and improve the standards of his calling and shares with his fellow-Realtors a common responsibility for its integrity and honor.

In the interpretation of his obligations, he can take no safer guide than that which has been handed down through twenty centuries, embodied in the Golden Rule:

"Whatsoever ye would that men should do to you, do ye even so to them."

Accepting this standard as his own, every Realtor pledges himself to observe its spirit in all his activities and to conduct his business in accordance with the following Code of Ethics:

Part I
Relations to the Public

ARTICLE 1.
The Realtor should keep himself informed as to movements affecting real estate in his community, state, and the nation, so that he may be able to contribute to public thinking on matters of taxation, legislation, land use, city planning, and other questions affecting property interests.

ARTICLE 2.
It is the duty of the Realtor to be well informed on current market conditions in order to be in a position to advise his clients as to the fair market price.

ARTICLE 3.
It is the duty of the Realtor to protect the public against fraud, misrepresentation or unethical practices in the real estate field.

He should endeavor to eliminate in his community any practices which could be damaging to the public or to the dignity and integrity of the real estate profession. The Realtor should assist the board or commission charged with regulating the practices of brokers and salesmen in his state.

ARTICLE 4.
The Realtor should ascertain all pertinent facts concerning every property for which he accepts the agency, so that he may fulfill his obligation to avoid error, exaggeration, misrepresentation, or concealment of pertinent facts.

ARTICLE 5.
The Realtor should not be instrumental in introducing into a neighborhood a character of property or use which will clearly be detrimental to property values in that neighborhood.

ARTICLE 6.
The Realtor should not be a party to the naming of a false consideration in any document, unless it be the naming of an obviously nominal consideration.

ARTICLE 7.
The Realtor should not engage in activities that constitute the practice of law and should recommend that title be examined and legal counsel be obtained when the interest of either party requires it.

ARTICLE 8.
The Realtor should keep in a special bank account, separated from his own funds, monies coming into his possession in trust for other persons, such as escrows, trust funds, client's monies and other like items.

ARTICLE 9.
The Realtor in his advertising should be especially careful to present a true picture and should neither advertise without disclosing his name, nor permit his salesmen to use individual names or telephone numbers, unless the salesman's connection with the Realtor is obvious in the advertisement.

ARTICLE 10.
The Realtor, for the protection of all parties with whom he deals, should see that financial obligations and commitments regarding real estate transactions are in writing, expressing the exact agreement of the parties; and that copies of such agreements, at the time they are executed, are placed in the hands of all parties involved.

Part II
Relations to the Client

ARTICLE 11.
In accepting employment as an agent, the Realtor pledges himself to protect and promote the interests of the client. This obligation of absolute fidelity to the client's interest is primary, but it does not relieve the Realtor from the obligation of dealing fairly with all parties to the transaction.

ARTICLE 12.
In justice to those who place their interests in his care, the Realtor should endeavor always to be informed regarding laws, proposed legislation, governmental orders, and other essential information and public policies which affect those interests.

ARTICLE 13.
Since the Realtor is representing one or another party to a transaction, he should not accept compensation from more than one party without the full knowledge of all parties to the transaction.

ARTICLE 14.
The Realtor should not acquire an interest in or buy for himself, any member of his immediate family, his firm or any member thereof, or any entity in which he has a substantial ownership interest, property listed with him, or his firm, without making the true position known to the listing owner, and in selling property owned by him, or in which he has such interest, the facts should be revealed to the purchaser.

ARTICLE 15.
The exclusive listing of property should be urged and practiced by the Realtor as a means of preventing dissension and misunderstanding and of assuring better service to the owner.

ARTICLE 16.
When acting as agent in the management of property, the Realtor should not accept any commission, rebate or profit on expenditures made for an owner, without the owner's knowledge and consent.

ARTICLE 17.
The Realtor should not undertake to make an appraisal that is outside the field of his experience unless he obtains the assistance of an authority on such types of property, or unless the facts are fully disclosed to the client. In such circumstances the authority so engaged should be so identified and his contribution to the assignment should be clearly set forth.

ARTICLE 18.
When asked to make a formal appraisal of real property, the Realtor should not render an opinion without careful and thorough analysis and interpretation of all factors affecting the value of the property. His counsel constitutes a professional service.

The Realtor should not undertake to make an appraisal or render an opinion of value on any property where he has a present or contemplated interest unless such interest is specifically disclosed in the appraisal report. Under no circumstances should he undertake to make a formal appraisal when his employment or fee is contingent upon the amount of his appraisal.

ARTICLE 19.
The Realtor should not submit or advertise property without authority and in any offering, the price quoted should not be other than that agreed upon with the owners as the offering price.

ARTICLE 20.
In the event that more than one formal written offer on a specific property is made before the owner has accepted an offer, any other formal written offer presented to the Realtor, whether by a prospective purchaser or another broker, should be transmitted to the owner for his decision.

Part III
Relations to His Fellow-Realtor

ARTICLE 21.

The Realtor should seek no unfair advantage over his fellow-Realtors and should willingly share with them the lessons of his experience and study.

ARTICLE 22.

The Realtor should so conduct his business as to avoid controversies with his fellow-Realtors. In the event of a controversy between Realtors who are members of the same local board, such controversy should be arbitrated in accordance with regulations of their board rather than litigated.

ARTICLE 23.

Controversies between Realtors who are not members of the same local board should be submitted to an arbitration board consisting of one arbitrator chosen by each Realtor from the real estate board to which he belongs or chosen in accordance with the regulations of the respective boards. One other member, or a sufficient number of members to make an odd number, should be selected by the arbitrators thus chosen.

ARTICLE 24.

When the Realtor is charged with unethical practice, he should place all pertinent facts before the proper tribunal of the member board of which he is a member, for investigation and judgment.

ARTICLE 25.

The Realtor should not voluntarily disparage the business practice of a competitor, nor volunteer an opinion of a competitor's transaction. If his opinion is sought it should be rendered with strict professional integrity and courtesy.

ARTICLE 26.

The agency of a Realtor who holds an exclusive listing should be respected. A Realtor cooperating with a listing broker should not invite the cooperation of a third broker without the consent of the listing broker.

ARTICLE 27.

The Realtor should cooperate with other brokers on property listed by him exclusively whenever it is in the interest of the client, sharing commissions on a previously agreed basis. Negotiations concerning property listed exclusively with one broker should be carried on with the listing broker, not with the owner, except with the consent of the listing broker.

ARTICLE 28.

The Realtor should not solicit the services of an employee or salesman in the organization of a fellow-Realtor without the knowledge of the employer.

ARTICLE 29.

Signs giving notice of property for sale, rent, lease or exchange should not be placed on any property by more than one Realtor, and then only if authorized by the owner, except as the property is listed with and authorization given to more than one Realtor.

ARTICLE 30.

In the best interest of society, of his associates and of his own business, the Realtor should be loyal to the real estate board of his community and active in its work.

CONCLUSION

The term *Realtor* has come to connote competence, fair dealing and high integrity resulting from adherence to a lofty ideal of moral conduct in business relations. No inducement of profit and no instructions from clients ever can justify departure from this ideal, or from the injunctions of this Code.

The Code of Ethics was adopted in 1913. Amended at the Annual Convention in 1924, 1928, 1950, 1951, 1952, 1955, 1956, 1961, and 1962.

CODE OF PRACTICES
OF THE
CALIFORNIA REAL ESTATE ASSOCIATION

1. It is the responsibility of a Realtor to offer equal service to all clients without regard to race, color, religion, or national origin in the sale, purchase, exchange, rental, or lease of real property.

   a. A Realtor should stand ready to show property to any member of any racial, creedal, or ethnic group.

   b. A Realtor has a legal and ethical responsibility to receive all offers and to communicate them to the property owner. The Realtor being but an agent, the right of decision must be with the property owner.

    c. A Realtor should exert his best efforts to conclude the transaction.

2. Realtors, individually and collectively, in performing their agency functions, have no right or responsibility to determine the racial, creedal, or ethnic composition of any neighborhood or any part thereof.

    a. A Realtor shall not advise property owners to incorporate in a listing of property an exclusion of sale to any such group.

    b. A Realtor may take a listing which insists upon such exclusions, but only if it is lawfully done at the property owner's insistance without any influence whatsoever by the agent.

3. Any attempt by a Realtor to solicit or procure the sale or other disposition in residential area by conduct intended to implant fears in property owners based upon the actual or anticipated introduction of a minority group into an area shall subject the Realtor to disciplinary action. Any technique that induces panic selling is a violation of ethics and must be strongly condemned.

4. Each Realtor should feel completely free to enter into a broker-client relationship with persons of any race, creed, or ethnic group.

    a. Any conduct inhibiting said relationships is a specific violation of the rules and regulations of the board, and shall subject the violating Realtor to disciplinary action.

The Broker is available to all GRANADA REALTY licensees at all times to help them in any way he can. Don't feel you are imposing upon him with your questions or problems. He welcomes the opportunity of meeting with you.

SALESMAN-SALESMAN RELATIONSHIP

The spirit of cooperation between GRANADA REALTY salesmen is an extraordinary benefit accruing to all licensees of the company. Be ready to help your fellow GRANADA REALTY salesman at all times. You can be certain the courtesy will be returned one hundred fold.

SALESMAN—CLIENT RELATIONSHIP

Personal problems or business problems of clients should be kept strictly confidential. Keep in touch with buyers and sellers after the close of an escrow. Building goodwill should be of paramount concern to every salesman. At least 50 per cent of an experienced salesman's prospects for both listing and selling are referrals from previous business associations.

ETHICS

As defined by Webster, the word "Ethics" means the "principles of ideal moral conduct." Such principles must govern every action in our associations with clients and fellow licensees.

By being constantly aware of our moral obligations, GRANADA REALTY has enjoyed the benefits that accrue to a real estate firm employing sound ethical practices as a standard sales procedure.

PERSONAL CONDUCT

All salesmen must have a professional attitude and demeanor. They must be well groomed, wear neat, clean, and well pressed clothing, maintain a neat desk, wear ties whenever working, and maintain a friendly and pleasant attitude with clients and the other personnel of GRANADA REALTY.

GENERAL CONDUCT

GRANADA REALTY will open for business at 9:00 AM and close at 9:00 PM daily, including Sundays. A floor schedule will be prepared recognizing each salesman's regular day off. Salesmen are expected to observe their floor assignments and arrange for substitute coverage when appointments or other matters require them to leave the office during their scheduled floor time.

In the office, the Golden Rule must be your guide. Each salesman is entitled to respect and must be allowed to conduct his business without unnecessary interruption. The office is intended for the conduct of business. A salesman who has no business to conduct in the office is advised to stay away and have the courtesy not to disturb others.

We are licensed only to sell real estate. Under no circumstances should you give legal or tax advice. If you are questioned on points of law or taxation, refer your client to an attorney or Certified Public Accountant. GRANADA REALTY retains well qualified real estate attorneys and Certified Public Accountants whose services are available to members of our firm.

If a salesman of GRANADA REALTY has taken even one alcoholic drink he will not make any further calls on buyers or sellers and will not return to the office. Even a faint trace of alcohol on the breath of a salesman will destroy the professional image so vital to success. Any salesman possessing, storing, or consuming any alcoholic beverage on the premises of GRANADA REALTY will be discharged.

Use telephones and office facilities only for business purposes.

MISCELLANEOUS POLICIES

Be courteous.

Respect the dignity of others in all your dealings.

"High pressure" salesmanship will not be tolerated.

Support our local Real Estate Board, be willing to serve on Board Committees, and attend as many Board functions as you can.

Do not criticize competing real estate firms.

Never qualify another salesman's prospect.

Never work on another Broker's "exclusive" until you have obtained his permission. (Multiple Listings are excepted.)

Never ask a seller when another Broker's exclusive listing will expire.

If you buy a property for yourself, you must advise the seller that you are a licensed real estate agent.

Always post the time of your return when leaving the office, and notify the floorman. When out of the office, call back each hour or so to assure prompt delivery of your messages.

In keeping with the GRANADA REALTY policy of professional performance by our licensees, all GRANADA REALTY salesmen must attend, and receive a passing grade in, at least one college real estate course yearly offered by the State Department of Higher Education (Diablo Valley College, University of California, or others).

NECESSITY FOR COMPLETE OFFICE RECORDS

Copies of all letters pertaining to real estate, whether they are written by the salesman or others, and copies of all contracts and agreements, shall be given to management to place in the office files.

OFFICE SUPPLIES

Office equipment, supplies, reference material, and so on shall not be removed from the office without permission. This includes the escrow files and original deposit receipts. It excludes the materials deemed necessary to complete a real estate transaction off the premises. However, management must be notified of the removal of such papers.

KEEP OFFICE IN ORDER

Each salesman is responsible to help keep the offices neat and orderly. It is mandatory that we, at all times, present an image of efficiency and attention to details.

VACATIONS
Each salesman is entitled to a vacation. Management should be consulted in advance of the individual's plans so necessary scheduling can be arranged.

DAYS OFF
Each salesman will be assigned one regular day off per week. Additional days off may be taken periodically upon notification to management provided the time off does not interfere with sales production of the office.

SECRETARIAL HELP
Secretarial help is available to perform regular secretarial duty necessary to complete a sale. In the event a salesman does his own typing or letter writing, a copy of all documents must be made and submitted to management for approval and filing so that a complete record may be kept of every transaction.

HEALTH INSURANCE
It is suggested that each salesman augment his insurance protection with a medical health policy. For example, health insurance is made available to all licensees of GRANADA REALTY by Kaiser Health Plan Memberships through the Contra Costa Board of Realtors Group Plan. Individual memberships are available periodically. Dues for membership are paid by each salesman.
An excellent major medical insurance policy, underwritten by a private company, is available through the California Real Estate Association Group Plan. The Contra Costa Board of Realtors has the details.

WITHHOLDING TAXES AND SOCIAL SECURITY
The Federal Internal Revenue Service has ruled that a real estate salesman is an independent contractor. Hence, it is necessary that the individual salesman file and pay income tax and social security payments as an independent businessman. The Broker will provide each salesman with an annual statement of earnings. The Broker will not deduct withholding from commissions.

EXPENDITURES OF OFFICES FUNDS
GRANADA REALTY shall not be liable to the salesman for any expenses incurred by him. The salesman shall not be liable to the

company for office help or expense except as otherwise stipulated in this manual.

No salesman has the right to spend the money of the company without the consent of management. This applies to cards, signs, advertising, and so forth.

WHO MAY OBLIGATE THE BROKER

Salesmen shall have no authority to bind the Broker by any promise or representation unless specifically authorized in writing by the Broker. In addition, salesmen shall not enter into any verbal or "side" agreement with buyers, sellers or other interested parties.

Expenses for attorney's fees, closing costs, revenue stamps, title insurance and the like, which must be paid from the commission, or are incurred in an attempt to collect the commission, shall be paid by the parties in the same proportion as provided for herein in their division of the commission.

ARBITRATION

Controversies between salesmen of GRANADA REALTY will be settled by management. The decision rendered will be as fair and just as can be rendered from the facts at hand, and will stand as final. However, salesmen are entitled to submit controversies to an arbitration board. The arbitration board shall include one salesman chosen by each of those involved and another one or two chosen by that board so the board shall be comprised of an uneven number. A member of management shall be chairman and will not vote. After hearing both sides of a dispute, there shall be a vote taken in writing and the majority of the vote shall decide the issue. All personnel must agree to abide by such decision.

Any controversy between a salesman and another office, or another office's salesman, must be turned over to the Broker for action *immediately.*

PERFECT ATTENDANCE AND PUNCTUALITY

GRANADA REALTY has always stressed the importance of perfect attendance and consistent punctuality. Such characteristics give an accurate indication of interest in the affairs of the company. Three unexcused absences from, or late arrivals at any regularly scheduled sales meeting will result in the termination of a salesman's association with the Company.

PUNCTUALITY POT

A salesman either late for, or absent from, a sales meeting or any other scheduled meeting will deposit $1.00 in the PUNCTUALITY POT as a fine for his tardiness. Periodically there will be a drawing among the licensees of GRANADA REALTY for the money in the "pot."

RETURN OF SUPPLIES ON TERMINATION

Upon termination of a salesman's association with GRANADA REALTY all equipment, supplies, reference material, policy books, reference books and other such material belonging to the company must be returned to the office.

PROCEDURE ON TERMINATION

The association created under the terms of this manual may be terminated by either party at any time upon written or verbal notice given to the other.

It is necessary under the law for a salesman to obtain an authorized release and transfer signature from the Broker before he leaves so he may submit it to the Real Estate Commissioner before joining another firm.

Any contracts started or revived by other salesmen of GRANADA REALTY after a salesman has left the company are to be considered new contracts and the departing salesman shall have no interest in them.

A salesman leaving GRANADA REALTY within the first 90 days of his association will reimburse the Broker $7.50 for business cards and miscellaneous expenses.

The salesman shall not, after said termination, use to his own advantage, or the advantage of any other person or corporation, any information gained from the files or business of this company.

BROKER—SALESMAN CONTRACT

GRANADA REALTY, hereinafter referred to as "Broker," and
                                        hereinafter referred to as "Salesman," hereby agree, subject to termination at the will of either party, to the following conditions and details of their relationship.

(1) FACILITIES:

Broker shall provide Salesman with advertising at Broker's discretion, and with necessary office equipment including desk space, telephone, signs, business cards and stationery, and shall assist and cooperate with Salesman in connection with his work.

(2) GENERAL CONDITIONS:

(a) Salesman shall read and shall govern his conduct by the Code of Ethics of the National Association of Real Estate Boards, the Real Estate Law of the State of California, the by-laws of the Contra Costa Board of Realtors, the regulations of the Multiple Listing Service of the Board of Realtors, and any future modifications or additions thereto.

(b) The schedule of customary commissions of the Contra Costa Board of Realtors shall be used in most transactions and any variation therefrom must first be approved by Broker. Salesman hereby confirms his knowledge of customary schedule of commissions as published by the Board of Realtors.

(c) Salesman shall furnish his own automobile and pay all exenses thereof. Salesman shall carry a minimum of $50,000/$110,000 bodily injury and property damage liability insurance and shall name GRANADA REALTY as additional insured and shall furnish Broker with a certificate of insurance from his individual carrier.

(d) Salesman must remain continuously licensed by the State of California to sell real estate and must become and remain a member in good standing of the Contra Costa Board of Realtors.

(e) Salesman shall not obligate Broker for materials or services without first obtaining consent of Broker.

(f) Salesman shall use only such real estate forms as have been approved first by the Broker.

(g) Salesman hereby acknowledges that he is an independent contractor, and is not a servant, employee, joint-adventurer or partner of the Broker.

(h) The Salesman has no authority, either express or implied, to represent anything to a prospective purchaser unless it is in the listing agreement or unless he receives specific written instructions from the Broker.

(3) COMMISSIONS:

All commissions resulting from real estate transactions negotiated by Salesman shall be divided between Broker and Salesman based on the schedule of commissions in paragraph (4). Any expenses incurred in negotiating the transaction, including Multiple Listing Service fees, shall first be deducted from the gross commission before such division. No commission shall be considered earned or payable to Salesman until the transaction has been completed and the commission collected by Broker.

(4) SCHEDULE OF COMMISSIONS:

(a) Upon sale and closing of transaction and receipt of commission by Broker, commission will be paid by Broker as indicated in this paragraph. All commissions are to be computed on total commission received by Broker.

(1) Property both listed and sold by GRANADA REALTY Salesmen:

20 per cent to listing Salesman

40 per cent to selling Salesman

60 per cent to Salesman selling his own listing

50 per cent to Salesman selling any open listing

(2) Property either listed or sold by cooperating Broker:

50 per cent to selling, or listing, GRANADA REALTY Salesman

(3) In certain specific transactions wherein an extended and unusual period of time will be required for close of escrow and consummation of the contract, and/or wherein the management of GRANADA REALTY will be required to devote an extraordinary amount of time and effort to effect the successful close of escrow, the commission percentage payable to Salesman and Company will be agreed upon and contracted for by Salesman and management.

(b) BONUS PAYMENTS

(1) Salesman will be paid an incentive bonus of 10 per cent on his individual earnings in excess of $7,500 paid during the calendar year. This sum is payable on December 31st. A Salesman terminating his association with GRANADA REALTY prior to December 31st forfeits his interest in any bonus monies accured.

(c) Upon termination of Salesman's association with GRANADA REALTY, Broker shall not be liable to Salesman for a commission on any listing secured by Salesman or on any sale of property unless an offer in writing has been obtained from a bona fide purchaser accompanied by a negotiable deposit and ratified in writing by the seller prior to the termination of association and the same transaction is later completed.

(d) Should Salesman terminate his association with Broker within his first six months of said association, before he has received commission payments from at least three closed GRANADA

REALTY escrows, or if Salesman associates with any other real estate firm in Contra Costa County, then Broker shall not be liable to Salesman for the payment of any commission on transactions which are not completed and commission collected by Broker prior to Salesman's termination. Said commissions, when collected by Broker, shall be deemed to have been earned by Broker as compensation for the expenses of association, training and providing office facilities to the terminating Salesman.

(e) Salesman may be discharged for conduct deemed, by the Broker, to be harmful to the Company. Upon such an occurrence, Broker shall not be liable to Salesman for the payment of any commission on transactions which are not completed and commission collected by Broker prior to Salesman's discharge. Said commissions, when collected by Broker, shall be considered to be forfeited to Broker as damages.

(5) ACCEPTANCE OF NOTES:

Promissory notes in lieu of commission payments will not be accepted unless expressly approved in advance by Broker. If a commission, or any part of a commission, is taken on a note, commission will not be considered collected by Broker until the entire note is paid in full.

(6) ESCROWS:

Salesman, under supervision and direction of Broker, shall order all title searches and handle all escrows.

(7) ADVERTISING:

All advertising must be approved by Broker before publication. All advertising shall be at Broker's expense unless some other prior agreement is made with Broker.

(8) TELEPHONE AND TELEGRAMS:

Do not accept collect telephone calls and telegrams! Salesman shall make no long distance telephone calls nor send any telegrams without the approval of Broker.

(9) LITIGATION OR DISPUTE:

In the event any transaction in which a Salesman is involved results in dispute, arbitration, litigation or legal expense, Salesman shall cooperate fully and abide by decision that is acceptable to Broker. Broker and Salesman shall share all expenses connected therewith in the same proportion as they would normally share the commission resulting from such transaction without a dispute or litigation. It is the policy of GRANADA REALTY to avoid litigation wherever possible and Broker reserves the sole right to determine whether or not any litigation or dispute shall be prosecuted, defended, settled, or whether or not legal expenses shall be incurred. If a dispute or litigation is anticipated by Broker in a transaction, Broker reserves the right to defer payment of commission to Salesman until a settlement acceptable to Broker is reached.

(10) DIVISION OF COMMISSIONS:

Any arrangement for division of commission with other Brokers must be approved by Broker. In the event that two or more Salesman licensed with Broker participate in a commission on the same transaction, the commission shall be divided between the participating Salesman according to a written agreement, by arbitration, by written Company policy, or by decision of Broker which shall be final.

(11) DEPOSITS:

All monies, documents, or property received by Salesman in connection with any transaction of Broker shall be delivered to Broker immediately. All checks must be made payable to GRANADA REALTY TRUSTEE or a title insurance company. In the event all or any portion of a deposit is forfeited, disbursement of Broker's portion shall be according to schedule in paragraph (4).

(12) CORRESPONDENCE:

All letters received, and a copy of all letters written by Salesman pertaining to the business of Broker, shall be delivered to Broker for his records. All letters are to be approved by Broker before mailing.

(13) SPECULATION:

The Company recognizes that in any real estate market there exists a genuine need for speculators. Should Salesman desire to speculate or invest in real property, he MUST review his proposal with Broker before submitting his offer to the property owner. Care must be exercised to protect the interests of our clients and assure that speculative activities will in no way reflect unfavorably upon the integrity and professional status of our salesman or the Company.

In speculative or investment ventures where a Salesman of this Company must obtain outside capital to make his purchase, the Company will be given first right of refusal to participate in the venture, and should the Company decline participation, then the Salesman is at liberty to obtain his capital elsewhere and share his speculation or investment as he chooses.

Upon speculation or investment by a GRANADA REALTY Salesman, the Company's share of the commission involved in the purchase will be credited to the Salesman's account. The Company will collect its normal commission on the sale of every property, including Salesmen's speculative properties and personal residences. All Salesmen's properties, when offered for sale, will be listed for sale through the Company. It is expected that Salesmen dealing in speculation or investment will uphold their office production and each must understand that failure to do so will be grounds for dismissal from the Company.

This entire paragraph (13) is applicable only after a Salesman has been associated with GRANADA REALTY for six months. If Salesman with less than six month's association wishes to purchase property for his own account, or if Salesman is working on a part time basis regardless of his tenure with the Company, the Company will collect its full share of the commission upon both purchase and sale.

This policy is designed to encourage the Salesman of GRANADA REALTY to build their estate through real estate investment. It is well to remember that this is a privilege to be earned. Do not take advantage of it.

(14) AFFIRMATION:

The undersigned understands and hereby agrees to abide by all of the foregoing specifications and to use skill and due diligence in his efforts to carry out the terms of this agreement for the mutual benefit of Broker and undersigned Salesman. Salesman acknowledges reading the POLICY BOOK of GRANADA REALTY and will abide by same.

Dated this_____ day of

_____,19 ___ .

By _____   _____
    for GRANADA REALTY, Broker   Salesman

DESCRIPTION OF SALESMAN'S JOB

QUALIFICATIONS FOR GRANADA REALTY SALESMEN

—California real estate salesman or broker license.

—Interest in attending real estate classes in salesmanship, appraisal,

listing, finance and other pertinent courses.
—Ability to learn appraising techniques.
—Familiarity with listing, sales and escrow techniques and procedures.
—Familiarity with financing sources and loan procedures.

SPECIAL REQUIREMENTS

GRANADA REALTY salesmen must have a car that is kept neat, clean and serviceable. They must be willing to work the hours necessary to secure listings, sales, and provide service to our customers.

SALESMAN'S OBLIGATIONS

The salesman agrees to work diligently to sell, lease, or rent all real estate listed with this office, to solicit additional listings and clients, and to otherwise promote the business of real estate in the best interests of all concerned.
The salesman agrees to conduct his business and regulate his habits so as to maintain and increase the goodwill and reputation of the Company.

TRAINING

Salesmen will receive sales training from the management of GRANADA REALTY. Salesmen are expected to learn the business of real estate, become professional in their attitudes and aptitudes, and work effectively with their time and talents on an organized, full time basis.

GENERAL ACTIVITY

GRANADA REALTY salesmen are expected to develop leads on properties for sale and to secure listings on properties.
They will develop leads on prospective buyers, show properties to prospective buyers, complete deposit receipt agreements, secure buyers' and sellers' signatures on closing instructions, and collect monies due to effect the close of a sale. All GRANADA REALTY salesmen are expected to follow their escrows closely and take all necessary action to bring about a successful close of escrow.
Salesmen shall report to the office each day at 9:00 AM unless they are excused.
Salesmen should keep their appointments promptly and should make their appointments so as not to interfere with floor duty or sales meetings.

Salesmen should regularly check the newspaper for listings and sales leads.

Sales meeting attendance by all personnel is mandatory.

It is imperative that all salesmen join in the weekly tour of new office listings which follows the sales meeting.

CONDUCT WHILE SHOWING PROPERTY

Salesmen must respect owners' requests for appointments before showing property. Always phone before going to inspect or show a home. Unfortunately, some real estate licensees think their license is a license to trespass. Be considerate of the privacy of home owners.

If, after making an appointment to show a home you find you will not be able to show the property, be sure to call the owner and so inform him.

If an appointment has been made and the prospect decides, after driving up to the front of the house, that he does not want to go in, let the owner know the appointment will not be kept.

When quoting prices on property, you must quote the price the seller is asking.

Be a self-starter! Be aggressive with *yourself*, but at all times respect the dignity of others. A gracious sales person is welcome in any home.

CONDUCT WHILE LOOKING AT OTHER BROKERS' LISTINGS

Don't oversell yourself and your office to another broker's principal. It is not necessary and is unethical. Remember you are only allowed there through the courtesy of your cooperating listing broker. Once in the property, inspect it and leave promptly. Don't give advice!

Never discuss financing or seek information from another broker's client. If you need additional information, call the listing broker.

COOPERATING WITH OTHER REALTORS

All real estate "for sale" may not be available on a cooperative basis.

If a property is not on Multiple, confirm with the listing office and always ask:

(1) Are you cooperating?
(2) What is the commission?
(3) What is the commission split?
(4) How can showing arrangements be made?
(Before attempting to show another listing, be sure listing office is cooperating.)

When another real estate firm asks for permission to work on the property of one of our clients, it is our policy to give all the assistance we can to fellow members of the Contra Costa Board of Realtors.

We cooperate with other brokers who are not members of the Contra Costa Board of Realtors, but who are members of some other real estate board, on a 50/50 commission basis. Generally we do not cooperate with brokers who are not members of some real estate board. The final decision on this rests with management.

LEAVE CARD IN HOME

A salesman using a key to enter a house or building shall leave his card in a conspicuous place so that the owner shall know he has been there.

PRECAUTIONS WHEN USING KEYS

Salesmen using keys to enter properties are required, before leaving the property, to check all doors and windows to determine that they are securely fastened or locked. Our possession of these keys represents a major responsibility. Don't neglect it!

PLAN YOUR WORK

Much time is wasted by most real estate salesmen. Such time is lost forever!

To accomplish the most and eliminate wasted time, the salesman should plan his day's work in advance, preferably at the close of the preceding day. Plan your work so there is as little lost motion as possible, so that you can devote the time between "showing" appointments to listing property, seeking new prospects, inspecting property, servicing listings, or contacting past customers.

FLOOR DUTY

Floor duty is the office time assigned to a salesman for the purpose of servicing phone calls and walk-ins regarding properties listed for sale by GRANADA REALTY. This is an excellent source of prospects.

The *floorman* is the person performing floor duty as specified on the office schedule.

The *floor schedule* is the monthly list of sales people who will perform floor duty. Management will provide a floor schedule giving all eligible salesmen their equal share of available floor time. It is the responsibility of each man to watch the posted schedule so that he may know when he is expected to cover the floor.

Salesmen are expected to take over their floor assignment promptly and to remain on duty for the full period. If called away, it is the floorman's responsibility to assure that substitute coverage is provided. If no "back-up" salesman is available, the floorman is to report to management before leaving the office unattended during business hours.

Should the floorman be late for his floor time or the floor is not covered for *any* reason other than being with a "walk-in" client, the assigned floorman shall be fined $5.00. If the assigned floorman neglects his floor time, his floor time will be taken away from him and assigned to another salesman.

FLOORMAN DUTIES AND RESPONSIBILITIES

The floorman is responsible for answering all incoming telephone calls, greeting all walk-in customers, taking messages, and generally maintaining the office in a neat and orderly way. The first man on the floor in the morning is expected to attend to all necessary "opening" procedures. The last man on duty in the evening is expected to assure that all doors are locked and that the heat and all lights (except night light) are turned off before securing the office. Particular attention must be given to turning off the radio and electric typewriters.

It will be the floorman's duty to acquaint himself with the properties currently advertised, and GRANADA REALTY properties with FOR SALE signs, so he can efficiently service inquiries on these properties. The floorman must also acquaint himself with advertised properties of competitive firms.

FLOOR CALLS

Only the scheduled floorman is authorized to receive floor calls. A floor call is determined as follows:

   —A prospect walks in or telephones, and at no time during the interview indicates that he wishes to see or talk to another specifically named salesman.

   —A prospect walks in or telephones and asks for a salesman no longer employed by this company.

   —The floorman is busy. A prospect walks in or telephones. *This call belongs only to the floorman.* It may NOT be assumed that it goes automatically to the next salesman on the floor schedule. The floorman MUST be consulted and *only he can designate* a substitute, which would be the next "back-up" man on the floor schedule.

—A prospective client walks in or telephones asking for a particular salesman. Every effort to locate the salesman is unsuccessful and there appears a danger of losing the customer entirely. In this case, the floorman may show the client property. If the salesman originally asked for by the client has previously shown property to the client, and the floorman sells this client a home the first time he shows him property, the salesman's commission will be split 50/50 between the selling floorman and the salesman who actually caused the customer to come to the office in the first place. However, if the customer does not buy the first time he is shown property and requests another appointment for a later date, the floorman and the client-motivating salesman must agree between themselves which salesman, or if both salesmen, will thereafter work with the client. If the client has not been shown property by the salesman asked for, the client is thereafter the customer of the floorman and the floorman will receive all the commission.

FLOOR ASSISTANCE

Any assistance that one salesman gives to another salesman in the office shall be considered as office courtesy unless prior commission arrangements between salesmen involved are mutually agreed upon, and approved and recorded with management.

MAKE FLOOR TIME PROFITABLE

Floor duty gives the salesman an excellent opportunity to make money. Make a list of potential purchasers, then make a list of possible sellers. Call ten of each and see how long it takes you to talk to 20 people. See how many prospects you get out of your ten calls and how many listings you can get out of your calls to property owners.

Floor time can be profitable even when there is little "floor activity." It is a good time to bring listings up to date, do telephone solicitation, or plan work for the following day. Do not read newspapers during floor time other than to check the real estate advertisements.

TELEPHONE TECHNIQUE

Incoming calls are to be answered "Good morning, Granada Realty." or "Granada Realty, Jack Wilson speaking".

When the call is for another salesman, everything possible must be done to secure the caller's name and phone number together with any message which should be properly recorded and left for the salesman called.

If it is a sales call, the answering salesman should use the telephone technique (Ten Questions) illustrated in the GRANADA REALTY Reference Book, under "Handling the Sales Call."

TAKING MESSAGES FOR OTHER SALESMEN

A message properly taken is often a sales commission. It is mandatory that all messages be taken with extreme care and accuracy, noting the date, time, and name of the person taking the message. Be certain telephone numbers and the caller's name are recorded accurately. Messages are the life blood of a successful real estate salesman. PAY ATTENTION WHEN YOU ARE TAKING AND RECORDING A MESSAGE!

ESCROW PROCEDURE

Salesmen of GRANADA REALTY may elect to open and handle all details of their own escrows under close supervision and direction of management. Escrow files are at all times to be stored in the file cabinet provided for that purpose and they are not to be kept on, or stored in, a salesman's desk or automobile. Salesmen should feel free to consult regularly with management on all escrow matters and should take all steps necessary to speed the close of their escrows.

LOKBOXES

Lokboxes must be checked in and out of the Lokbox Register. The office maintains a record by serial number of each lokbox. It is the responsibility of the listing salesman to be certain that lokboxes are returned to the office upon the listing expiration or sale of a property. Failure to return the lokbox within five days after its use is no longer required will be considered sufficient cause for Broker to charge the cost of the lokbox against the salesman's commission account and to deduct this amount from the next commission payment the salesman receives. The current cost of lokboxes is $4.00 each. This sum will be refunded to the salesman upon return of the lokbox if such a deduction has been made.

LISTING PROCEDURES

Read *Real Estate Listing Magic* and *The Listing Master* by Gael Himmah.
These texts will serve as an excellent guide for real estate success.

GENERAL LISTING PROCEDURES

Each GRANADA REALTY salesman is expected to maintain a minimum of eight saleable listings at all times. If you observe this faithfully, your success is assured.

All listings are the property of the Broker. All listings secured by a GRANADA REALTY salesman must be given to the Broker immediately. Listings will not be transferred to another real estate firm. A salesman, upon leaving the company, is not entitled to any fees from listings he secured and which are sold after his termination.

Verbal listings are not recognized by this company as they have no legal justification.

A listing salesman who does not attend the sales meeting will not have his new listings toured by the office staff unless prior arrangements are made with management.

NET LISTINGS

Net listings will not be accepted by the company. Refer to the 90 per cent COMMISSION LISTINGS in *Real Estate Listing Magic* as an acceptable alternative.

OPEN LISTINGS

While the taking of open listings is generally discouraged, it is recognized that there are certain occasions when acceptance of an open listing is beneficial. This applies usually to commercial, residential-income and unimproved acreage properties commonly referred to as "Commercial Properties."

Recognizing the need to encourage all types of listing activity, GRANADA REALTY will treat an acceptable open listing as an exclusive and will protect the listing salesman's commission accordingly. However, the acceptability of an open listing will be judged solely by the company and will be evidenced by the publishing of a GRANADA REALTY listing card in the normal manner. Salesmen with questions about the acceptability of an open listing should consult with the Broker *before* giving information on the listing to other salesmen. At no time will any salesmen of the company offer to cooperate with another office on an open listing unless the listing is his own and he is satisfied that the other office will recognize him as the listing agent and protect his normal listing commission.

SERVICING THE LISTING

Good public relations between seller and company depends upon service. Your reputation and your company's reputation depends on service.

The longer a salesman must service his listing, the more expensive it becomes. Therefore, good judgment must be exercised. Get saleable listings. Service them regularly, and renew them until they are sold.

MAKE A SERVICE CALL

If a property is not sold within 30 days of listing there is usually some reason that has become evident by them.

Make a call on the owner. Take along your listing file, mart opinion (Realtor's Estimated Value sheet) and comparables. Go over your progress with the seller. Now is the time to take a definite stand! The property owner is relying on you for advice. DON'T WAIT FOR HIM TO ADVISE YOU! Try to get the owner to cooperate in removing the obstacles for a sale (price, location or condition). In the next 15 days, follow the same procedure. Make your second service call and discuss your reasons why the property has not sold. Give the owner information on the sales of comparable properties.

Your third call should not be later than two days prior to the expiration of the listing. Get the renewal listing at that time.

CANCELLING LISTINGS

No listing can be cancelled without the consent of the Broker. If a commission is paid by the listing party for such cancellation, the listing salesman shall receive a commission on the same percentage basis as if he sold his own listing.

LISTING KIT

Each salesman shall have a listing kit which is readily available to him. It should include:

    —3 sets of Exclusive listing forms (2 to a set)
    —3 Multiple Listing forms (3 to a set)
    —3 Mart listing cards—homes

—3 Mart listing cards—lots

—2 sets of Authorization to change terms or extend listing forms (3 to a set)

—2 sets of Notice forms for MLS (3 to a set)

SELLING PROCEDURES

Read *Real Estate Selling Magic* by Gael Himmah.
This text will serve as an excellent guide for real estate success.

DO IT NOW

Time is of the essence in servicing any client. Many sales are lost because of improper servicing. *Delay in making contact is responsible for losing more sales than any other single act or omission.* If your client feels you are actively working for him, you will obtain greater cooperation from him. Any lead you produce is expected to be serviced promptly. If you are not able to follow up a lead within 24 hours, turn it back to the company and it will be assigned to another salesman.

PERSONAL INTERVIEW WITH PROSPECTS

Of cardinal importance is the salesman's prospect file. The information included therein will be gained from a personal interview with the client. The accuracy and care with which he compiles, adds to, and maintains his prospect record has a direct relation to his success. The prospect records show detailed information about the prospect. Every call should be recorded, with the date and precise outcome of the interview; i.e., what was said, how the client reacted, what sales points were used, what sales efforts were unsuccessful. Only by reviewing each previous call can the salesman plan his next call.

The salesman who shrugs off prospect records, or whose files are inaccurate and poorly documented, will rarely succeed.

LEARN THE MOTIVE

To sell a home to a prospect, learn his motives for buying, his wishes, his needs, his urgency to complete a sale, his ability to fulfill his needs. When interviewing a prospect, get as much detailed information as possible.

MATCHING PROPERTY WITH PROSPECT

Whenever a new listing is received in the office, the salesmen should inspect this listing as soon as possible. Study and analyze the listing, then try to match it with the needs of your various prospects.

If the listing seems to meet the requirements of any of your prospects, arrange an appointment to show the property immediately. Don't hesitate and wait for someone else to sell the property. Call, and sell it NOW!

SEEK OUT PROSPECTS

There are many sources of prospects. In fact, it is nearly impossible to find anyone who is not interested in talking about real estate. That is all you need for a start.

If you were to go out "cold canvassing" for an hour a day, merely knocking on doors in any neighborhood, asking the occupants if they knew of anyone interested in buying or selling real estate, you would rapidly have more good prospects than you could handle. Do not rely upon the office to furnish you clients. You are an independent businessman. The office will support your activity, but your success in real estate depends upon your own initiative.

More obvious sources of prospects are:

    —Lodge and church members
    —Motel clerks who know of guests wanting to purchase homes
    —Newspaper articles of marriages, divorces, promotions, etc.
    —Attorneys
    —Apartment house owners whose tenants may want to purchase
    —Neighbors in the vicinity of a newly acquired listing
    —Service clubs

Tell everyone you meet you are in real estate. Give everyone you meet a business card. It will repay you handsomely.

TAKE A DEPOSIT

A deposit of at least 2 per cent of the purchase price should be received at the time the purchaser signs the deposit receipt. This will demonstrate to the seller the good faith of the buyer. All deposits on offers must be deposited with the company as soon as obtained. Trustee checks will be cashed immediately. We will not hold checks or accept post-dated checks.

When it is necessary to take a deposit of less than 2 per cent of the purchase price, it should be included as a condition in the deposit receipt that an amount equal to 2 per cent of the purchase price will be deposited by the buyer immediately upon acceptance of the offer by the seller.

SUGGESTED PROGRAM FOR SUCCESS

Salesmen should devote a portion of each day to the following:
  —Show properties to prospects
  —Solicit new listings
  —Call expired listings and For-Sale-By-Owner ads
  —Secure new prospects
  —Inspect new listings
  —Service your listings
  —Follow your leads tenaciously and promptly
  —Keep prospect cards up to date

SALES KIT

Each salesman shall have a sales kit. It should include:
  —3 sets of deposit receipt forms
  —3 sets of FHA amendment forms (4 to a set)
  —3 sets of Structural Pest Control Agreement forms (4 to a set)
  —3 Promissory notes (straight)
  —3 Counter checks
  —3 sets of Personal Property Transfer forms (4 to a set)
  —Loan amortization book
  —FHA slide rule
  —Title Insurance rate card
  —1 Lease deposit receipt set (4 to a set)
  —Carbon paper
  —Prospect cards
  —100-foot measuring tape
  —2-pound sledge hammer (for installing signs)
  —Claw hammer
  —Map of our marketing area

BE AWARE THAT YOU ARE A PROFESSIONAL!

AMENDMENTS

I

A GRANADA REALTY listing becomes available to all GRANADA salesmen to relist for their own account during the final week of the listing's term. Listing agents should be careful to extend the term of their listings before this final 7 day period. A salesman who intends to pursue such a listing should inform the current listing agent that he plans to work on the listing during the final week of its term.

II

If a GRANADA salesman wants to make a bulk (multiple) mailing from the office, he must first receive approval from management. The Company will pay the cost of stationery. The salesman will pay the cost of postage.

III   **PROCEDURES FOR CLOSING AT NIGHT**

1. Lock back door.
2. Unplug radio and electric typewriters.
3. Turn heat down to 65.
4. Make sure the front table is cleared of newspapers, dirty ashtrays and so on.
5. Bring in Granada sign from the sidewalk.
6. Turn off all lights with the exception of the fixture over the table.

AFFIRMATION:

The undersigned understands and hereby agrees to abide by all of the policies contained in this manual.

NAME   DATE

_____

_____

_____

_____

_____

_____

_____

_____

_____

_____

_____

_____

_____

APPENDIX B

THE REFERENCE BOOK

Often a salesman hesitates to make direct, personal contact with prospective clients due to his lack of knowledge of the various forms and contracts used in selling real estate. Many salesmen hesitate to "close" sales due to this handicap.

A conscientious study of the material in this Reference Book will remove this obstacle to success. All the sales forms used in the normal course of general brokerage business are completed. You can use them as a guide in preparing your own contracts.

Just as a lawyer selects a book from his library to check a reference, you should feel free to refer to this Reference Book at any time. Its use will impress your clients with your attention to detail and desire for accuracy.

Throughout your real estate career you can amend, keep current, and constantly refer to this Reference Book as an invaluable aid in your profession.

HANDLING THE SALES CALL

IO MAGIC QUESTIONS

1- ARE YOU A BROKER?

2- ARE YOU CALLING LONG DISTANCE?

3- ARE YOU FAMILIAR WITH OUR AREA?

4- WAS IT THE __(ie. seclusion)__ ASPECT THAT ATTRACTED YOUR ATTENTION?

5- HOW SOON DO YOU NEED A HOME?

6- DO YOU OWN YOUR OWN HOME NOW?

7- HAVE YOU HAD AN OPPORTUNITY TO LOOK AT ANY PROPERTY IN THIS AREA?

8- WOULD YOU LIKE AN UNUSUAL HOME?

9- WHAT PORTION OF YOUR SAVINGS WILL YOU USE AS A DOWN PAYMENT?

10-WOULD __(day & time)__ BE CONVENIENT FOR YOU TO INSPECT THIS PROPERTY?

Exhibit B-1
Ten Questions for Telephone Client

CLIENT INTERVIEW SHEET

NAME_____

ADDRESS_____PHONE(res.)_____(bus.)_____

HOW LARGE IS FAMILY? BOYS_____ GIRLS_____ TOTAL_____

DO YOU OWN HOME?_____ WHERE?_____

MUST YOU SELL IT BEFORE YOU BUY?_____

DO YOU OWN OTHER REAL ESTATE?_____ WHERE?_____

HAVE YOU OWNED MANY PROPERTIES IN THE PAST?_____ HOW MANY?_____

IS ANY OF YOUR PROPERTY CURRENTLY FOR SALE?_____ DESCRIBE IT_____

HOW LONG HAVE YOU BEEN LOOKING FOR A HOME?_____

WHY DO YOU WANT TO BUY?_____

HAVE YOU SEEN ANYTHING YOU LIKE?_____

DESCRIBE IT_____

WHAT HOBBIES DO YOU HAVE?_____

WHAT DID YOU LIKE MOST ABOUT YOUR LAST PROPERTY?_____

WHAT DID YOU LIKE LEAST ABOUT YOUR LAST PROPERTY?_____

WHAT STYLE HOME DO YOUR LIKE?(ranch, colonial, etc.)_____

DO YOU WANT A LARGE LOT?_____

MUST YOU HAVE 2 BATHROOMS?_____

DO YOU WANT A SWIMMING POOL?_____

WHAT OTHER REQUIREMENTS HAVE YOU?_____

WHAT IS THE MAXIMUM CASH INVESTMENT YOU CAN MAKE IN A HOME?_____

DO YOU HAVE THIS SUM OF MONEY AVAILABLE NOW?_____

DO YOU HAVE ANY TRUST DEEDS, TRAILERS, BOATS, ETC. TO TRADE?_____

HOW MUCH RENT OR MONTHLY PAYMENTS DO YOU MAKE NOW?_____

HOW MUCH COULD YOU SPEND MONTHLY?_____

WHAT AREA DO YOU WORK IN?_____

MONTHLY INCOME (gross)_____(net)_____EXTRA INCOME_____

AUTO_____YEAR_____PAYMENT_____BALANCE DUE_____

ANY OTHER PAYMENTS?_____BALANCE DUE_____

Exhibit B-2
Client Interview Sheet

PROSPECT CARD

DATE		Salesman	
		HOW OBTAINED	
NAME		Ad	
Res. Add.	Res. Phone	Sign	
Bus. Add.	Bus. Phone	Office	
Business Connection		Personal	
		PROSPECT FOR	
Approximate Income		Rental	
Down Payment	Monthly Payments	House	
REQUIREMENTS		Lot	
		Business	
		Apts.	
		Number In Family	
REMARKS		Number Of Children	
		Boys	Girls
		Ages	

Exhibit B-3
Prospect Card

Promissory Note

(STRAIGHT)

$ 1,000.00 .... Lafayette ...., California, ... June 1 ...., 19--....
For value received,.... Johl L.Jones and Mary V. Jones, his wife
....promise...... to pay to
.... GRANADA REALTY TRUSTEE
or order, at............ P.O.BOX 697 Lafayette, California ....,
the sum of........... One Thousand and no/100---------------------------DOLLARS,
with interest from........ June 7, 19--.... (*)...until paid at the rate of
...... 10 ...... per cent per annum; interest payable.... with principal ....;
principal payable.... on or before June 7, 19--.
....
....
....

Should interest not be so paid it shall thereafter bear like interest as the principal. Should default be made in payment of interest when due the whole sum of principal and interest shall become immediately due, at the option of the holder of this note. Principal and interest payable in lawful money of the United States. If action be instituted on this note, I promise to pay such sum as the Court may fix as attorney's fees.

This note is an earnest money deposit for purchase of lot and improvements commonly known as 119 Oak Street, Lafayette, as shown on Deposit Receipt dated June 1, 19--.

John L. Jones
Mary V. Jones

* This is the agreed upon redemption date.

If you cannot get a cash deposit—take a personal check or either one of these two forms.

Counter Check

Bank Name *Bank of America*

Branch *Lafayette*   No. _____

City *Lafayette, Calif* State _____   *June 1* 19--

PAY TO THE ORDER OF *Granada Realty Trustee* $ *1,000 xx* —

One Thousand and no/100 _____ DOLLARS

FOR VALUE RECEIVED I CLAIM THAT THE ABOVE AMOUNT IS ON DEPOSIT IN SAID BANK IN MY NAME SUBJECT TO THIS CHECK AND IS HEREBY ASSIGNED TO PAYEE OR HOLDER HEREOF.

John L. Jones

2115 17th Ave   Lafayette Calif
ADDRESS

Exhibit B-4

172

AUTHORIZATION TO SELL

_____ Walnut Creek _____, California, July 1, 19--

In consideration of the services of _____ **GRANADA REALTY** _____
hereinafter called the agent, I hereby list with said agent, exclusively and irrevocably, for a period of time beginning
_____ July 1 _____, 19 -- and ending December 31 _____, 19 --, and grant said agent the
exclusive and irrevocable right to sell within said time for Twenty One Thousand and no/100---
($ 21,000.00--- _____) Dollars, and to accept a deposit thereon, the following described property in the
City of Walnut Creek _____ County of Contra Costa _____ State of California, to-wit:

Lot and improvements commonly known as 115 Olive Drive, including living
room carpets and drapes.

The purchase price shall be payable as follows: all cash to seller.

Property may be placed on Board of Realtors Multiple Listing Service at
agent's option.

This is an EXCLUSIVE AGENCY listing from date until July 10, 19-- during
which time seller is not obligated to the commission statement for
purchasers he should secure through his own efforts.

I hereby agree to pay the agent as commission SIX (6) _____ per cent of the selling price herein named,
whether said property is sold by said agent, or by me, or by another agent, or through some other source, or if said property
is transferred, conveyed, leased or withdrawn from sale during the time set forth herein.

If within ten days after the termination of this listing, said agent notifies me in writing personally, or by mail, that
during its life, he negotiated with persons named by him, and sale is made within 365 days after the termination
of this contract to any person so named, I agree to pay the agent the commission provided for herein.

If a deposit is forfeited, one-half thereof shall go to said agent as commission and one-half to me, provided, however
the agent's share shall not exceed the amount of the above named commission.

Evidence of title to be in the form of a policy of Title Insurance issued through **any responsible Title Company
and paid for by the buyer.**

Thirty days allowed for examination of title, following receipt of the deposit. Taxes (July 1 basis), interest, insurance,
loan trust funds (if indebtedness is being assumed) and rents to be prorated. Insurance may be cancelled. When sold as
herein provided, I will convey said property to the buyer by a grant deed, and when notified of sale I will immediately
upon request deposit with said Title Company for delivery, said deed and any other documents and instructions necessary
to complete the transaction. If objection to title is reported, I agree to take immediate steps to clear title and buyer shall
within five days after title is reported cleared by the Title Company, deposit the full purchase price in escrow.

Notice of sale hereunder may be given to me by telephone, orally, or by mail to the address given below, or by
personal service.

Time is of the essence hereof. In the event of the failure of a buyer to perform any of the terms hereof, all rights
of such buyer shall immediately cease and terminate.

We hereby acknowledge receipt of a copy of this contract.

Address 115 Olive Drive

Walnut Creek, California

Telephone 934-2367

Thomas T. Poole

Wilma L. Poole

Seller.

In consideration of the above listing, the undersigned agent agrees to use diligence in procuring a buyer.

GRANADA REALTY

By _____

Real Estate Agent.

Exhibit B-5
Exclusive Agency Listing

EXCLUSIVE LISTING DATED .... July 1 19--

Subject to conditions hereinafter set forth

NO LISTING ACCEPTED FOR LESS THAN 90 DAYS

The Mart Copy of This Listing Must Be Turned in to the Multiple Office by the Listing Office Within 48 Hours After Being Signed by the Owner

Date 7/1/-- .... HOME Listing #

Address 84 GRAN VIA, ALAMO

Area or Subd. off Ridgewood ...... Lot No. .... Unit No ....

Occupied by owner .... Phone ....

Owner L.G. Franklin .... Phone 817-2517

Address same

Listing Office GRANADA (Himmah) ...... Phone 285-5555

How Shown phone for appointment - LOKBOX

Reason for Selling transferred

Occupancy Date by agreement .... Zoning ....

Terms of Sale cash to best loan

Present Loan $ 12,565.10 for 20 yrs. @ 6 %Pmt. $ 145.00

Pmt. inc. $ no Ins.; $ no Taxes; $ Assmt.

Loan Commitment $ coming for yrs. @ %Pmt. $

Sewer There? yes Connected yes Bal. Assmt. $ none

Lot Size ½ acre F R S Contour

Remarks Gorgeous, estate setting in orchard of mature walnut trees. Large areas of lawn and gardens. Swimming pool (15 X 30), heated badminton court. Carpets & drapes included.

Price $ 45,000
Sq. Ft. (House) 1900
Style ranch
Ext. wood & brick
Roof shake
Gar. dbl att
Floors hdwd
Fireplace 2
Heat cent FA
Dining room
Brkfst nook
Laundry room
Shower st-ot
Elect. Kit. X R&O X
Dspl. X D.W. X Ref.
Fmly Rm yes
Taxes 950
Vet. Ex. no

ADDRESS	CITY	STORY	ROOMS	BED RMS	BATH	AGE	PRICE
84 GRAN VIA	A	1	6	3	2	12	$ 45,000

TERMS AND CONDITIONS

In consideration of services to be performed by GRANADA REALTY , hereinafter called Broker, I hereby employ Broker as my sole and exclusive agent to sell for me that certain real property situated in the City of Alamo area , County of , California, as above described. I hereby grant said Broker the exclusive and irrevocable right to sell the same, and to accept a deposit thereon, for the price of $ 45,000 on the following terms: $ all cash; balance payable $

This authority shall continue irrevocably from date until terminated on December 31 19--

I agree to pay Broker 6 per cent of the selling price in the event that during the period of this contract:

Broker secures a purchaser ready, able and willing to purchase said property on the above terms, or at any other price or terms acceptable to me, or said property is sold or exchanged or leased by said broker or any other person, including myself. I agree to pay Broker said per cent of the listing price if I withdraw said property from sale or exchange, or otherwise prevent performance hereunder by Broker

I agree to pay Broker said percent of the selling price if said property be sold or exchanged within three months after the termination of this contract to any person with whom Broker has negotiated or to whose attention he has called said property and whose name has, during the life hereof or within ten days after its termination, been submitted to me in writing personally or by mail to me at my address given below, in which case Broker shall be conclusively deemed the procuring cause of such sale or lease or exchange to such person.

It is understood Broker is a realtor member of Board of Realtors. Members of said Board may act in association with Broker in procuring or attempting to procure a purchaser. This shall not be construed as making the Board my agent for any purpose, or as making any members sub-agents of the Board or of Broker. In the event a sale or exchange shall be made or a purchaser procured by a member of the Board other than Broker, all of the terms of this agreement shall apply to the transaction, subject to the rights of Broker. Payment for commission or compensation hereunder shall be made by me only to Broker.

Evidence of merchantable title shall be in form of policy of title insurance by a responsible title company, same to be paid for by purchaser.

Interest, insurance, taxes, expenses and rent shall be pro-rated through escrow as of date of recording of deed, unless otherwise herein designated.

In case deposit is forfeited, one-half of same shall be retained by or paid to Broker as his compensation, and one-half to me, provided Broker's portion of any forfeiture shall not exceed the amount of the above named commission.

RECEIPT OF A COPY OF THIS LISTING IS HEREBY ACKNOWLEDGED. (IN TRIPLICATE)

(Signed) *John C. Franklin* , Owner

Mary M. Franklin , Owner

(Dated July 1, 19-- .... same as above .... Address

IN CONSIDERATION OF THE ABOVE EMPLOYMENT, BROKER AGREES TO USE DILIGENCE IN PROCURING A PURCHASER.

Broker GRANADA REALTY .... Address P.O. BOX 697 Lafayette, Calif.

By

HOME LISTING

BOARD COPY

Exhibit B-6
Multiple Listing Residential

EXCLUSIVE LISTING DATED .... **July 1** .... 19__

Subject to conditions hereinafter set forth

Lot Listing

NO LISTING
ACCEPTED
FOR LESS THAN
90 DAYS

The Mart Copy
of This Listing Must
Be Turned in to
the Multiple
Office by the Listing
Office Within 48
Hours After Being
Signed by the
Owner

Date **7/1/--** ACREAGE or LOT #	
Address/Location **Lot 15, Parcel 2, Lafayette Homesites**	Price $ **10,000**
Directions **Adjacent to 10 Oak Street, sign on property**	Acres **½**
	Contour **level**
Owner **Jordan, W.D.** Phone **234-9982**	Trees **oak**
Address **10 Oak Street, Lafayette**	Creek **no**
Listing Office **GRANADA REALTY (Himmah)** Phone **284-9550**	Zoning **R 20**
Improvements **none**	View **terrific**
Legal Description: Lot No. **15, Parcel 2** Subdv. **Lafayette Hmsts**	Fenced **no** (acres)
Dimension: F **200** S **120** R **200** S **120**	Street **paved**
Planted in **grass**	Curb **no**
Terms **all cash to seller**	Sidewalks **no**
Exchange for **money**	Sewer **in st.**
Loan **clear** Taxes **$85.00/year**	Gas **avail.**
Sewer Location **in street** Bal. Assmt. $ **none**	Elect. **yes**
Remarks **Terrific building site. Many large oak trees. View for miles. Very secluded setting in area of $50,000 homes. Seller will NOT subordinate.**	Water **in st.**

LOCATION	SIZE	ZONE	PRICE
Lot 15, Oak St., Laf.	½ acre	R 20	$ 10,000

TERMS AND CONDITIONS

In consideration of services to be performed by **GRANADA REALTY**,
hereinafter called Broker, I hereby employ Broker as my sole and exclusive agent to sell for me that certain real property situated in the
City of **Lafayette area** County of ____ California, as above described. I hereby grant said Broker the exclusive
and irrevocable right to sell the same, and to accept a deposit thereon, for the price of $ **10,000** on the following
terms: $ **all** cash; balance payable $ ____

This authority shall continue irrevocably from date until terminated on ____ **December 31** ____ 19__
I agree to pay Broker **10** per cent of the selling price in the event that during the period of this contract:
Broker secures a purchaser ready, able and willing to purchase said property on the above terms, or at any other price or terms acceptable to me, or said property is sold or exchanged or leased by said Broker or any other person, including myself. I agree to pay Broker said
per cent of the listing price if I withdraw said property from sale or exchange, or otherwise prevent performance hereunder by Broker.
I agree to pay undersigned Broker said percent of the selling price if said property is not relisted exclusively with another R.E. Broker
and said property is sold or exchanged within three months after the termination of this contract to any person with whom Broker has negotiated or to whose attention he has called said property and whose name has, during the life hereof or within ten days after its termination,
been submitted to/me in writing personally or by mail to me at my address given below, in which case Broker shall be conclusively deemed
the procuring cause of such sale or lease or exchange to such person.
It is understood Broker is a realtor member of ____ Board of Realtors. Members of said Board may act in association with Broker
in procuring or attempting to procure a purchaser. This shall not be construed as making the Board my agent for any purpose, or as making
any members sub-agents of the Board or of Broker. In the event a sale or exchange shall be made a purchaser procured by a member
of the Board other than Broker, all of the terms of this agreement shall apply to the transaction, subject to the rights of Broker. Payment for
commission or compensation hereunder shall be made by me only to Broker.
Evidence of merchantable title shall be in form of policy of title insurance by a responsible title company, same to be paid for by purchaser.
Interest, insurance, taxes, expenses and rent shall be pro-rated through escrow as of date of recording of deed, unless otherwise herein
designated.
In case deposit is forfeited, one-half of same shall be retained by or paid to Broker as his compensation, and one-half to me, provided
Broker's portion of any forfeiture shall not exceed the amount of the above named commission.
RECEIPT OF A COPY OF THIS LISTING IS HEREBY ACKNOWLEDGED. (IN TRIPLICATE)

(Signed) _____ , Owner
_____ , Owner

(Dated ____ **July 1, 19__**   **same as above** _____ Address

IN CONSIDERATION OF THE ABOVE EMPLOYMENT, BROKER AGREES TO USE DILIGENCE IN PROCURING A PUR-
CHASER.

Broker **GRANADA REALTY**   Address **3333 Mt. Diablo Blvd., Lafayette**

By _____

LOT LISTING
OWNER'S COPY

MULTIPLE LISTING SERVICE

Exhibit B-7
Multiple Listing—Lot

Date_____ HOME Listing #_____		Price $_____
Address_____		Sq. Ft.
Area or Subd._____		House_____
Occupied by_____ Phone_____		Style_____
Owner _____ Phone_____		Ext. _____
Address_____		
Listing Office_____ Phone_____		Roof _____
How Shown_____		Gar. _____
Reason for Selling_____		Floors_____
Occupancy Date_____ Zoning_____		Fireplace_____
Terms of Sale_____		Heat _____
Present Loan $_____ for_____yrs.@_____%Pmt. $_____		Dining _____
Pmt. inc. $_____Ins.; $_____Taxes; $_____Assmt.		Brkfst _____
Loan Commitment $_____ for_____yrs.@_____%Pmt. $_____		Laundry_____
Sewer There?_____Connected_____Bal. Assmt. $_____		Shower _____
Lot Size_____ _____F_____S_____R_____S_____Contour_____		Elect.K.t.____R&O____
Remarks_____		Dsp.:___D.W.___Ref.___
_____		Fmiy Rm_____
_____		Taxes_____
_____		Vet.Ex._____

Address	City	Story	Rooms	Bedrms	Bath	Age	PRICE
							$

RESIDENCE

Exhibit B-8
Listing Information Cards

UNIMPROVED PROPERTY

Date _____ ACREAGE or LOT #		
Address		
Location_____		
Directions_____		Price $_____
_____		Acres _____
Owner _____ Phone_____		Contour_____
Address_____		Trees _____
Listing Office_____ Phone_____		Creek _____
Improvements_____		Zoning_____
Legal Description: Lot No._____Subdv._____		View _____
Dimension: F_____S_____R_____S_____		Fenced_____(Acres)___
Planted in_____		Street _____
Terms_____		
Exchange for_____		Curb _____
Loan_____Taxes_____		Sidewalks_____
Sewer Location_____Bal. Assmt. $_____		Sewer _____
Remarks_____		Gas _____
_____		Elect. _____
_____		Water_____

LOCATION	SIZE	ZONE	PRICE
			$

Date 4/6/-- HOME Listing # GR#97 (EXCL)	Price $ 29,500
Address 2212 Rainbow Avenue, Lafayette	
Area or Subd. Off Mt. Diablo Blvd. (NO SIGN)	Sq. Ft. House 2100
Occupied by owner Phone	Style ranch
Owner Murley, Eugene & Nancy Phone 284-7995	Ext. brick
Address same	redwood
Listing Office GRANADA (Cane) Phone 284-9550	Roof shake
How Shown Call first--then LokBox	Gar. 2 att.
Reason for Selling Moving from area	Floors Hdwd
Occupancy Date coe + 20 days Zoning	Fireplace 2
Terms of Sale All cash to seller-Will consider second	Heat F/A
Present Loan $ clear for yrs.e %Pmt. $	Dining yes
Pmt. inc. $ Ins.; $ Taxes; $ Assmt.	Brkfst area
Loan Commitment $ for yrs.e %Pmt. $	Laundry yes
Sewer There? yes Connected yes Bal. Assmt. $	Shower ST&OT
Lot Size 3/4 ac. F s R s Contour level	Elect.Kit. X R&O X
Remarks Beautifully landscaped, surrounded by many	Dsp.: X D.W. X Ref.
towering pines. Very secluded with circular drive-	Fmly Rm huge
way. ½mile from bus close to schools excellent	Taxes 690
for family with young children.	Vet.Ex.

Address	City	Story	Rooms	Bedrms	Bath	Age	PRICE
2212 Rainbow Ave.	L	1½	8	3+den	2	8	$ 29,500

Exhibit B-9
Listing Information Card (Completed)

Open House Invitation

A FANTASTIC HOME

OPEN FOR INSPECTION FROM 1 to 3:30 P.M. ON
              SATURDAY, JUNE 28th.

2212 RAINBOW AVENUE, LAFAYETTE

This beautifully constructed ranch house covers
2100 sq. feet, in the midst of towering pines, a
country setting which all will find irresistible.
It also offers a breath taking view of the scenic
Rheem Valley.

WE INVITE YOU TO COME SEE THIS BUY OF A LIFETIME,
PRESENTED TO YOU EXCLUSIVELY THROUGH GRANADA REALTY.

                    ROBERT CANE, GRANADA REALTY

Exhibit B-10
"Listing Magic" Review Information

WHY HOME OWNERS ATTEMPT TO SELL BY THEMSELVES:

1—Save 6 per cent commission.
2—Afraid of salesmen in general.
3—Confident of their own ability to sell.
4—Uncertain about mechanics of selling through agent.

TEN MAGIC QUESTIONS:

1—How much are you asking?
2—Have you had any offers?
3—How long has your home been on the market?
4—Have you been advertising in the newspaper?
5—Have you seen our ads?
6—May I see the inside of your home?
7—Why are you selling?
8—Do you have any loan commitments?
9—Do you have deposit receipts and promissory notes?
10—Will your husband be home at 6 PM?

EXCLUSIVE AGENCY STATEMENT:

"This is an EXCLUSIVE AGENCY listing from date until ....,
during which term seller is not obligated to the commission statement for
buyers he should secure through his own efforts."

LISTING LETTERS:

STANDARD LISTING LETTER

Dear Mr. Jacobs,
Pursuant to our telephone conversation this evening, I am writing this
brief letter to acquaint you with my firm.
We have a sales staff composed of five experienced Real Estate salesmen
who are thoroughly familiar with Moraga properties.
You can see our style of advertising in the *Oakland Tribune* and the
Contra Costa Times. It is effective advertising.
Given the opportunity to work for you, we'll do a fine job.
I will stop by in the near future and discuss our services in more detail.
Please accept my thanks for your courtesy during our telephone con-
versation.
With kindest regards, I am

                                     Very truly yours,

THE EXCLUSIVE AGENCY LETTER

Dear Mr. Baylor,
I am writing this letter soliciting a listing on your home. This afternoon
your wife was so kind as to give me 15 or 20 minutes to explain something about my firm and the sale of your home in particular. I am

writing this letter in response to her suggestion. I fully understand how irritating it is to be pestered continually by real estate salesmen trying to list your home.

I am certain Mrs. Baylor will discuss the suggestions I made today. However, I would like to outline in detail a proposal of mine which she felt would interest you.

It is axiomatic in the real estate business that very few professional real estate salesmen will ever show a home to a prospective purchaser unless that home is listed with some Broker. A listing is the only protection the salesman has and, of course, all of us in this business live on commissions. I don't blame you one bit for trying to sell your home yourself. I'd probably consider doing the same thing if I were you.

However, there are reasons too numerous to mention here explaining why a purchaser seldom buys direct from an owner. But still there is that slim chance that you might sell direct to a buyer.

Due to the exceptional sales-to-listings ratio our sales staff enjoys, GRANADA offers an unusual type of listing arrangement to a seller who still wants to try to sell his home himself. This is known as an EXCLUSIVE AGENCY listing.

There is a statement on the listing form which reads, "Sellers are not obligated to the commission statement for purchasers they should secure through their own efforts."

That is self-explanatory. You do not lose any of your privileges as a seller under the terms of this listing. If you sell your home to one of your buyers, at any price you desire, you pay us no commission at all. You can advertise and do anything you are doing right now to promote the sale of your home.

GRANADA would be competing with you, in a sense, to bring you an acceptable sales contract before you can secure one yourself. Of course, we would net you at least as much money as you would net if you sold the home yourself. Buyers are willing to pay at least 6 per cent more for the security of buying through a licensed real estate firm.

Under the terms of such a listing you are, in fact, hiring an entire staff of full time professional salesmen to work for you at no expense to you.

In addition, should you find a buyer during the term of this Exclusive Agency listing, at your request, we would be happy to act as your personal Real Estate Broker; write the appropriate sales contracts, qualify the buyers, place the loan, handle all the escrow work, etc., all at NO EXPENSE TO YOU!

We do this because an owner very seldom beats us in our "race" to bring in an acceptable offer first. Also, the few times we have lost the "race," the sellers were so pleased with the calibre of the work we did for them in completing their sales, that they most kindly recommended several other persons to us whose homes we listed and sold.

Considering the loan information Mrs. Baylor gave me, I believe we can net you approximately $3,000 at a sales price of $21,500.

I would appreciate an opportunity to meet with you personally and discuss the sale of your home in more detail.

Mr. Baylor, please accept my thanks for your courtesy and graciousness this afternoon.

With kindest regards, I am

Very truly yours,

....

A FLATTERING LETTER:

Dear Mrs. Dixon,

I have just returned to the office after my visit to your charming home. I want to thank you for being so gracious. It was very considerate of you to invite me in.

I was so impressed with the appearance of your home that I was moved to write this short letter. The beautiful setting, the quiet country lane, the flowering trees and cool green lawn make your home a veritable paradise.

The exterior elevation of your home is particularly appealing. The rustic front makes it appear to be solid and well built. It blends very well with your landscaping. I can see many hours of hard work that you must have spent on landscaping and maintenance.

The interior has a spaciousness, due, I am certain, to the exceptionally well conceived floor plan and the light, bright rooms.

Those large windows surely make a difference! There is a picture view from each one.

(The balance of this letter was a basic listing letter describing the number of salesmen in my office, etc.)

**Exhibit B-11
Bulletin Notice to Members
of Multiple Listing Service**

BULLETIN NOTICE

2957 $ 30,950

(Owner) S. L. MORRISETTE

(Address of Property) 59 HILLCREST AVE. (CONCORD)

(L.O.) GRANADA (SHAW)

SELLER WILL CONSIDER SECOND TO WELL QUALIFIED BUYER.

8/7/--

AUTHORIZATION TO CHANGE PRICE AND/OR EXTEND LISTING

I/We hereby authorize _GRANADA REALTY_ (Broker) to make the
following changes in Multiple Listing Contract # _2957_
covering property located at _59 HILLCREST AVE (CONCORD)_

Price as listed _31,500_ _____ New Price _30,950_
Present expiration date _9/5/--_ _____ Extend to _____

Additional changes or remarks: _____

_____

Date: _7/17/--_ _____ Signed _L.L. Morrisette_ (Owner)

L.Salesman: _T. Shaw_ _____ Signed _D.R. Morrisette_ (Owner)

This form must be signed by all parties signing original listing
and must reach the board office prior to the expiration of the
listing. Mail original copy to _____ Board of Realtors,
P.O. Box _____ , _____ , Calif.

Exhibit B-12

If your listing doesn't sell, get the price reduced!

We report sales or mart listings promptly.

SOLD OR LEASED NOTICE _____ DATE SOLD _8/11/--_

LISTING # _2957_

OWNER'S NAME _MORRISETTE, L._

PROPERTY ADDRESS _10 OLIVE RD, CONCORD_

LISTING OFFICE _GRANADA (RANDLE)_
Salesman

SELLING OFFICE _GRANADA (GESTER)_
Salesman

LISTED PRICE _30,950_ _____ SELLING PRICE _30,500_

FIRM SALE _YES_ LEASE _____ LGTH. OF LEASE _____

CONTINGENT SALE _____

CONTINUE TO SHOW: _____ (Show Clause & Length)
DOWN PAYMENT _____

RELEASE CLAUSE (How Long) _NO_ _____

The listing office is responsible for notification of sales to the
Board Office, within 24 hours after the deposit is taken. Mail to
Board Of Realtors, P.O. Box _____ , _____ , Calif.

FINANCING
SINGLE FAMILY RESIDENCES

CASH DOWN	LOAN AMOUNT	INTEREST RATE	2ND ALLOWED	TERM (YEARS)	MAX. LOAN	LOAN FEE
5%	95%	10½%	—	30	$35,000	3% + $50
10%	90%	10%	—	30	$45,000	2% + $50
10%	80%	9¾%	10%	30	$45,000	1½% + $50
20%	80%	9½%	—	30	$60,000	1% + $50
25%	75%	9¼%	—	30	$40,000	1%

Exhibit B-13
Conventional Loan Information Card
A salesman should keep a similar schedule of current available financing.

Exhibit B-14
Key to Writing Deposit Receipts

DEPOSIT RECEIPT

A PROPERLY COMPLETED DEPOSIT RECEIPT WILL INCLUDE ATTENTION GIVEN TO THE FOLLOWING:

1. City or town where Deposit Receipt is signed by purchaser.
2. Date Deposit Receipt is signed by purchaser.
3. Purchaser(s) name(s) as to be shown on Grant Deed. (It's a good idea at this point to determine exactly how purchaser wishes to take title, i.e., Joint Tenants, Tenants in Common, etc.).
4. The amount of deposit should be indicated both in writing and in Arabic numbers followed by notation of the form of deposit, ie., (promissory note), (personal check), (cash), or whatever.
5. Location of property being purchased is best described as Lafayette *area,* Concord *area,* etc., inasmuch as so much of the property we deal in is not actually within a city but is within an unincorporated county area.
6. Most of our sales are in the County of Contra Costa.
7. Property description should read: LOT AND IMPROVEMENTS KNOWN AS 1444 ANCHOVY ST. Care should be taken, especially in the case of sales requiring government

insured financing, to omit any reference to "extras" such as drapes, furniture, and so forth, which may be included in the sale at the contract price. It is for this situation that the Personal Property Transfer form is used.

8. The buyer's offer should be indicated both in writing and in Arabic numbers.

9. The amount of the deposit is often increased after seller's acceptance.

10. The amount of time indicated for completion of payment will depend upon several considerations. Among these are: a.) the length of time required to process financing for purchaser; b.) how long it will take purchaser to arrange his cash down payment; c.) how soon seller is prepared to deliver title.

11. TERMS OF PURCHASE ARE DISCUSSED SEPARATELY.

12. The number of days inserted in this blank is governed entirely by the circumstances under which salesman is working. Ordinarily, the salesman should use only the minimum number of days he knows will allow him to make contact with and obtain acceptance from the seller.

13. Pro-rations are usually made to date of close of escrow.

14. Existing bonds or assessments are normally PAID BY SELLER. However, any exceptions should be noted here.

15. When selling an occupied property, you should allow the seller from 7-10 days after close of escrow to give possession of property. (As a general rule, when more than 10 days is given after close of escrow it would be proper to provide for rental payment from seller to buyer by including an Interim Occupancy Agreement clause in the Terms of Purchase section of the Deposit Receipt.)

16. Selling Salesman should SIGN the Deposit Receipt.

17. Only one signature is necessary to purchase a home.

18. Don't forget what we work for—because counter offers or sales prices can always change, it's a good idea to use "6 per cent OF SELLING PRICE" rather than a dollar amount.

19. Signatures of both husband and wife are necessary to sell property.

20. Dating the seller's acceptance could be an extremely important factor in the case of a disputed Deposit Receipt.

21. If seller is required to pay FHA or GI Points, commit him in writing following the commission statement. SELLER AGREES TO PAY A MAXIMUM OF TWO POINTS FOR FHA FINANCING.

☐ BROKER'S COPY   ☐ COPY FOR_____
☐ SELLER'S COPY
☐ BUYER'S COPY   ☐ COPY FOR_____

AGREEMENT OF SALE AND
DEPOSIT RECEIPT

(1)

(2)

_____, California_____ 19____

CITY

Received from_____ (HEREIN CALLED PURCHASER)

(3)

CHECK ☐   NOTE ☐

CASH ☐   In the sum of_____ (4) _____($) Dollars.

(5)

as a deposit on account of the purchase price of the following described property, situated in the City of

(6)

County of_____ State of California; known as:

(7)

For the total purchase price of_____Dollars.

(8)

Deposit to be increased to $_____ (9) _____within_____(10)_____days of acceptance of this offer by seller.

The balance of the purchase price is to be paid within_____days from date of acceptance hereof, as follows,

(11)

AND IT IS HEREBY AGREED: (1st) Undersigned real estate agent shall have_____(12)_____days to obtain acceptance of seller.

(2nd) That should the purchaser fail to pay the balance of the purchase price, or fail to complete the purchase, as herein provided, the amounts paid hereon may, at the option of the seller, be retained as the consideration for the execution of this agreement by the seller.

(3rd) Title is to be free of liens and encumbrances, other than (1) Current taxes, not yet due or payable (2) recorded tract restrictions, (3) set back lines and utility easements set forth on recorded maps or in recorded tract restrictions. (4) zoning regulations (5) any other items set forth herein. That the evidence of title shall be a Policy of Title Insurance issued by_____INSURANCE COMPANY, to be furnished and paid for by the purchaser. That in the event the improvements on said property shall be destroyed or materially damaged between the date hereof and delivery of final deed or contract, or should the title to said property prove defective or unmerchantable, and should the seller be unable to perfect the same within ninety days from date hereof, all amounts paid hereon shall be returned to the purchaser upon demand, unless the purchaser elects to accept the title in said condition.

(4th) That the taxes for the fiscal year ending June 30th and the rents, insurance, if policies are satisfactory to purchaser, and other expenses of said property shall be prorated as of date of delivery of deed or final contract, or within_____(13)_____days from said recordation.

(5th) Any existing assessments and/or improvement bonds are to be_____(14)_____by_____provided any delinquencies shall be paid by seller.

(6th) That the essence of this agreement is time and the undersigned real estate broker may, without notice, extend the time for an additional period of thirty days should said broker deem the extension advisable, except the time for the acceptance hereof by seller and date of possession. That the property is sold subject to the approval of the seller.

(7th) Possession of premises to be given upon recordation of Deed or Final Contract or within_____(15)_____days from date of said recordation.

(8th) No representations, guarantees or warranties of any kind or character have been made by any party hereto or their representatives which are not herein expressed.

Real Estate Broker_____ By_____(16)_____

Address_____ Phone No._____

I agree to purchase the above described property on the terms and conditions herein stated, and acknowledge receipt of a copy hereof.

(17)

PURCHASER   PURCHASER

Address_____ Phone No._____

I agree to sell the above described property on the terms and conditions herein stated and agree to pay the above named broker as commission the

sum of_____(18)_____% of the purchase price, or one-half the deposit in case same is forfeited by the purchaser, provided the same shall not exceed the full amount of the commission. and I hereby authorize the escrow holder to pay said commission from escrow upon closing. The undersigned acknowledges receipt of copy hereof.

(20)   (21)   (19)

Acceptance Date_____19____   SELLER

SELLER

Exhibit B-15
Deposit Receipt

BLANK SAMPLE (REFERS TO KEY)

**AGREEMENT OF SALE AND
DEPOSIT RECEIPT**

☐ BROKER'S COPY   ☐ COPY FOR _____
☐ SELLER'S COPY
☐ BUYER'S COPY   ☐ COPY FOR _____   Lafayette _____, California July 15 ___ 19 __
                                             CITY

Received from **JOHN J. WILSON AND MARTHA M. WILSON, his wife** _____ (HEREIN CALLED PURCHASER)

CHECK ☒X NOTE ☐

CASH ☐ In the sum of **One Thousand and no/100------** ($ **1,000.00---**) Dollars.

as a deposit on account of the purchase price of the following described property, situated in the City of **Walnut Creek**

County of **Contra Costa** . State of California; known as:

Lot and Improvements commonly known as 27 Oak Hill Road, including living room carpets and drapes.

For the total purchase price of **Twenty Thousand and no/100 ($20,000.00)----** _____ Dollars.

Deposit to be increased to $ _____ within _____ days of acceptance of this offer by seller.

The balance of the purchase price is to be paid within **30** _____ days from date of acceptance hereof, as follows,

1-Buyers to make a cash down payment of $5,000 including above deposit.

2-Buyers and property to qualify for a new conventional loan of $15,000 for a term of approximately 30 years with interest at approximately 6%.

3-Standard termite form attached.

AND IT IS HEREBY AGREED: (1st) Undersigned real estate agent shall have **2** _____ days to obtain acceptance of seller.

(2nd) That should the purchaser fail to pay the balance of the purchase price, or fail to complete the purchase, as herein provided, the amounts paid hereon may, at the option of the seller, be retained as the consideration for the execution of this agreement by the seller.

(3rd) Title is to be free of liens and encumbrances, other than (1) Current taxes, not yet due or payable (2) recorded tract restrictions, (3) set back lines and utility easements set forth on recorded maps or in recorded tract restrictions. (4) zoning regulations (5) any other items set forth herein. That the evidence of title shall be a Policy of Title Insurance issued by **INSURANCE COMPANY**, to be furnished and paid for by the purchaser. That in the event the improvements on said property shall be destroyed or materially damaged between the date hereof and delivery of final deed or contract, or should the title to said property prove defective or unmerchantable, and should the seller be unable to perfect the same within ninety days from date hereof, all amounts paid hereon shall be returned to the purchaser upon demand, unless the purchaser elects to accept the title in said condition.

(4th) That the taxes for the fiscal year ending June 30th and the rents, insurance, if policies are satisfactory to purchaser, and other expenses of said property shall be prorated as of date of delivery of deed or final contract, or within **0** _____ days from said recordation.

(5th) Any existing assessments and/or improvement bonds are to be **paid** _____ by **seller** _____ provided any delinquencies shall be paid by seller.

(6th) That the essence of this agreement is time and the undersigned real estate broker may, without notice, extend the time for an additional period of thirty days should said broker deem the extension advisable, except the time for the acceptance hereof by seller and date of possession. That the property is sold subject to the approval of the seller.

(7th) Possession of premises to be given upon recordation of Deed or Final Contract or within **5** _____ days from date of said recordation.

(8th) No representations, guarantees or warranties of any kind or character have been made by any party hereto or their representatives which are not herein expressed.

Real Estate Broker **GRANADA REALTY**   By _____

Address **P.O. BOX 697 Lafayette, California**   Phone No. **284-3555**

I agree to purchase the above described property on the terms and conditions herein stated, and acknowledge receipt of a copy hereof.

_____   _____
    PURCHASER   PURCHASER

Address **1001 Sutter St. San Francisco**   Phone No. **YU 7-4010**

I agree to sell the above described property on the terms and conditions herein stated and agree to pay the above named broker as commission the sum of **6** _____ % of the purchase price, or one-half the deposit in case same is forfeited by the purchaser, provided the same shall not exceed the full amount of the commission. and I hereby authorize the escrow holder to pay said commission from escrow upon closing. The undersigned acknowledges receipt of copy hereof.

Acceptance Date **July 16** ___ 19 __

_____
SELLER

_____
SELLER

CONVENTIONAL LOAN

185

☐ BROKER'S COPY   ☐ COPY FOR_____

☐ SELLER'S COPY

☐ BUYER'S COPY   ☐ COPY FOR_____

AGREEMENT OF SALE AND DEPOSIT RECEIPT

Lafayette _____ , California July 15 ___ 19--

CITY

Received from   JOHN J. WILSON, a single man

CHECK ☒   NOTE ☐   (HEREIN CALLED PURCHASER)

CASH ☐   In the sum of One Thousand and no/100--- ($ 1,000.00---) Dollars.

as a deposit on account of the purchase price of the following described property, situated in the City of Walnut Creek

County of Contra Costa . State of California; known as:

Lot and improvements commonly known as 27 Oak Hill Road, including living room carpets and drapes.

For the total purchase price of Twenty Thousand and no/100 ($20,000.00)----- Dollars.

Deposit to be increased to $_____ within_____ days of acceptance of this offer by seller.

The balance of the purchase price is to be paid within_____30_____ days from date of acceptance hereof, as follows,

1—Buyer to make a cash down payment of $2,000 including above deposit.

2—Buyer to give and seller to take back a note secured by a deed of trust in the approximate amount of $2,000 with monthly payments of approximately $20.00 or more including 7% interest. Said note due and payable in full 5 years from date of making.

3—Buyer and property to qualify for a new conventional loan in the approximate amount of $16,000 for a term of approximately 30 years with interest at approximately $6\frac{1}{4}\%$.

4—Stardard termite form attached.

AND IT IS HEREBY AGREED: (1st) Undersigned real estate agent shall have_____I_____days to obtain acceptance of seller.

(2nd) That should the purchaser fail to pay the balance of the purchase price, or fail to complete the purchase, as herein provided, the amounts paid hereon may, at the option of the seller, be retained as the consideration for the execution of this agreement by the seller.

(3rd) Title is to be free of liens and encumbrances, other than (1) Current taxes, not yet due or payable (2) recorded tract restrictions, (3) set back lines and utility easements set forth on recorded maps or in recorded tract restrictions. (4) zoning regulations (5) any other items set forth herein. That the evidence of title shall be a Policy of Title Insurance issued by **INSURANCE COMPANY**, to be furnished and paid for by the purchaser. That in the event the improvements on said property shall be destroyed or materially damaged between the date hereof and delivery of final deed or contract, or should the title to said property prove defective or unmerchantable, and should the seller be unable to perfect the same within ninety days from date hereof, all amounts paid hereon shall be returned to the purchaser upon demand, unless the purchaser elects to accept the title in said condition.

(4th) That the taxes for the fiscal year ending June 30th and the rents, insurance, if policies are satisfactory to purchaser, and other expenses of said property shall be prorated as of date of delivery of deed or final contract, or within____I____days from said recordation.

(5th) Any existing assessments and/or improvement bonds are to be_____paid_____by_____seller_____provided any delinquencies shall be paid by seller.

(6th) That the essence of this agreement is time and the undersigned real estate broker may, without notice, extend the time for an additional period of thirty days should said broker deem the extension advisable, except the time for the acceptance hereof by seller and date of possession. That the property is sold subject to the approval of the seller.

(7th) Possession of premises to be given upon recordation of Deed or Final Contract or within_____7_____days from date of said recordation.

(8th) No representations, guarantees or warranties of any kind or character have been made by any party hereto or their representatives which are not herein expressed.

Real Estate Broker   GRANADA REALTY

Address P.O. BOX 697 Lafayette, California   Phone No. 284-5555

I agree to purchase the above described property on the terms and conditions herein stated, and acknowledge receipt of a copy hereof.

PURCHASER   PURCHASER

Address 840 California St., Salinas, California   Phone No. 297-5407

I agree to sell the above described property on the terms and conditions herein stated and agree to pay the above named broker as commission the

sum of_____6_____% of the purchase price, or one-half the deposit in case same is forfeited by the purchaser, provided the same shall not exceed the full amount of the commission. and I hereby authorize the escrow holder to pay said commission from escrow upon closing. The undersigned acknowledges receipt of copy hereof.

Acceptance Date____July 16____19--

SELLER

SELLER

CONVENTIONAL LOAN WITH 2ND DEED OF TRUST

Exhibit B-17
Deposit Receipt

AGREEMENT OF SALE AND
DEPOSIT RECEIPT

Lafayette_____, California__July 15____19--

City

Received from __JOHN J. WILSON, a single man_____

CHECK ☒X   NOTE ☐   (HEREIN CALLED PURCHASER)

CASH ☐   In the sum of __One Thousand and no/100---_____ ($1,000.00---__) Dollars.

as a deposit on account of the purchase price of the following described property, situated in the City of __Walnut Creek__ County of __Contra Costa__   State of California; known as:

Lot and improvements commonly known as 27 Oak Hill Road.

(NOTE: Personal property is listed on separate form for GI and FHA sales.
     See Exhibit B-31)

For the total purchase price of __Twenty Thousand and no/100 ($20,000.00)---_____ Dollars.

Deposit to be increased to $_____within_____days of acceptance of this offer by seller.

The balance of the purchase price is to be paid within _____90_____ days from date of acceptance hereof, as follows,

1-Buyer and property to qualify for a GI loan of $20,000 for a term of 30 years with monthly payments of approximately $110.45 including principal and interest.

2-Standard termite form attached.

3-Seller agrees to pay necessary "points" to secure GI loan.

AND IT IS HEREBY AGREED: (1st) Undersigned real estate agent shall have_____2_____days to obtain acceptance of seller.
(2nd) That should the purchaser fail to pay the balance of the purchase price, or fail to complete the purchase, as herein provided, the amounts paid hereon may, at the option of the seller, be retained as the consideration for the execution of this agreement by the seller.
(3rd) Title is to be free of liens and encumbrances, other than (1) Current taxes, not yet due or payable (2) recorded tract restrictions, (3) set back lines and utility easements set forth on recorded maps or in recorded tract restrictions. (4) zoning regulations (5) any other items set forth herein. That the evidence of title shall be a Policy of Title Insurance issued by **INSURANCE COMPANY**, to be furnished and paid for by the purchaser. That in the event the improvements on said property shall be destroyed or materially damaged between the date hereof and delivery of final deed or contract, or should the title to said property prove defective or unmerchantable, and should the seller be unable to perfect the same within ninety days from date hereof, all amounts paid hereon shall be returned to the purchaser upon demand, unless the purchaser elects to accept the title in said condition.

(4th) That the taxes for the fiscal year ending June 30th and the rents, insurance, if policies are satisfactory to purchaser, and other expenses of said property shall be prorated as of date of delivery of deed or final contract, or within_____0_____days from said recordation.

(5th) Any existing assessments and/or improvement bonds are to be __paid__ by __seller__ provided any delinquencies shall be paid by seller.

(6th) The essence of this agreement is time and the undersigned real estate broker may, without notice, extend the time for an additional period of thirty days should said broker deem the extension advisable, except the time for the acceptance hereof by seller and date of possession. That the property is sold subject to the approval of the seller.

(7th) Possession of premises to be given upon recordation of Deed or Final Contract or within_____2_____days from date of said recordation.

(8th) No representations, guarantees or warranties of any kind or character have been made by any party hereto or their representatives which are not herein expressed.

Real Estate Broker __GRANADA REALTY__

Address __P.O. BOX 697 Lafayette, California__   Phone No. __284-5555__

I agree to purchase the above described property on the terms and conditions herein stated, and acknowledge receipt of a copy hereof.

_____   _John J. Wilson_
PURCHASER   **PURCHASER**

Address __840 California St., Salinas, California__   Phone No. __297-5407__

I agree to sell the above described property on the terms and conditions herein stated and agree to pay the above named broker as commission the sum of_____6_____% of the purchase price, or one-half the deposit in case same is forfeited by the purchaser, provided the same shall not exceed the full amount of the commission. and I hereby authorize the escrow holder to pay said commission from escrow upon closing. The undersigned acknowledges receipt of copy hereof.

Acceptance Date___July 16___19--   _Thad J. Bryan_
                              SELLER
                              Emily J. Bryan
                              SELLER

NO-DOWN-PAYMENT GI LOAN

Exhibit B-18
Deposit Receipt

☐ BROKER'S COPY   ☐ COPY FOR_____

☐ SELLER'S COPY

☐ BUYER'S COPY   ☐ COPY FOR_____   Lafayette____, California July 15____ 19 --

CITY

Received from FRANK L. RYAN AND LOUISE V. RYAN, his wife

CHECK ☒X   NOTE ☐   (HEREIN CALLED PURCHASER)

CASH ☐   In the sum of Five Hundred and no/100---   ($ 500.00---) Dollars

as a deposit on account of the purchase price of the following described property, situated in the City of Pleasant Hill

County of Contra Costa , State of California; known as:

Lot and improvements commonly known as 2228 Serena Lane

For the total purchase price of Twenty Thousand and no/100 ($20,000.00)---- ____ Dollars.

Deposit to be increased to $ 1,000.00 ____ within 5 days of acceptance of this offer by seller.

The balance of the purchase price is to be paid within 90 days from date of acceptance hereof, as follows,

1-Buyer to make a cash down payment of $3,000 including above deposit.

2-Buyer and property to qualify for a new GI loan in the amount of $17,000
for a term of 30 years with monthly payments of approximately $93.88
including principal and interest.

3-Standard termite form attached.

AND IT IS HEREBY AGREED: (1st) Undersigned real estate agent shall have_____2_____days to obtain acceptance of seller.
(2nd) That should the purchaser fail to pay the balance of the purchase price, or fail to complete the purchase, as herein provided, the amounts paid hereon may, at the option of the seller, be retained as the consideration for the execution of this agreement by the seller.
(3rd) Title is to be free of liens and encumbrances, other than (1) Current taxes, not yet due or payable (2) recorded tract restrictions, (3) set back lines and utility easements set forth on recorded maps or in recorded tract restrictions. (4) zoning regulations (5) any other items set forth herein. That the evidence of title shall be a Policy of Title Insurance issued by **INSURANCE COMPANY,** to be furnished and paid for by the purchaser. That in the event the improvements on said property shall be destroyed or materially damaged between the date hereof and delivery of final deed or contract, or should the title to said property prove defective or unmerchantable, and should the seller be unable to perfect the same within ninety days from date hereof, all amounts paid hereon shall be returned to the purchaser upon demand, unless the purchaser elects to accept the title in said condition.

(4th) That the taxes for the fiscal year ending June 30th and the rents, insurance, if policies are satisfactory to purchaser, and other expenses of said property shall be prorated as of date of delivery of deed or final contract, or within____0____days from said recordation.
(5th) Any existing assessments and/or improvement bonds are to be paid by seller provided any delinquencies shall be paid by seller.
(6th) That the essence of this agreement is time and the undersigned real estate broker may, without notice, extend the time for an additional period of thirty days should said broker deem the extension advisable, except the time for the acceptance hereof by seller and date of possession. That the property is sold subject to the approval of the seller.

(7th) Possession of premises to be given upon recordation of Deed or Final Contract or within____5____days from date of said recordation.

(8th) No representations, guarantees or warranties of any kind or character have been made by any party hereto or their representatives which are not herein expressed.

Real Estate Broker GRANADA REALTY

Address P.O. BOX 697 Lafayette, California   Phone No. 284-5555

I agree to purchase the above described property on the terms and conditions herein stated, and acknowledge receipt of a copy hereof.

Frank L. Ryan   *Louise V. Ryan*

PURCHASER   PURCHASER

Address 121 Monument Blvd., Alamo, Calif.   Phone No. 887-9904

I agree to sell the above described property on the terms and conditions herein stated and agree to pay the above named broker as commission the

sum of_____6_____% of the purchase price, or one-half the deposit in case same is forfeited by the purchaser, provided the same shall not exceed the full amount of the commission, and I hereby authorize the escrow holder to pay said commission from escrow upon closing. The undersigned acknowledges receipt of copy hereof.

Acceptance Date July 16 ____ 19 --

Thomas T. Tumas

SELLER

Susan O. Tumas

SELLER

GI LOAN WITH DOWN PAYMENT

Exhibit B-19
Deposit Receipt

☐ BROKER'S COPY   ☐ COPY FOR_____
☐ SELLER'S COPY
☐ BUYER'S COPY   ☐ COPY FOR_____

AGREEMENT OF SALE AND DEPOSIT RECEIPT

Lafayette, California _July 15_ 19__
CITY

Received from_ JOHN J. WILSON AND MARTHA M. WILSON, his wife _

CHECK ☒X   NOTE ☐   (HEREIN CALLED PURCHASER)

CASH ☐   In the sum of_One Thousand and no/100---_ ($1,000.00--) Dollars.

as a deposit on account of the purchase price of the following described property, situated in the City of _Walnut Creek_
County of _Contra Costa_   State of California; known as:

Lot and improvements commonly known as 27 Oak Hill Road

For the total purchase price of _Twenty Thousand and no/100 ($20,000.00)---_ Dollars.

Deposit to be increased to $_____ within_____ days of acceptance of this offer by seller.

The balance of the purchase price is to be paid within_____90_____ days from date of acceptance hereof, as follows:

1—Buyer to make a cash down payment of $1,000 including above deposit.

2—Buyer and property to qualify for a FHA loan in the amount of $19,000 for a term of 30 years with monthly payments of approximately $112.94 including principal and interest.

3—Standard termite form attached.

AND IT IS HEREBY AGREED: (1st) Undersigned real estate agent shall have____1____days to obtain acceptance of seller.

(2nd) That should the purchaser fail to pay the balance of the purchase price, or fail to complete the purchase, as herein provided, the amounts paid hereon may, at the option of the seller, be retained as the consideration for the execution of this agreement by the seller.

• (3rd) Title is to be free of liens and encumbrances, other than (1) Current taxes, not yet due or payable (2) recorded tract restrictions, (3) set back lines and utility easements set forth on recorded maps or in recorded tract restrictions. (4) zoning regulations (5) any other items set forth herein. That the evidence of title shall be a Policy of Title Insurance issued by **INSURANCE COMPANY**, to be furnished and paid for by the purchaser. That in the event the improvements on said property shall be destroyed or materially damaged between the date hereof and delivery of final deed or contract, or should the title to said property prove defective or unmerchantable, and should the seller be unable to perfect the same within ninety days from date hereof, all amounts paid hereon shall be returned to the purchaser upon demand, unless the purchaser elects to accept the title in said condition.

(4th) That the taxes for the fiscal year ending June 30th and the rents, insurance, if policies are satisfactory to purchaser, and other expenses of said property shall be prorated as of date of delivery of final contract, or within____1____days from said property.

(5th) Any existing assessments and/or improvement bonds are to be _paid_ by _seller_ provided any delinquencies shall be paid by seller.

(6th) That the essence of this agreement is time and the undersigned real estate broker may, without notice, extend the time for an additional period of thirty days should said broker deem the extension advisable, except the time for the acceptance hereof by seller and date of possession. That the property is sold subject to the approval of the seller.

(7th) Possession of premises to be given upon recordation of Deed or Final Contract or within____5____days from date of said recordation.

(8th) No representations, guarantees or warranties of any kind or character have been made by any party hereto or their representatives which are not herein expressed.

Real Estate Broker_ GRANADA REALTY _

Address_ P.O. BOX 697 Lafayette, California _ Phone No._ 284-5555 _

I agree to purchase the above described property on the terms and conditions herein stated, and acknowledge receipt of a copy hereof.

John J. Wilson   _Martha M. Wilson_
PURCHASER   PURCHASER

Address_ 840 California St., Salinas, California _ Phone No._ 297-5407 _

I agree to sell the above described property on the terms and conditions herein stated and agree to pay the above named broker as commission the sum of___6___% of the purchase price, or one-half the deposit in case same is forfeited by the purchaser, provided the same shall not exceed the full amount of the commission. and I hereby authorize the escrow holder to pay said commission from escrow upon closing. The undersigned acknowledges receipt of copy hereof.

SELLERS AGREE TO PAY A MAXIMUM OF 3 FHA POINTS.

Acceptance Date_ July 16 _ 19__

Thad J. Bryan
SELLER

Emily J. Bryan
SELLER

FHA LOAN

Exhibit B-20
Deposit Receipt

189

**AGREEMENT OF SALE AND
DEPOSIT RECEIPT**

Lafayette , California July 15 19--
CITY

Received from EDWARD F. MURPHY, a married man

(HEREIN CALLED PURCHASER)

CHECK ☒ NOTE ☐
CASH ☐ In the sum of Five Hundred and no/100--- ($ 500.00--) Dollars.

as a deposit on account of the purchase price of the following described property, situated in the City of Walnut Creek
County of Contra Costa State of California, known as:

Lot and improvements commonly known as 1559 Solano Court

For the total purchase price of Thirteen Thousand Five Hundred and no/100 ($13,500.00)-- Dollars.
Deposit to be increased to $_____ within_____days of acceptance of this offer by seller.
The balance of the purchase price is to be paid within_____90_____days from date of acceptance hereof, as follows,

1-Property to obtain an FHA valuation of $13,500.

2-Buyer and property to qualify for a FHA loan of $13,500 under Section 221.d2.

3-Buyers cash payment to be at least 3% of acquisition cost which is the sum
of the sales price plus normal closing costs.

4-Buyers cash payment to be applied to his normal closing costs. Seller
agrees to pay all of buyers closing costs in excess of 3% of acquisition
cost.

5-Standard termite form attached.

AND IT IS HEREBY AGREED: (1st) Undersigned real estate agent shall have_____2_____days to obtain acceptance of seller.
(2nd) That should the purchaser fail to pay the balance of the purchase price, or fail to complete the purchase, as herein provided, the amounts paid hereon may, at the option of the seller, be retained as the consideration for the execution of this agreement by the seller.
(3rd) Title is to be free of liens and encumbrances, other than (1) Current taxes, not yet due or payable (2) recorded tract restrictions, (3) set back lines and utility easements set forth on recorded maps or in recorded tract restrictions. (4) zoning regulations (5) any other items set forth herein. That the evidence of title shall be a Policy of Title Insurance issued by **INSURANCE COMPANY**, to be furnished and paid for by the purchaser. That in the event the improvements on said property shall be destroyed or materially damaged between the date hereof and delivery of final deed or contract, or should the title to said property prove defective or unmerchantable, and should the seller be unable to perfect the same within ninety days from date hereof, all amounts paid hereon shall be returned to the purchaser upon demand, unless the purchaser elects to accept the title in said condition.

(4th) That the taxes for the fiscal year ending June 30th and the rents, insurance, if policies are satisfactory to purchaser, and other expenses of said property shall be prorated as of date of delivery of deed or final contract, or within_____0_____days from said recordation.
(5th) Any existing assessments and/or improvement bonds are to be_____paid_____by_____seller_____provided any delinquencies shall be paid by seller.
(6th) That the essence of this agreement is time and the undersigned real estate broker may, without notice, extend the time for an additional period of thirty days should said broker deem the extension advisable, except the time for the acceptance hereof by seller and date of possession. That the property is sold subject to the approval of the seller.
(7th) Possession of premises to be given upon recordation of Deed or Final Contract or within_____1_____days from date of said recordation.
(8th) No representations, guarantees or warranties of any kind or character have been made by any party hereto or their representatives which are not herein expressed.

Real
Estate Broker_____GRANADA REALTY_____
Address P.O. BOX 697 Lafayette, California Phone No. 284-5555

I agree to purchase the above described property on the terms and conditions herein stated, and acknowledge receipt of a copy hereof.

_____Edward F. Murphy_____
PURCHASER
Address 14 Valencia Road, Alamo, Calif. Phone No. 255-8867

PURCHASER

I agree to sell the above described property on the terms and conditions herein stated and agree to pay the above named broker as commission the
sum of_____6_____% of the purchase price, or one-half the deposit in case same is forfeited by the purchaser, provided the same shall not exceed the full amount of the commission. and I hereby authorize the escrow holder to pay said commission from escrow upon closing. The undersigned acknowledges receipt of copy hereof.

Acceptance Date_____July 15_____19 --

_____Wilbert K. Cassady_____
SELLER
_____Violet B. Cassady_____
SELLER

SECTION 221.D2 FHA LOAN

**Exhibit B-21
Deposit Receipt**

AGREEMENT OF SALE AND
DEPOSIT RECEIPT

_____Lafayette_____, California, July 15 19--
City

Received from KEITH F. JOHNSON AND ALVINA M. JOHNSON, his wife

CHECK ☒X   NOTE ☐   (HEREIN CALLED PURCHASER)

CASH ☐   In the sum of Five Hundred and no/100---   ($ 500.00---) Dollars.

as a deposit on account of the purchase price of the following described property, situated in the City of Walnut Creek

County of Contra Costa   State of California; known as:

Lot and improvements commonly known as 449 Acacia Street, including all carpets and drapes and patio furniture.

For the total purchase price of Twenty Five Thousand and no/100 ($25,000.00)--- Dollars.

Deposit to be increased to $ 1,000.00   within 10 days of acceptance of this offer by seller.

The balance of the purchase price is to be paid within 100 days from date of acceptance hereof, as follows,

1-Buyer to make a cash down payment of $10,000 including above deposit.

2-Buyer and property to qualify for a new Cal Vet loan in the amount of $15,000 for a term of approximately 22 years with interest at the approximate rate of 3 3/4%.

3-Standard termite form attached.

AND IT IS HEREBY AGREED: (1st) Undersigned real estate agent shall have 2 days to obtain acceptance of seller.

(2nd) That should the purchaser fail to pay the balance of the purchase price, or fail to complete the purchase, as herein provided, the amounts paid hereon may, at the option of the seller, be retained as the consideration for the execution of this agreement by the seller.

(3rd) Title is to be free of liens and encumbrances, other than (1) Current taxes, not yet due or payable (2) recorded tract restrictions, (3) set back lines and utility easements set forth on recorded maps or in recorded tract restrictions. (4) zoning regulations (5) any other items set forth herein. That the evidence of title shall be a Policy of Title Insurance issued by INSURANCE COMPANY, to be furnished and paid for by the purchaser. That in the event the improvements on said property shall be destroyed or materially damaged between the date hereof and delivery of final deed or contract, or should the title to said property prove defective or unmerchantable, and should the seller be unable to perfect the same within ninety days from date hereof, all amounts paid hereon shall be returned to the purchaser upon demand, unless the purchaser elects to accept the title in said condition.

(4th) That the taxes for the fiscal year ending June 30th and the rents, insurance, if policies are satisfactory to purchaser, and other expenses of said property shall be prorated as of date of delivery of final contract, or within 1 days from said recordation.

(5th) Any existing assessments and/or improvement bonds are to be paid by seller provided any delinquencies shall be paid by seller.

(6th) That the essence of this agreement is time and the undersigned real estate broker may, without notice, extend the time for an additional period of thirty days should said broker deem the extension advisable, except the time for the acceptance hereof by seller and date of possession. That the property is sold subject to the approval of the seller.

(7th) Possession of premises to be given upon recordation of Deed or Final Contract or within 0 days from date of said recordation.

(8th) No representations, guarantees or warranties of any kind or character have been made by any party hereto or their representatives which are not herein expressed.

Real Estate Broker GRANADA REALTY   By _[signature]_

Address P.O. BOX 697 Lafayette, California   Phone No. 234-5555

I agree to purchase the above described property on the terms and conditions herein stated, and acknowledge receipt of a copy hereof.

[signature] PURCHASER   _[signature]_ PURCHASER

Address 265 Gloria Terrace, Walnut Creek, Calif.   Phone No. 995-2480

I agree to sell the above described property on the terms and conditions herein stated and agree to pay the above named broker as commission the sum of 6 % of the purchase price, or one-half the deposit in case same is forfeited by the purchaser, provided the same shall not exceed the full amount of the commission. and I hereby authorize the escrow holder to pay said commission from escrow upon closing. The undersigned acknowledges receipt of copy hereof.

Acceptance Date July 16   19--

[signature] SELLER

[signature] SELLER

CAL VET LOAN

Exhibit B-22
Deposit Receipt

191

AGREEMENT OF SALE AND
DEPOSIT RECEIPT

Lafayette , California July 15 19__
CITY

Received from ELVY F. MAZZONI, a single man

(HEREIN CALLED PURCHASER)

CHECK ☒X   NOTE ☐

CASH ☐   In the sum of   Five Hundred and no/100--- ($ 500.00---) Dollars.

as a deposit on account of the purchase price of the following described property, situated in the City of Concord

County of Contra Costa   State of California; known as:

Unimproved property known as Lot 16, Parcel 21 as shown in Book 554 on page 316 in the records of Contra Costa County, said parcel being approximately 6.37 acres in size and vested in the name of John J. Valdez.

For the total purchase price of Eighteen Thousand and no/100 ($18,000.00)---- Dollars

Deposit to be increased to $ 1,000.00--- within 10 days of acceptance of this offer by seller.

The balance of the purchase price is to be paid within 120 days from date of acceptance hereof, as follows:

1-Buyer to give and seller to take back a note secured by a deed of trust in the amount of $17,000 with interest at 7% and monthly payments of $200.00 including interest. Seller agrees, upon buyers request, to subordinate said note and deed of trust to a new construction loan in the amount not to exceed $100,000 with interest of not more than 7% for a term not to exceed 25 years. Said note is due and payable in full 18 months from the date of its making or upon sale of any portion of this property by buyer, whichever occurs first.

2-This offer subject to buyers approval of survey of property to be provided by buyer at buyer's expense.

AND IT IS HEREBY AGREED: (1st) Undersigned real estate agent shall have_____2_____days to obtain acceptance of seller.
(2nd) That should the purchaser fail to pay the balance of the purchase price, or fail to complete the purchase, as herein provided, the amounts paid hereon may, at the option of the seller, be retained as the consideration for the execution of this agreement by the seller.
(3rd) Title is to be free of liens and encumbrances, other than (1) Current taxes, not yet due or payable (2) recorded tract restrictions, (3) set back lines and utility easements set forth on recorded maps or in recorded tract restrictions. (4) zoning regulations (5) any other items set forth herein. That the evidence of title shall be a Policy of Title Insurance issued by **INSURANCE COMPANY**, to be furnished and paid for by the purchaser. That in the event the improvements on said property shall be destroyed or materially damaged between the date hereof and delivery of final deed or contract, or should the title to said property prove defective or unmerchantable, and should the seller be unable to perfect the same within ninety days from date hereof, all amounts paid hereon shall be returned to the purchaser upon demand, unless the purchaser elects to accept the title in said condition.

(4th) That the taxes for the fiscal year ending June 30th and the rents, insurance, if policies are satisfactory to purchaser, and other expenses of said property be prorated as of date of delivery of deed or final contract, or within 0 days from said recordation.

(5th) Any existing assessments and/or improvement bonds are to be paid by seller provided any delinquencies shall be paid by seller.

(6th) That the essence of this agreement is time and the undersigned real estate broker may, without notice, extend the time for an additional period of thirty days should said broker deem the extension advisable, except the time for the acceptance hereof by seller and date of possession. That the property is sold subject to the approval of the seller.

(7th) Possession of premises to be given upon recordation of Deed or Final Contract or within 1 days from date of said recordation.

(8th) No representations, guarantees or warranties of any kind or character have been made by any party hereto or their representatives which are not herein expressed.

Real Estate Broker GRANADA REALTY

Address P.O. BOX 697 Lafayette, California   Phone No. 284-5555

I agree to purchase the above described property on the terms and conditions herein stated, and acknowledge receipt of a copy hereof.

PURCHASER _____ PURCHASER

Address 10 Grammercy Road, Weed, California   Phone No. 335-8895

I agree to sell the above described property on the terms and conditions herein stated and agree to pay the above named broker as commission the sum of 6 % of the purchase price, or one-half the deposit in case same is forfeited by the purchaser, provided the same shall not exceed the full amount of the commission. and I hereby authorize the escrow holder to pay said commission from escrow upon closing. The undersigned acknowledges receipt of copy hereof.

Acceptance Date July 16 19__

SELLER

SELLER

LAND PURCHASE WITH LOAN SUBORDINATION

Exhibit B-23
Deposit Receipt

☐ BROKER'S COPY   ☐ COPY FOR_____
☐ SELLER'S COPY
☐ BUYER'S COPY   ☐ COPY FOR_____

AGREEMENT OF SALE AND
DEPOSIT RECEIPT

__Lafayette__, California, __August 1__ 19__
CITY

Received from __RALPH SANTINI AND RENA S. SANTINI, his wife__
CHECK ⊠ NOTE ☐ (HEREIN CALLED PURCHASER)
CASH ☐ In the sum of __One Hundred and no/100----__ ($100.00---) Dollars.
as a deposit on account of the purchase price of the following described property, situated in the City of __Walnut Creek__
County of __Contra Costa__ State of California; known as:

Lot 15, Wildwood Acres, together with home to be constructed thereon.

For the total purchase price of __approximately Twenty Nine Thousand and no/100 ($29,000.00)--__ Dollars.
Deposit to be increased to $_____ within _____ days of acceptance of this offer by seller.
The balance of the purchase price is to be paid within __180__ _____ days from date of acceptance hereof, as follows,

THIS IS A LOT RESERVATION

Buyer will pay all cash to seller subject to:

1—Buyer and builder agreeing upon plans, specifications and price of home.

2—Buyers' ability to obtain required financing.

3—Buyer and builder agree that this LOT RESERVATION shall automatically terminate 30 days from above date unless agreement is reached on items #1 & #2 above and a specific purchase-sales agreement is executed between them.

4—If agreement cannot be reached by buyer and seller (builder), buyers' deposit shall be refunded in full except that any charges incurred by buyer for architectural services shall be deducted from deposit.

5—If agreement is reached, buyer shall increase deposit to 10% of purchase price before construction begins.

AND IT IS HEREBY AGREED: (1st) Undersigned real estate agent shall have___1___ days to obtain acceptance of seller.
(2nd) That should the purchaser fail to pay the balance of the purchase price, or fail to complete the purchase, as herein provided, the amounts paid hereon may, at the option of the seller, be retained as the consideration for the execution of this agreement by the seller.
(3rd) Title is to be free of liens and encumbrances, other than (1) Current taxes, not yet due or payable (2) recorded tract restrictions, (3) set back lines and utility easements set forth on recorded maps or in recorded tract restrictions. (4) zoning regulations (5) any other items set forth herein. That the evidence of title shall be a Policy of Title Insurance issued by **INSURANCE COMPANY**, to be furnished and paid for by the purchaser. That in the event the improvements on said property shall be destroyed or materially damaged between the date hereof and delivery of final deed or contract, or should the title to said property prove defective or unmerchantable, and should the seller be unable to perfect the same within ninety days from date hereof, all amounts paid hereon shall be returned to the purchaser upon demand, unless the purchaser elects to accept the title in said condition.

(4th) That the taxes for the fiscal year ending June 30th and the rents, insurance, if policies are satisfactory to purchaser, and other expenses of said property shall be prorated as of date of delivery of deed or final contract, or within __0__ days from said recordation.
(5th) Any existing assessments and/or improvement bonds are to be __paid__ by __seller__ provided any delinquencies shall be paid by seller.
(6th) That the essence of this agreement is time and the undersigned real estate broker may, without notice, extend the time for an additional period of thirty days should said broker deem the extension advisable, except the time for the acceptance hereof by seller and date of possession. That the property is sold subject to the approval of the seller.
(7th) Possession of premises to be given upon recordation of Deed or Final Contract or within __0__ days from date of said recordation.
(8th) No representations, guarantees or warranties of any kind or character have been made by any party hereto or their representatives which are not herein expressed.

Real Estate Broker __GRANADA REALTY__
Address __P.O. BOX 697 Lafayette, California__ Phone No. __284-5555__

I agree to purchase the above described property on the terms and conditions herein stated, and acknowledge receipt of a copy hereof.

Ralph Santini
PURCHASER
Rena S. Santini
PURCHASER
Address __55 Clemson Ct., Walnut Creek, Calif.__ Phone No. __934-6583__

I agree to sell the above described property on the terms and conditions herein stated and agree to pay the above named broker as commission the sum of __6__ % of the purchase price, or one-half the deposit in case same is forfeited by the purchaser, provided the same shall not exceed the full amount of the commission. and I hereby authorize the escrow holder to pay said commission from escrow upon closing. The undersigned acknowledges receipt of copy hereof.

Acceptance Date __August 2__ 19__

Wembley Homes, Inc.
SELLER
Colombo Jones, Pres.
SELLER

Exhibit B-24
Deposit Receipt

AS A LOT RESERVATION, CUSTOM BUILDING JOB TO FOLLOW

Summary of Deposit Receipt Clauses

FOLLOWING IS A CHECK LIST OF ITEMS THAT MAY APPEAR IN A NORMAL DEPOSIT RECEIPT
FOR A HOME SALE:

1. INCREASE OF DEPOSIT (& CONDITIONS UNDER WHICH REFUND WILL BE MADE)
2. SPECIFIED CASH DOWN PAYMENT
3. BUYER/SELLER TO PAY CLOSING COSTS
4. LOAN SPECIFICATIONS (NEW LOAN OR ASSUMPTION OF EXISTING LOAN)
5. SECONDARY FINANCING
6. CONTINGENCY CLAUSE
7. RELEASE CLAUSE
8. TERMITE CLAUSE

IN ADDITION TO THE ABOVE, THERE FOLLOWS THE PROPER PHRASEOLOGY FOR THE NOT-
SO-COMMON SITUATIONS WHICH HAVE SPECIAL APPLICATION. THESE WOULD BE:

9. SUBORDINATION CLAUSE
10. CONTRACT OF SALE
11. INTERIM OCCUPANCY AGREEMENT
12. LOT RESERVATION
13. PERSONAL PROPERTY TRANSFER
14. EQUITY PURCHASE CONSIDERATION.

IN THE PAGES THAT FOLLOW, EACH OF THE ABOVE CLAUSES AND THEIR APPLICATION
WILL BE DISCUSSED IN DETAIL.

Exhibit B-25
Summary of Deposit Receipt Clauses

EXPLANATION OF DEPOSIT RECEIPT CLAUSES

1. ### INCREASE OF DEPOSIT

   When the initial deposit is less than $500 ($1,000 for sales of $20,000 or more), the first paragraph of the terms of purchase should read as follows:

   > Buyer to increase deposit to $500 within 2 days of sellers' acceptance of this contract. If required financing cannot be obtained by buyer within term hereof, deposit monies will be returned to buyer upon demand.

2. ### SPECIFIED CASH DOWN PAYMENT

   This clause spells out the total cash down payment to be made by the buyer within the time period allowed by the contract. Buyer to make a cash down payment of $2,500 including above deposit.

3. ### BUYER/SELLER TO PAY CLOSING COSTS

   Although customary for the buyer to pay those closing costs which are known as "usual buyers closing costs", it is not unusual for a seller to agree to pay a portion or all of the buyers closing costs. While several options are possible, the first of the following (a) is the most commonly used.

   (a) Buyer to pay usual closing costs.

   (b) Seller to pay all of buyers' usual closing costs.

   (c) Seller to pay $400 of buyers' usual closing costs.

   (d) Seller to pay buyers' non-recurring closing costs.

4. ### LOAN SPECIFICATIONS (NEW LOAN OR ASSUMPTION OF EXISTING LOAN)

   In general, the many types of loans and their description are limited only by the imagination of the salesman. Most of the more common types, and their description are listed here.

   #### NEW FHA

   "Buyer and property to qualify for new FHA insured loan of $12,500.00 repaying at approximately $78.18 monthly including principal and interest for a term of 30 years."
   (Salesman: Don't forget FHA Amendment forms)

   #### NEW CONVENTIONAL

   "Buyer and property to qualify for new conventional loan of

Exhibit B-26
Explanation of Deposit Receipt Clauses

EXPLANATION OF DEPOSIT RECEIPT CLAUSES (Continued)

$12,500.00 repaying at approximately $80.54 monthly including
principal and 6% annual interest for a term of 25 years."

NEW GI

"Buyer and property to qualify for a new GI loan of $12,500.00
repaying at approximately $69.03 monthly including principal
and interest for a term of 30 years."

(If a no down payment purchase - add the following)
"Buyers' deposit to be applied to usual closing costs."

NEW CAL-VET

"Buyer and property to qualify for new Cal-Vet loan of $12,500.00
repaying at approximately $75.75 monthly including principal and
3 3/4% annual interest for a term of 20 years."

SELLER CARRY-BACK FIRST LOAN

Buyer to give and seller to take back a note, secured by 1st deed
of trust in the amount of $17,500 repaying $125.38 or more monthly
including 6% interest for a term of 20 years.

ASSUMPTION OF EXISTING LOAN

Buyer to assume existing loan of approximately $17,500 repaying
at approximately $163 monthly including principal and interest.

(It is important to remember to use the word "approximately"
after the cash down payment amount when your buyer is assuming
a loan as the existing loan balance will vary dependent upon
the day the escrow closes.)

OVERLAPPING DEED OF TRUST

Buyer to give and seller to take back a note for $17,500.00
secured by an overlapping deed of trust repaying $125.38 or more
monthly including 6½% interest for a term of 20 years.

5. SECONDARY FINANCING

An invaluable tool for making sales that are often overlooked. Especially
helpful to the buyer with a low or medium sized down payment and a poor
loan qualifying ability.

STRAIGHT SECOND

Buyer to give and seller to take back a note, secured by 2nd deed
of trust, in the amount of $2,500 repaying at $25 or more monthly
including 7% interest with the entire unpaid principal due in full
3 years from making of the note.

EXPLANATION OF DEPOSIT RECEIPT CLAUSES (Continued)

BLANKET SECOND

Buyer to give and seller to take back a note secured by a blanket second deed of trust in the amount of $2,500 on this property and on buyers' property at 110 Oak Street, Walnut Creek, California, repaying $25 or more monthly including 7% interest with the entire unpaid principal due in full 3 years from making of the note or upon resale of either property, whichever first occurs.

6. CONTINGENCY CLAUSE

While there are many types of contingencies, such as "approval of wife", special financing, zoning, etc., the most common is probably that which requires the sale of a buyers' present home. This is the example given.

> This offer is contingent upon the close of escrow of the sale of buyers' property at 110 Oak Street, Walnut Creek, California.

> (When the home to be sold is in the area we serve, add:)

> Buyer agrees to list said property with GRANADA REALTY immediately upon sellers' acceptance of this contract.

7. RELEASE CLAUSE

Whenever a contract contains a contingency (other than normal financing) which is not required by the terms of the contract to be removed within 7-10 days of the sellers' acceptance, a release clause must be included with the contingency clause.

> Should seller receive another acceptable offer within the term of this contract, buyer will have 3 days from written notification to remove this contingency or this entire agreement will become null & void.

8. TERMITE FORM

Required by VA for all sales which will apply for a new GI loan. In other sales, it is always a good idea to recommend a termite inspection for buyers' protection.

The Termite Form says that sub-structure of main building shall be examined. Seller is responsible for work to repair damage caused by wood destroying organisms and work to correct conditions that caused the infestation or infection. Conditions deemed likely to cause infestation or infection will be pointed out to buyer in report but will not be sellers' responsibility to correct.

9. SUBORDINATION CLAUSE

Usually used when seller carries back financing on a land sale.

EXPLANATION OF DEPOSIT RECEIPT CLAUSES (Continued)

Upon buyers' request, seller will subordinate his note
and deed of trust to a construction loan which will not
exceed $20,000 at 6½% interest for 30 years, providing
that buyer shall pay sellers' loan in full upon resale
of the property but not later than the due date hereto-
for established.

(The specific amount, interest rate and term of the construction loan must be specified.)

10. CONTRACT OF SALE

Use of this instrument is not recommended as it offers little protection to either buyer or seller. If the purchaser defaults in
a contract of sale, it can take the seller a year or more to recover
his property through court action. If the seller fails to make payments on the existing first note, the property can be awarded to
the lender at a Trustee Sale and the buyer loses all his investment.

11. INTERIM OCCUPANCY AGREEMENT

Whenever a buyer desires to occupy, or is given possession of, property before close of escrow, or, whenever seller is permitted to
remain in property for a period of longer than 10 days after the
close of escrow, there should be a provision in the contract for
payment of rent. Example of the clause providing for an Interim-
Occupancy by buyer is given.

Upon lender's approval of buyers' credit, buyer and seller
agree to execute an Interim-Occupancy Agreement for payment
of $5.00 per day by buyer to seller from date of buyers'
occupancy of property to close of escrow. Use the PRE-
RECORDATION or POST-RECORDATION RENTAL AGREEMENT as the
form for this agreement.

12. LOT RESERVATION

This form is used to reserve a specific lot in a subdivision pending
buyer and builder agreement as to plans, specifications and price of
new home to be constructed.

13. PERSONAL PROPERTY TRANSFER

An addendum to deposit receipt spelling out specific personal property
that will be included with house upon buyers' completion of purchase.
It is especially important to use this form in connection with sales
requiring new Government Insured Loans because any personal property
transfer shown on the deposit receipt itself will effect the property
appraisal. No reference to the personal property transfer form is
made on the deposit receipt.

EXPLANATION OF DEPOSIT RECEIPT CLAUSES (Continued)

14. EQUITY PURCHASE CONSIDERATION

This is an excellent money making tool. Its use eliminates the necessity of contingent sales. For example: If a customer wants to
purchase a new home but he must sell his present home first, he can
give the seller a note secured by a deed of trust on his present home.
as all, or part,of the down payment. The note will be payable in full
6 months from the date of making, or upon sale of his present home,
and has no monthly payments. He will make certain his present home
is priced to sell for he must get the money to pay off the note from
the proceeds of the sale of his home. The following clause would
replace the usual "specified cash down payment" clause.

> Buyer to give as down payment and seller to take back a note,
> secured by a second deed of trust in the amount of $2,500
> on property commonly known as 110 Oak Street, Walnut Creek,
> California, due in full including 7% interest 6 months from
> date of making or upon close of escrow of sale of the buyers'
> Walnut Creek property, whichever occurs first.

SECURITY TRANSACTIONS
SUBORDINATION PROVISIONS

Since January 2, 1964, the California Civil Code (sections 2953.1-2953.5) has required certain specific language in all agreements containing subordination provisions affecting subordination of loans up to $25,000.

Under the provisions of the code the title of any such agreement must contain in either 10-point bold face type or capitalized and underlined typewriting the words

"SUBORDINATED" or "SUBORDINATION AGREEMENT"

Immediately following the title in either eight-point bold type or capitalized typewriting the following is required:

"NOTICE: THIS (TITLE OF AGREEMENT) CONTAINS A SUBORDINA-TION CLAUSE WHICH MAY RESULT IN YOUR SECURITY INTEREST IN THE PROPERTY BECOMING SUBJECT TO AND OF LOWER PRIORITY THAN THE LIEN OF SOME OTHER OR LATER SECURITY INSTRUMENT."

If the subsequent loan may be utilized for a purpose other than construction on or improvement of the property securing the loan, then over the signature of the party agreeing to subordinate must appear the following wording in eight-point bold type or Capitalized typing:

"NOTICE: THIS (TITLE OF AGREEMENT) CONTAINS A SUBORDINATION CLAUSE WHICH ALLOWS THE PERSON OBLIGATED ON YOUR REAL PROPERTY SECURITY INSTRUMENT TO OBTAIN A LOAN A PORTION OF WHICH MAY BE EXPENDED FOR OTHER PURPOSES THAN THE IMPROVEMENT OF THE LAND."

Failure to comply with the foregoing requirements allows the party who agreed to subordinate to avoid the subordination provisions of the agreement without avoiding the remaining provisions.

Exhibit B-27
Contract Subordination Provisions

FHA REQUIRED AMENDATORY LANGUAGES

This rider amends Deposit Receipt dated _6/25/--_ covering property
located at _21 BELLE AVE, PLEASANT HILL_, California.

"It is expressly agreed that, notwithstanding any other provisions of this contract,
the BUYER shall not be obligated to complete the purchase of the property described
herein or to incur any penalty by foreiture of earnest money deposits or otherwise
unless the SELLER has delivered to the BUYER a written statement issued by the
Federal Housing Commissioner setting forth the appraised value of the property for
mortgage insurance purposed of not less than $_20,000_, which statement the
SELLER hereby agrees to deliver to the BUYER promptly after such appraised value
statement is made available to the SELLER."

"The BUYER shall, however, have the privilege and option of proceeding with the consummation of this contract without regard to the amount of the appraised valuation
made by the Federal Housing Commissioner."

William B. Douglas	_David S. Robinson_
Buyer's Signature	Seller's Signature
Sally A. Douglas	_Carol M. Robinson_
Buyer's Signature	Seller's Signature

Date _6/25/--_

This form is required on all FHA sales.

Exhibit B-29
Pre-Recordation Rental Agreement

PRE-RECORDATION RENTAL AGREEMENT

Effective date ——————————

In consideration of the payment of $ per diem beginning
on the above date, Seller grants permission to the undersigned, hereinafter known as Purchaser, to hereby take possession of the premises
known as , prior to recordation of deed
and necessary loan papers thereof. The undersigned understand and
agree to the following terms and conditions:

1. That purchaser's possession of said home shall not be deemed to be
a tenancy under the laws of the State of California, but merely an interim
occupancy pending the completion of arrangements for financing the
purchase of said home pursuant to the agreement set forth in the Deposit
Receipt, and purchasers waive all requirements of the State of California
regarding prior notice by a landlord to tenant requiring the tenant to
move from the premises, or any other notice required by such laws in
connection with unlawful detainer actions.

2. That upon taking possession of the subject premises and in the event
anything arises from any source whatsoever thereby making it impossible
for the mortgagor to issue a first trust deed against the subject premises,

the purchaser agrees to vacate the subject premises within fiive days from the date of notification by registered mail or pay $10 per day as rent alone.

3. That purchaser hereby agrees that he has inspected the premises and accepts said premises in their present condition and agrees not to request any further corrections or adjustments, subject to any exceptions listed on the reverse side.

4. That in the event it becomes necessary for purchaser to vacate said premises due to any reason, purchaser understands and agrees to leave said premises in perfect condition as agreed on at the time of possession. In the event damage has been caused to the premises as a direct result of the purchaser's possession, the purchaser agrees to repair the same, or to reimburse the seller for costs and expenses incurred in the repair of same. If purchaser fails to promptly reimburse the seller, it is understood and agreed that the seller may use any or all monies purchaser has on deposit including down payment, closing costs and impounds to repair damage in connection with the subject transaction, it being further understood and agreed that the amount of damage is not necessarily limited to the monies on deposit to the seller.

5. That purchaser agrees that until title is transferred to him and this escrow closed, he will make no improvements to this property. However, in the event that he improves said property in any way, and is required to vacate said property, for any reason, said improvements become a part of the real property and belong completely and wholly to the seller. All terms and conditions of the Sales Agreement or Deposit Receipt executed by the purchaser are to remain in full force and effect, and purchaser agrees to execute any documents required by the seller, lender, VA, FHA, title company or   on the day such papers are presented. If purchaser refuses to sign same, purchaser hereby agrees to pay $10 per day until papers are signed.

6. That should seller fail to sign those documents necessary to the close of the escrow within forty-eight hours of the time they are available, the purchaser shall remain in possession and the per diem rate will be terminated.

7. That the per diem rate is to be paid monthly in advance and pro-rated as of the date of the close of escrow.

The above terms and conditions are hereby concurred in, approved and accepted.

Title Company   Escrow Number

Buyer   Seller

Buyer   Seller

Date   Agent

GRANADA REALTY

GRANADA REALTY
P.O. Box 697
Lafayette, California

Phone 284-5555

POST-RECORDATION RENTAL AGREEMENT

AGREEMENT entered into this ____15____ day of ____July____ 19--

between __John & Mary Franks__ hereinafter referred to as

SELLERS and __William & Evelyn Watson__ hereinafter referred to as BUYERS:

WITNESSETH

WHEREAS, under the date of __June 1, 196____ the undersigned entered into an agreement for the sale by SELLERS to BUYERS of the real property hereinafter described as follows:

ALL of that real property known as __119 Oak St., Lafayette, California__ and that such sale would be consummated immediately following completion of the arrangements for the buyers to finance the purchase of said property. NOW, THEREFORE, IT IS HEREBY AGREED THAT SELLER AGREES AS FOLLOWS:

1. That seller will pay to buyer as compensation for the use of said dwelling the sum of $ 50.00 at $5.00 per diem from close of escrow until __July 25, 196__ when they agree to vacate said premises, however, should the seller for any reason fail to vacate on or before the date agreed upon, then said payment shall be increased to double the agreed per diem during the period of such delay.

2. That seller will not commit any waste upon the property during their occupancy thereof and that they will remove all of their possessions forthwith and will leave the premises in the same condition as of the time that the sale of the property was consummated.

3. That in case suit is instituted by buyer to enforce the provisions of this agreement, seller shall pay, in addition to all other sums which may be due, such sums as the Court may adjudge reasonable as attorney's fees in said action.

4. Seller waives all requirements of the laws of the State of California regarding prior notice by landlord and tenant in connection with unlawful detainer actions.

The said real property is in the County of ____Contra Costa____

State of California, commonly known as __119 Oak St., Lafayette, Calif.__

__Colonial Title Company__	____#6911____
Title Company	Escrow Number

William V Watson
Buyer

John E Franks
Seller

Evelyn Watson
Buyer

Mary O. Franks
Seller

Date __July 15, 19--__

[signature]
Agent
GRANADA REALTY

Exhibit B-30
Post-Recordation Rental Agreement

PERSONAL PROPERTY TRANSFER

ADDENDUM to Deposit Receipt dated _May 10, 19—_

Between _Thomas Pillsbury a single man_ (BUYER)

and _Willard L. Wine and Theresa Y. Wine his wife_ (SELLER)

Concerning Real Property known as _3333 Clem Ct, Walnut Creek_

When sale is successfully concluded according to the terms of the Deposit Receipt, SELLER shall deliver to BUYER, at no extra cost, the following items of Personal Property:

1 - Wall to wall carpets in living room and hall

2 - Drapes in living room

3 - Chandelier in dining room

4 - all swimming pool maintenance equipment

5. all garden furniture

BUYER _Thomas Pillsbury_   SELLER _Willard J Wine_

Theresa J Wine

BROKER _Granada Realty_   By _Gale A Leninad_

(A copy of this form should be attached to each copy of Deposit Receipt.)

Exhibit B-31
Personal Property Transfer Form

BEFORE THE
DEPARTMENT OF INVESTMENT
DIVISION OF REAL ESTATE
OF THE
STATE OF CALIFORNIA

In the matter of the application of	FINAL SUBDIVISION
ARCADY HOMES, INC., a corporation STEVE RUBOTTOM, President	PUBLIC REPORT
for a final subdivision public report on	FILE NO. 4448 OAK

SUBDIVISION 3068
BROOKWOOD VALLEY
CONTRA COSTA COUNTY,
CALIFORNIA

This Report Is Not a Recommendation or Endorsement of the Subdivision But Is Informative Only.

Buyer or Lessee Must Sign That He Has Received and Read This Report.

THIS REPORT EXPIRES FIVE YEARS FROM DATE OR UPON A MATERIAL CHANGE.

MAY 4, 19--

SPECIAL NOTE

YOUR ATTENTION IS ESPECIALLY DIRECTED TO THE PARAGRAPHS BELOW HEADED: *STREETS, FILLED GROUND.*

ADDITIONAL INFORMATION FOLLOWS IN NARRATIVE FORM:

LOCATION AND SIZE: On Hannibal Drive, North of Withers Avenue, one mile west of Pleasant Hill. Approximately six acres, divided into 15 lots.

TITLE: Title is subject, among other things, to: Easements affecting certain lots for utility, drainage, pipeline, sanitary sewer, and other purposes. These easements as they affect individual lots may

Exhibit B-32
State Subdivision Report

be determined by an examination of the title report and the recorded map of this tract.

ZONING: The property is to be sold for residential purpose.

PURCHASE MONEY HANDLING WILL BE AS FOLLOWS: All funds received from each purchaser will be impounded in an escrow depository until a release is obtained from any blanket encumbrance applying to this subdivision and the legal title is delivered to the purchaser. (Ref. Section 11013.2(a) Business and Professions Code).

NOTE: A blanket encumbrance is one which affects more than one parcel of subdivided land; it can concern money or matters of agreement.

FILLED GROUND: The subdivider's engineer reports that: Some lots will contain filled ground to a maximum depth of 13 feet, and are to be properly compacted for intended use under the supervision of a state licensed engineer or firm.

WATER: Water will be supplied by the East Bay Municipal Utility District.

FIRE PROTECTION: Central County Fire Protection District.

ELECTRICITY and GAS: Electricity and gas will be supplied by the Pacific Gas and Electric Company, whose facilities are presently located adjacent to the subdivision.

TELEPHONE: Telephone service will be supplied by the Pacific Telephone & Telegraph Company, whose facilities are presently located adjacent to the subdivision. Lot purchasers will be required to pay the costs for normal connection charges.

SEWERAGE DISPOSAL: Public sewers will be installed by the subdivider. Sewers will discharge into the Central Contra Costa Sanitary District sewer.

STREETS AND ROADS: Streets within this subdivision have been offered for dedication and have not yet been accepted by the County for public use and maintenance.

PUBLIC TRANSPORTATION: Public transportation consists of Greyhound Bus three miles from the subdivision.

PUBLIC SCHOOLS WHICH SERVICE THIS SUBDIVISION: The Pleasant Hill Elementary School is approximately 5½ miles from the subdivision. The Pleasant Hill Junior High School is approximately 5½ miles from the subdivision.

The Pleasant Hill High School is approximately 5½ miles from the subdivision.

School bus service is available to all schools.

Note: Purchasers should contact the local school board if they desire information regarding school facilities and bus service.

SHOPPING FACILITIES: Shopping facilities are approximately three miles from the subdivision located in downtown Walnut Creek, consisting of general shopping facilities.

MFS: ABW

FILE NO. 4448 OAK
Page 2

REQUIRED RECEIPT FOR PUBLIC REPORT

"2795.1. *Approved Form for Receipt for Public Report.* The following form shall be used by the owner, subdivider or agent as the receipt to be taken from prospective purchasers for the copy of the Public Report which must be given to prospective purchasers."

RECEIPT FOR PUBLIC REPORT

The owner, subdivider, or his agent is required to give you an opportunity to read the public report before demanding or accepting any deposit, consideration or written offer to purchase or lease lots or parcels in a subdivision.

Do not sign unless you have read the report.

I have read the Commissioner's Public Report on:

4448 OAK   #3068 - BROOKWOOD VALLEY
_____   _____
File No.   Tract No. or Name

The date of the copy of said report which I received and read is:

Tom Huffy
_____
Name

3399 Center St, Concord
_____
Address

8/21/--
_____
Date

Subdivider is required to retain this receipt for three years.

Exhibit B-33
Agent's Receipt for State Subdivision Report

GRANADA REALTY

LIABILITY RELEASE FORM

The undersigned Sellers hereby consent to return, release and refund the
deposit to Buyers heretofore made under the terms of that certain deposit
receipt or contract dated _____August 5_____, _19‑‑_, and said Sellers
do hereby agree to the cancellation and termination of said agreement; and
that in consideration thereof the undersigned Buyers do hereby agree to the
cancellation and termination of said deposit receipt or agreement; and that
in consideration of mutual promises and conditions herein contained the
Buyers, Sellers and Brokers (including all agents connected herewith) do
hereby jointly and severally release each other from all claims of every
kind and character arising from or connected with the foregoing deposit
receipt and contract.

DATED _October 2_ , 19‑‑

Fred Smith
            Buyer

Mary Smith
            Buyer

By _Wm. a. Stark_
       For Selling Broker

Jack Toms
            Seller

Ellie Toms
            Seller

By _____
      For Listing Broker

Exhibit B-34
Liability Release Form

EXCHANGE AGREEMENT

(NOT TO BE RECORDED)

THIS AGREEMENT ENTERED INTO BETWEEN

Franklin F. Farmer and Joan J. Farmer, his wife

HEREIN CALLED THE FIRST PARTY, AND

Simon S. Secory and Marilyn M. Secory, his wife

HEREIN CALLED THE SECOND PARTY; WITNESSETH THAT THE FIRST PARTY DOES HEREBY OFFER TO EXCHANGE THE
FOLLOWING PROPERTY, IN THE City of Concord COUNTY OF Contra Costa
STATE OF CALIFORNIA, TO-WIT:

Lot and improvements commonly known as 840 California Street

FOR THE PROPERTY OF SAID SECOND PARTY IN THE City of Walnut Creek
COUNTY OF Contra Costa STATE OF CALIFORNIA, TO-WIT:

Lot and improvements commonly known as 10 Mildred Lane

UNDER THE FOLLOWING TERMS AND CONDITIONS:

1-Second party agrees to pay First Party $3,000.00 cash.
2-Second party will assume existing first loan on Concord property
in the approximate amount of $15,000, payable $96.65 per month including
6% interest for a term of 25 years.
3-First party and Walnut Creek property to qualify for a new conventional
loan in the amount of $20,000.00 with interest not to exceed 6% for a
term of at least 25 years.

Exhibit B-35
Exchange Agreement

Each party hereto at his own expense shall furnish a policy of title insurance through the   Title Guaranty Company Contra Costa County Division, for the respective properties they are acquiring, by first obtaining a preliminary report therefor within

15   days from the date this offer is accepted by the second party, showing the titles to said properties to be merchantable and free from encumbrances, except taxes and the encumbrances herein mentioned, and the hereinafter named agent is authorized to procure and deliver said preliminary reports and policies of title insurance.

Each party hereto shall execute and deliver, within   **30**   days from the date this offer is accepted, all instruments in writing necessary to transfer the titles to said properties and complete and consummate this exchange.

In the event defects appear in the titles to either or any of said properties, then this agreement shall be extended for a reasonable time that the same may be corrected. In the event any such defects cannot be corrected within said reasonable time, this agreement shall be null and void, except as to the payment of commissions, unless the title to the property affected is accepted subject thereto.

All taxes (on July 1 basis) and the insurance, rents and other expenses affecting said properties shall be prorated to the date this exchange is consummated. Any act required to be done may be extended not longer than thirty days by the hereinafter named agent.

(a) **GRANADA REALTY**   whose address is **3333 Mt. Diablo Blvd., Lafayette** California, is hereby authorized to act as agent for all parties hereto and may accept commission therefrom and should this offer be accepted by the second party the undersigned agrees to pay said agent $**1,500.00----------**   commission for services rendered to become due on the execution of this agreement by all parties hereto.

The word "party" wherever used in this instrument shall be construed respectively to include the plural as well as the singular.

Dated **August 3**   , 19--   *Franklin F. Farmer*

                                                    Joan J. Farmer

ACCEPTANCE

The foregoing offer is hereby accepted upon the terms and conditions stated, and the undersigned, hereinbefore called the second party, agrees to pay (a) **GRANADA REALTY** $**1,440.00------** commission for services rendered to become due on the execution of this agreement by all parties hereto.

Dated **August 4**   , 19--   *Session S. Secory*

                                                    Marilyn M. Secory

(a) Name of agent **GRANADA REALTY,** 3333 Mt. Diablo Blvd., Lafayette
By: *[signature]*   284-9550
THIS FORM SHOULD BE EXECUTED IN TRIPLICATE. ORIGINAL SHOULD BE HELD BY BROKER AND THE DUPLICATE AND TRIPLICATE SHOULD BE DELIVERED TO THE FIRST AND SECOND PARTIES.

Note: On exchanges, commissions are divided 50/50 between cooperating real estate offices.

GRANADA REALTY
P.O. Box 697
Lafayette, California

Phone 284-5555

STRUCTURAL PEST CONTROL AGREEMENT

Property located at _211 PINE ST. , CONCORD_

SECTION 1. Substructure of the main building (unless otherwise indicated
herein) shall be examined by a State licensed pest control inspector at
the expense of the BUYER. All work to repair damage from infestation or
infection by wood destroying organisms, and all work to correct conditions
that caused infestation or infection shall be done at the expense of the
SELLER. Any work to correct conditions usually deemed likely to lead to
infestation or infection (where no infestation or infection is found)
shall NOT be the responsibility of the SELLER, and shall be segregated
in the report. Funds for work to be done at the expense of the SELLER
shall be held in escrow and disbursed upon issuance of certificate of
completion by the State licensed pest control operator.

SECTION 2. If further Inspection Recommended in Report: BUYER has
option of accepting the report or of requiring further inspection at his
expense. If further inspection is made and infestation, infection or
damage is found, correction will become a part of Section 1, above. If
no further inspection is requested by the BUYER prior to completion of
sale, all factors as they pertain to this agreement will be satisfied.

EACH PARTY SIGNATORY HERETO ACKNOWLEDGES THAT HE IS HEREBY GIVEN WRITTEN
NOTICE OF HIS RIGHT, AS PROVIDED IN SECTION 8614 OF THE BUSINESS AND
PROFESSIONS CODE OF CALIFORNIA, TO OBTAIN DIRECTLY FROM THE STRUCTURAL
PEST CONTROL BOARD, 1020 "N" STREET, SACRAMENTO, CALIFORNIA, A CERTIFIED
COPY OF ALL INSPECTION REPORTS AND COMPLETION NOTICES PREPARED AND FILED
BY ANY STRUCTURAL PEST CONTROL OPERATOR DURING THE PRECEDING TWO YEARS.
(FEE $2.00)

> Sec. 8614, Calif. B & P Code: Any person, whether or not a
> party to a real estate property transaction, has a right to
> request and, upon payment of the required fee, to obtain di-
> rectly from the board a certified copy of all inspection re-
> ports and completion notices prepared and filed by any
> structural pest control operator during the preceding two
> years.

THIS AGREEMENT is hereby made a part of that certain deposit receipt
dated _8/10/--_ .

Date approved and accepted _8/10/--_ .

BUYER _John Thomas_   SELLER _Frank F. Bell_
BUYER _Martha S. Thomas_ SELLER _Sally Y. Bell_
....

INSTRUCTION TO PEST CONTROL OPERATOR
Name of Operator _B. J. Termite Co._   Date _8/10/--_
Address   _W.C._

You are instructed to make a structural pest control inspection and
report to comply with the agreement between BUYER AND SELLER noted
above, and a quotation of cost of recommended work shall be given for
each Section, above.

Report ordered by _Granada (C.M.)_

Colonial   Escrow Number _T-2229_
Title Company

Exhibit B-36
Structural Pest Control Agreement

Copies of this and other reports may, on payment of prescribed fee, be obtained from:

Structural Pest Control Board
1021 O Street
Sacramento, Calif. 95814

STANDARD INSPECTION REPORT FORM

This form is prescribed by the Structural Pest Control Board, with whom a copy must be filed, by licensee.

FIRM NAME AND ADDRESS	
XTERMITE COMPANY 1955 DORA AVE. P.O. BOX 793 WALNUT CREEK, CALIFORNIA	CO. REPORT NO. (if any)

AFFIX STAMP TO BOARD COPY ONLY

FIRM LICENSE NUMBER	STAMP NUMBER	DATE OF INSPECTION
2757	17711A	11-29--

FOR STATE CODING ONLY: LICENSEE SHALL INDICATE INFESTATIONS, INFECTIONS, AND CONDITIONS SHOWN BELOW BY AN X IN THE PROPER SQUARE	S	K	F	R	FG	EC	Z	SL
	X			X				

THIS IS AN INSPECTION REPORT ONLY
NOT A NOTICE OF COMPLETION

CITY CODE	ADDRESS OF PROPERTY INSPECTED	BLDG.NO.	STREET	CITY
07-3093		156	Lancaster Road	walnut Creek

Inspection Ordered By .... Granada Realty, 3678 Mt Diablo Blvd., Lafayette, California
Report Sent To and Date .... same, Transamerica Title Co., Lafayette # 14734
Owner's Name and Address .... Mary Bernhard   Buyer - Donald VanDurgen
Name and Address of a Party in ....
Interest as per Sec. 8516(b)3 ....

INSPECTED BY: L.S. Moffett	LICENSE NO. 2757	This is an Original Report X	This is a Supplemental Report ☐	Number of Pages of this Report 1

Symbols to be used for State Coding Only

FINDINGS — To Be Explained In Detail Below

EVIDENCE OF: (ALSO SEE DIAGRAM AND EXPLANATION BELOW)	YES	1	2	3	4	5	6	7	8	9	10	11	12	13	14	15	16	17	18
S–Subterranean Termites	X	X			X														
K–Dry-wood Termites																			
Z–Dampwood Termites																			
F–Fungus or Dry Rot																			
B–Beetles–Other Wood Destroying Insects	X		X																
FG–Faulty Grade Levels																			
EC–Earth-wood Contacts																			
SL–Shower Leaks																			
Cellulose Debris	X		X	X															
Excessive Moisture Conditions																			
Insufficient Ventilation																			
Structural Damage																			
Attic																			
Inaccessible Areas																			
Further Inspection Recommended ➔ NO ☐																			

If further inspection is warranted under Section 8516 (8) and 1990 (i) and (j) (see below) indicate locations above and explain in detail below.*

DIAGRAM AND EXPLANATION OF FINDINGS AND METHODS OF RECOMMENDED CORRECTIONS

(This report is limited to structure or structures shown on diagram per Section 1995.) *

General Description .... 1 story, wood shingle exterior, 2x8 joists

*As is customary in this area, this report as requested by Granada Realty is limited to the substructure of the main building shown on the diagram unless otherwise indicated herein.

Exhibit B-37
Structural Pest Control Report

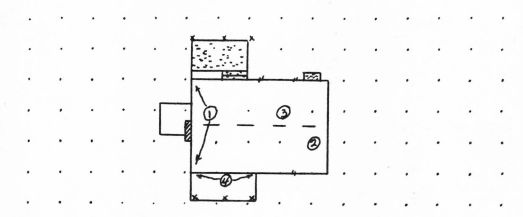

1. Termites have tubed from ground over foundation to the substructure on this side of house. Treat with a chemical toxic to termites, the subsoil adjacent to this foundation.
2. Remove foundation footing form boards.
3. Clear out from under house all wood and cellulose products.
4. Drill through the front porch on approx. 16 inch centers adjacent to house and pressure treat the soil under the porch with a chemical toxic to termites. Termites are in evidence in the substructure adjacent to the front porch. No evidence of structural damage as yet.

To complete the above recommendations the cost would be $115.00

Signature

* 1990 (i): Areas normally subject to damage which are inaccessible or for other reasons not inspected. The Board recognizes the following areas as inaccessible for the purposes of this subdivision: inaccessible attics or portions thereof; the interior of hollow walls; spaces between a floor or porch deck and the ceiling or soffit below; such structural segments as porte cocheres, enclosed bay windows, buttresses, and similar areas to which there is no access without defacing or tearing out lumber, masonry, or finished work; areas behind stoves, refrigerators, and built-in cabinet work; floors beneath coverings; areas where storage conditions or locks make inspection impracticable.

1990 (j): The report shall indicate or describe any area which is not inspected because it is inaccessible, or which is not inspected for any other reason, and shall either recommend inspection of such areas if inspection is practicable or state the reason inspection is not practicable.

See reverse side for other applicable sections of Structural Pest Control Act and Regulations.

NOTE: *Size of report form must be - 8½ x 17¼ inches.*

Exhibit B-37
Structural Pest Control Report

Standard Notice Of Work Completed

This form is prescribed by the Structural Pest Control Board, with whom a copy must be filed by licensee within 5 days after completion of work under a contract.

THIS IS A NOTICE OF COMPLETION ONLY, NOT AN INSPECTION REPORT.

Structural Pest Control Board
1021 O Street
Sacramento, California 95814

LICENSEE FIRM NAME AND ADDRESS:		
XTERMITE COMPANY 1955 DORA AVE. P.O. BOX 793 WALNUT CREEK, CALIFORNIA		**AFFIX STAMP TO BOARD COPY ONLY**

LICENSEE FIRM LICENSE NUMBER:	COMPLETION STAMP NUMBER:	DATE OF COMPLETION: *
2757	11728A	12-6--

CITY CODE:	ADDRESS OF PROPERTY INSPECTED:	BLDG. NO.	STREET:	CITY:
07-8093		156	Lancaster Road	Walnut Creek

Notice of Completion
Sent To and Date: { Granada Realty, 3678 Mt Diablo Blvd., Lafayette, California
Transamerica Title Co., Lafayette # 14234   12-8--

Owner's Name and Address: Mary Bernhard
Buyer's Name and Address: Donald VanDurgen

This is to certify that the recommendations on the above designated property, as outlined in STANDARD INSPECTION REPORT NO. ...., dated ......11-29--......, REGISTRATION STAMP NO. ......17711A......, have been completed with exceptions as noted below:

The following recommendations have been completed and are considered secondary measures under Section 1992 of the Structural Pest Control Board's Rules and Regulations: ....

COST OF THE COMPLETED WORK - $ ......115.00......

The following recommendations were not completed by this Company: ....

ESTIMATED COST OF WORK RECOMMENDED BUT NOT COMPLETED BY THIS COMPANY - $ ....

REMARKS: The substructure of this dwelling is free from any indication of wood infestation and fungus infection.

Signature _Lumum ? myft_

* Use numbers, i.e.: 9-1-64

Exhibit B-38
Notice of Pest Control Work Completed

TAX DATES YOU SHOULD KNOW

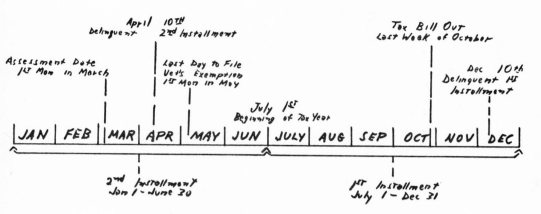

Exhibit B-39
Property Tax Dates

TAX RESERVES

Impounds for tax reserves are based on the month the first payment is due. This is usually the second month after escrow closes. On late-in-the-month closes, check with the lender to see when the first payment is due.

1st payment due:		No. Months taxes required:
January	-	4
February	-	5
March	-	0
April	-	1
May	-	2
June	-	3
July	-	4
August	-	5
September	-	6
October	-	7
November	-	8
December	-	3

An additional $2.00 per month are collected in the monthly payment to stabilize disbursements. Adjustments in payments are made as new tax bills are receided. This is important for estimating closing costs on GI and FHA sales.

Exhibit B-40
Tax Reserve Schedule

ESTIMATING CLOSING COSTS

(Rules of Thumb)

BUYERS' CLOSING COSTS

CONVENTIONAL SALES:

Normal closing costs will be about 3% of sales price.

Policy of title insurance=	1% of sales price
Loan fee=	1% of sales price
Pro-ration of taxes & insurance=	1% of sales price
	3% of sales price

GI and FHA SALES:

Normal closing costs will be a bit under 4% of sales price.

Policy of title insurance=	1% of sales price
Loan fee=	1% of sales price
Pro-ration of taxes and insurance=	1% of sales price
Loan trust fund impounds=	1% of sales price
	4% of sales prece

SELLERS' CLOSING COSTS

Tax pro-rations
Revenue stamps
Recording fees
Drawing fees
Pre-payment penalty (if applicable)
Termite damage repair (if applicable)
Realtor's commission
Loan discount fee "Points" (if applicable)

Exhibit B-41
Estimating Closing Costs

MONTH TO MONTH TENANCY AGREEMENT

THIS IS TO CERTIFY THAT _Gordon Jones_

hereinafter called Tenant has this _11_ day of _August_, 19___ rented from

Carl Curtis hereinafter called Owner.

ALL THAT CERTAIN _single family dwelling_ known and designated as

No. _1110 Topper St._ _Lafayette_ California.

TO HAVE AND TO HOLD the same as Tenant from month to month at the monthly rent of

$_200.00_ and $_____ for garage payable monthly in advance at _55 Smith_

Lane, _Concord_ California or such other place as the Owner

may designate, on the _10_ day of _Sept_, 19___, and continuing thereafter on the

_10_ day of each month during this tenancy in Lawful Money of the United States.

SAID PREMISES are rented for the occupancy of _2_ adults and _2_ children,

and an extra charge of $_40.00_ per month in addition to above rental for each and every other person. Payable at same time as above rent is paid.

1st: Tenant agrees that no alteration or repairs shall be made at the expense of Owner; nor shall the cost of any repairs, made by Tenant, be deducted from the rent, and Tenant hereby expressly waives all right to make repairs at the expense of the Owner, as provided for in Section 1942 of the Civil Code of California.

2nd: Tenant hereby acknowledges the premises to be in first class, satisfactory, tenantable condition and agrees the Owner shall not be liable for any damage to the furniture, goods or effects, or property, in or on said property, by leakage from the roof, or any cause whatsoever and Tenant further agrees to hold the Owner harmless from any claim for damages for personal injury by reason of any defects in said building, or any other cause whatsoever.

3rd: Tenant agrees that in the event of vacating said premises to give the Owner at least THIRTY DAYS NOTICE IN WRITING of such intention, before terminating payment of rent, and Owner reserves the right to demand possession of said premises at the end of THIRTY DAYS NOTICE IN WRITING, delivered to Tenant or either of them.

4th: Upon vacating said premises Tenant agrees to leave same broom clean, and in as good condition as they now are, reasonable wear and tear and damage by the elements excepted, and to remove any and all rubbish and/or garbage therefrom, or pay for such cleaning and/or removal before ceasing to pay rent. Rent therefore shall be paid until delivery of all keys and possession is accepted by Owner or Owner's Agent.

5th: Tenant agrees that Owner or Owner's Agent shall have the right to enter the herein demised premises at all reasonable hours for the purpose of examining or inspecting the same for the proper protection of same and/or for other lawful purposes.

6th: Tenant agrees to pay the rent in the manner hereinabove stipulated and upon failure to do so agrees to pay the sum of ONE DOLLAR in addition to any rent due and unpaid for each call made by Owner or Owner's Agent as is required to collect same.

7th: In the event rent be not paid when due, or should Tenant default in any agreement herein contained, landlord may re-enter said premises and remove all persons and property therefrom. Tenant agrees to pay the Owner all reasonable attorney's fees, together with all costs, which may be incurred by the Owner in any action or actions, instituted by Owner, against Tenant to enforce the payment of any rent from Tenant or to enforce any of the terms, covenants and conditions herein contained or to recover possession of the herein demised premises or any part hereof.

8th: Tenant agrees to pay for all utilities used by tenant during this tenancy, and to notify Owner or Owner's Agent of any leaks in roof, pipes, or elsewhere. Owner reserves the right to waive any term or condition herein contained, at any time or times, without invalidating this agreement.

9th: Tenant agrees that this lease contains all the agreements made in all matters pertaining to the renting of said premises and that the grounds surrounding said premises shall be cleaned of all rubbish and weeds and kept clear during this tenancy.

10th: It is agreed that Tenant shall not sublet any portion or all of said premises without the written consent of Owner, first had and obtained, nor to keep or allow to be kept any animals or pets of any kind on said premises.

WITNESS OUR HANDS, the day, month and year first above written.

TENANT _Gordon Jones_ OWNER _Carl Curtis_

TENANT _____

Exhibit B-42
Monthly Rental Agreement

                                    August 15   19 --

Received from   John e. Parker, a single man

the sum of Ten Thousand and no/100 ($10,000.00)---------------- *dollars.*

as part payment for the following described   real   *property situated*

in   area of Lafayette

County of Contra Costa   *State of* California   .

to wit: Unimproved lot at the North-East corner of the Intersection of Mt. Diablo Blvd. and Clark Street consisting of approximately 40,000 square feet and vested in the name of George and Mary Bunder.

        The entire price to be paid for said above described real   *property*

is Two Hundred Ten Thousand and no/100 ($210,000.00)-------- *dollars*

($ 210,000.00------), *payable as follows:*

1-Buyer pays $10,000.00 herewith as option money for 1 year from
  date of acceptance of this contract.
2-Balance to be paid all cash at the end of 1 year.

        Title to be perfect. Grant   *deed to be executed*

and delivered by the said George and Mary Bunder

to John E. Parker   , *or* his

assigns, on or before the 15   *day of* August   , *19 --,*

together with a policy of Title Insurance   *showing a good merchantable title*

provided, however, that the sum of $ 200,000.00------------------

is paid at said date; but if said sum is not paid on or before the said 15

day of August   , *19 --, then this contract is to be of no effect, and in that*

event the said sum of $ 10,000.00------   *is to be retained by*

        George and Mary Bunder

        Time is of the essence of this contract.

        August 15, 19 --

LEASE

(For Corporation or Individual Use)

ORDER NO._____

THIS INDENTURE, made in duplicate * this **10** day of **August**   A.D. 19 --

between **George and Vida Moyal**

hereinafter called the lessor

and **Frank and Jane Turner**

hereinafter called the lessee

WITNESSETH, that the lessor does by these presents, lease and demise unto the lessee all that certain property situate in the

Lafayette area   County of **Contra Costa**   , State of California, described as follows, to-wit:

Lot and Improvements commonly known as 557 Walnut Court

for the term of **Twelve (12) months**
beginning **September 1**   , 19 --   and ending **August 31**   , 19 --
for the total rent or sum of **Twenty Four Hundred and no/100 ($2,400.00)------**   Dollars,

in lawful money of the United States of America payable as follows, to-wit:

1—**$500.00 payable in advance as first two months rent in advance plus $100.00 damage deposit. Receipt for said $500.00 is hereby acknowledged.**
2—**$200.00 payable October 1, 1965 and a like sum on the first day of each successive month until the entire principal balance is paid in full.**
3—**Damage deposit will be refunded at termination of lease if property is vacated in same condition as it was at commencement of lease, reasonable wear and tear excepted.**
4—**Lessee shall have option to purchase said property within the term of this lease for $28,000.00, all cash to seller. If lessee exercises option, lessor will credit lessee $50 toward purchase price for each lease payment made.**

All of said rent shall be paid at the office of **Granada Realty**

the agent of the lessor **3333 Mt. Diablo Blvd.**   Street, **Lafayette**
California, or at such other place as may be designated by the lessor.

AND IT IS HEREBY AGREED AS FOLLOWS, TO WIT:

First: That if any rent shall be due and unpaid, or if default shall be made in any of the covenants herein contained, or if this lease is affected by the lessee becoming legally involved, that the lessor or representative or agent may reenter said premises and remove all persons therefrom;

Second: That the lessee shall pay the lessor said rent in the manner hereinbefore specified, and shall not let or underlet the whole or any part of said premises, nor sell or assign this lease, either voluntarily or by operation of law, nor allow any person, persons or corporation to occupy the same or any part thereof, without written consent of the lessor;

Third: That the lessee shall personally occupy said demised premises and shall keep the same in good repair, including all improvements which may hereafter be added, damage by the elements excepted, and shall not make any alterations therein without the written consent of the lessor and shall not commit or suffer to be committed any waste upon said premises;

Fourth: That said premises shall not be used by the lessee, nor anyone else, during the term hereof or any extension thereof, for the sale of any intoxicating or spirituous liquors, nor for any illegal or immoral purpose, and that possession of said premises by the lessee or successors or assigns shall not be construed as conveying any title thereto or ownership thereof;

Fifth: That the lessee waives all rights under Section 1942 of the Civil Code of California and releases the lessor for any and all damages which may be sustained by the lessee during the time lessee may be in possession of said premises;

Sixth: That the lessee shall not use said premises for any purpose which will cause the lessor to pay an additional or added expense, without obtaining the written consent of said lessor;

Seventh: That all Governmental laws and ordinances shall be complied with by the lessee;

Eighth: That should the lessor be compelled to commence or sustain an action at law to collect said rent or parts thereof or to dispossess the lessee or to recover possession of said premises, the lessees shall pay all of the cost in connection therewith including counsel fees of the attorney of said lessor;

Ninth: That the waiver, by the lessor, of any covenant herein contained shall not vitiate the same or any other covenant contained herein and that the terms and conditions contained herein are to apply to and bind the heirs, successors, and assigns of each of the parties hereto;

Tenth: That should the lessee occupy said premises after the date of expiration of this lease, with the consent of the lessor, expressed or implied, such possession shall be construed to be a tenancy only from month to month and the said lessee shall pay said lessor for said premises the sum of $ **200.00** per month for such period as said lessee may hold possession of said premises;

Eleventh: That the lessee shall use the premises for **single family residential dwelling** and for no other purpose, except upon the written consent of the lessor;

Twelfth: That at the expiration of said term or the sooner determination thereof, the lessee shall peacefully quit and surrender possession of said premises in as good condition as reasonable use and wear thereof will permit;

Thirteenth: The words "lessor" and "lessee" wherever used in this instrument, shall be construed respectively to include the plural as well as the singular.

IN WITNESS WHEREOF, the lessor and the lessee have hereunto subscribed their names the day and year in this indenture first above written.

NOTE: LEASE COMMISSIONS ARE—
7% 1st year
5% 2-3rd yrs.
4% 4-5th yrs.
2½% thereafter

George Moyal
Vida Moyal
Frank Turner
Jane Turner

Exhibit B-44
Lease with Option to Purchase

SQUARE FOOT APPRAISAL FORM

for use with the **RESIDENTIAL COST HANDBOOK**

1. Measure the building; make a sketch in right-hand space; mark dimensions on it. Also, note dimensions of Porches and Basement.

2. From overall appearance note:

Quality	Type	Number of Stories
☐ Low	☒ Conventional	☒ One
☐ Fair	☐ Modern	☐ Two
☐ Average	☐ Rustic	☐
☒ Good		
☐ Very Good	☐	

3. Enter Exterior Wall Material: STUCCO

4. Note Roofing and enter on line 12 below under *House Adjustments.*

5. Examine the Interior, noting the type of floor and heating. Count the Plumbing fixtures and note any miscellaneous features.

6. Review your estimate of Quality, mentally comparing each element of the specifications for that Quality and noting any significant differences.

7. Age NEW **Condition** EXCELLENT

OWNER: FRANK L. JOHNSON
STREET ADDRESS: 110 OAK ST.
CITY: LAFAYETTE
APPRAISER: G. HIMMAH
DATE: 10/1/--

AREAS: House 1600 □   Garage 400 □   Porch 100 □

Other _____

AREAS AND UNIT COSTS		
8. Compute total area of all floors above basement in square feet	1600	
9. Compute area of porches in sq. ft.	100	
10. Compute area of basement	---	
11. Select House square foot cost	10.77	
HOUSE ADJUSTMENTS		
12. Roofing SHAKES	+.22	
13. Floor HARDWOOD	BASE	
14. Heat FORCED AIR GAS	BASE	
15. Insulation CEILING	BASE	
16. Total Sq. Ft. Adjustment	+.22	
17. Plumbing 10 FIXTURES		+170
18. Miscellaneous 1 FIREPLACE	BASE	
GARBAGE DISPOSAL	BASE	
EXHAUST FAN	BASE	
6 CORNERS		−108
19. Porch: Line 9 × Cost 3.47		+347
WITH STEPS- COVERED		
20. Basement: Line 10 × Cost	NONE	
21. Multiply Line 8 × (Line 11 + 16) 10.99		17,584
22. Preliminary Replacement Cost (Total Lines 17 through 21)		17,993

GARAGE		
23. Base Cost STUCCO	3.24	
24. Adjustment (Roofing)	+.22	
25. Area 400 × Adjusted Cost	3.46	1,384
26. Attached Garage Wall NONE Deduct L.F. _____ × Cost _____		
27. Total Garage (line 25 − 26)		1,384
28. Total House and Garage (Lines 22 + 27)		19,377
29. Local Multiplier 1.03		
30. Total Replacement Cost of buildings (Line 28 × Line 29)		19,958
31. Depreciation NONE		
32. Sound Value of Building (Line 30 − Line 31)		19,958
YARD IMPROVEMENTS		
33. Fence 6' RDWD-200' @ 2.00/FT		400
34. Paving		
35. Landscape 5,000' LAWN @ .05		250
36. Miscellaneous		
37. Land		6,500
38. Total Property Value		27,108

FORM 1001   Copies of this form may be purchased from MARSHALL AND STEVENS, 1645 Beverly Blvd, Los Angeles 26, Calif, for $1.75 per pad
California subscribers add 4% sales tax

Exhibit B-45
Square Foot Appraisal Form

GUIDES TO APPRAISALS

(NOTE: The following Guides to Appraisals should be used
only as "Rule of Thumb" techniques to give an
approximate value to residential property. In
order to appraise property with precision, much
study is necessary.)

1-The value of an improved, residential lot (curbs, gutters,
utilities and graded ready for construction) should be
approximately $\frac{1}{4}$ the value of the property fully improved
with a completed home.

(ie. If a house would sell for $40,000, the value of the
lot is approximately $10,000.)

2-To determine the fair market sales price of a residential
property of average quality of construction, multiply the
number of square feet of living area of the home times $18
and add the value of the lot.

If the construction is very good, allow $30 per square foot.

3-Add $4,000 for a swimming pool regardless of size.

Remember - the single most important factor in determining
the value of real estate is

LOCATION.

You must adjust your appraisal figures dependent upon the
location of the property and the sales prices of comparable
properties in the area.

Exhibit B-46
Guides to Appraisals

PRELIMINARY REPORT for a policy of title insurance in the sum of $
to be issued by

FPC/ge

TO
Granada Realty   Escrow Order No. L-400321
3678 Mt. Diablo Boulevard
Lafayette, California   Escrow Officer:
Four copies of this report sent to
Bankers Mortgage Company, P. O.
Box 2948, San Francisco, California
Mr. Mower

WESTERN TITLE GUARANTY COMPANY Contra Costa County Division, a corporation, hereby
reports that title to the real property hereinafter described is on September 16, 1966 at 8:00 a.m.
vested in:

OTTO NEAL   and OLIVE E.   , his wife, as joint
                          tenants

SUBJECT TO:

1- 1966-67 County taxes: 1st. due November 1, 1966, delinquent December
   12, 1966; 2nd. due February 1, 1967, delinquent April 10, 1967:
            1st. $92.31   Real Estate $700
            2nd. $92.30   Improvements $1240
            Tax Bill 375-213-011   Code Area 76006
   The premises are assessed separately.

2- Deed of trust securing payment of $6800.00, and other sums and
   obligations
            Dated: August 23, 1962
            Recorded: September 7, 1962
            Book of Official Records: 4198
            Page: 617
            Trustor: Robert R. Baker and Geraldine Z. Baker, his wife
            Trustee: Lafayette Co., a California corporation
            Beneficiary: Lafayette Federal Savings and Loan Association.
   Notice of default by Lafayette Federal Savings and Loan Association
            Recorded: July 14, 1966
            Book of Official Records: 5161
            Page: 128.
                              -over-

Exhibit B-47
Preliminary Title Report

3- Deed of trust securing payment of $1000.00, and other sums and
   obligations
           Dated: March 5, 1963
           Recorded: March 13, 1963
           Book of Official Records: 4321
           Page: 370
           Trustor: Otto Neal   and Olive E.   , his wife
           Trustee: Western Title Guaranty Company Contra Costa County
           Division, a corporation
           Beneficiary: M. B.   and LaDene
    Said beneficial interest was assigned to Contra Costa Solano Invest-
   ment Corporation
           Recorded: June 7, 1963
           Book of Official Records: 4382
           Page: 340.

      That parcel of land in the County of Contra Costa, State of
California, described as follows:

      Lot 6, Block 9, map of Martinez Land Company Tract No. 2,
filed September 21, 1915, Map Book 14, page 285, Contra Costa County
records.

MARTINEZ LAND COMPANY
TRACT NO. 2 VOL. 14 PG. 285

THIS PLAT IS A PRINT OF THAT PART OF THE
RECORDED MAP REFERRED TO IN THE DESCRIPTION
HEREIN WHICH SHOWS THE RECORD SIZE AND
LOCATION OF THE PREMISES.
IF THE SIZE AND LOCATION ON THE GROUND
DIFFER FROM THE DATA DISCLOSED BY THIS PLAT,
THE ATTENTION OF THE TITLE COMPANY SHOULD
BE CALLED THERETO BEFORE THE ESCROW IS
CLOSED

BUYER'S INSTRUCTIONS

Escrow No. 1000

Date August 23, 19--

Enclosed herewith are the following:

CHECK in the amount of $ see below CASH in the amount of $

DEED of TRUST and NOTE Bankers Mortgage Company

(Documents and terms thereof have been examined and approved by buyer)

You are hereby authorized to deliver and/or record all of said documents and disburse said funds, together with the proceeds of any deed of trust mentioned below, on account of the purchase price for the real property described in your above numbered escrow and on account of the other costs, fees and adjustments in that connection, when you can issue your Standard Coverage form Title Insurance Policy in the amount of $ 18,000, insuring title as vested in the name of: Peter H. Ealy and Simone D. Ealy, his wife as joint tenants

SUBJECT TO:

COUNTY and/or CITY TAXES not delinquent; BONDS and/or SPECIAL ASSESSMENTS not delinquent; and COVENANTS, CONDITIONS, RESTRICTIONS, RIGHTS of WAY, EASEMENTS and RESERVATIONS now of record.

DEED of TRUST in favor of Bankers Mortgage Company

DEED of TRUST in favor of

Pro-rate as of Close , 19 -- ; ☒ Taxes (based on the latest available tax bills) ; ☐ Fire Insurance premiums; ☐ Interest on existing loan; ☐Rents (based on statements provided by seller) ; ☐ Upkeep charge.

☐ Credit to seller existing loan trust fund.

ESTIMATED STATEMENT

		DEBITS	CREDITS	
(27)	Purchase price	$ 18,000.00	$	(27)
(28)	Deposit paid by Buyer to: Broker		400.00	(28)
(29)	Deposit paid by Buyer to:			(29)
(30)	Paid to Seller outside of escrow			(30)
(31)	Existing loan balance			(31)
(32)	First Deed of Trust Bankers Mortgage Company		17,200.00	(32)
(33)	Second Deed of Trust			(33)
(34)				(34)
(35)	Taxes pro-rata $146.41 for ½ yr. pd. to 7/1/6		43.04	(35)
(36)	Fire Insurance: ☐ pro rata ☐ new Amount $ required before close please advise			(36)
(37)	Interest pro-rata			(37)
(38)	Rents pro-rata			(38)
(39)	Upkeep Charge pro-rata			(39)
(40)	Loan Trust Fund			(40)
(41)	Title Ins. Prem.: Standard $ 154.00 ATA $ 30.80	184.80		(41)
(42)	Recording Fees	8.40		(42)
(43)	Drawing Fees to:	1.00		(43)
(44)	Notary Fees to:			(44)
(45)	Termite Report	35.00		(45)
(46)	New Loan Charges: Fee $172.00 Interest $20.08 Tax Res. $231.00 Ins. Res. $ 5.52 FHA Mtge. Ins. $ 7.12 Appr. Fee $35.00 Tax Serv. $ 15.00 Credit Rep. $ 8.50 Total	494.22		(46)
(47)	Assumption Fee			(47)
(48)	Municipal Tax Report			(48)
(49)				(49)
(50)				(50)
(51)	Balance due this escrow (Estimated)		1,080.38	(51)
(52)	Balance due Buyer (Estimated)			(52)
TOTALS		$ 18,723.42	$ 18,723.42	

I hereby agree to pay all my proper costs and fees, including any adjustments, and request you to remit balance to me at the address shown below.

Received , 19

Buyers *Peter H. Ealy*
Peter H. Ealy
Simone D. Ealy
Simone D. Ealy

Address

By

City Phone No.

Exhibit B-48
Buyer's Instructions to Title Company

SELLER'S INSTRUCTIONS

Escrow No. 1000

Date August 23, 19--

Enclosed herewith are the following:

DEED FROM: Miller TO: Ealy

(Covering the property described in your above numbered escrow)

FIRE INSURANCE POLICIES: Yes ☐ No ☐

Which you may deliver and/or record when you have collected for me the sum of $ 18,000.00 as follows:

Less debits as shown below

Pro-rate as of Close , 19--; ☒ Taxes (based on the latest available tax bills); ☐ Fire Insurance premiums; ☐ Interest on existing loan; ☐ Rents (based on statements provided by seller);

☐ Credit to seller existing loan trust fund.

ESTIMATED STATEMENT

		DEBITS	CREDITS	
(1)	Purchase price	$	$ 18,000.00	(1)
(2)	Paid to Seller outside of escrow			(2)
(3)	Existing loan balance			(3)
(4)	Deed of Trust (First ☐, Second ☐, Third ☐)			(4)
(5)	Taxes pro-rata $146.41 for ½ yr. pd. to 7/1/6	48.80		(5)
(6)	Fire Insurance pro-rata			(6)
(7)	Interest pro-rata			(7)
(8)	Rents pro-rata			(8)
(9)	Upkeep charge pro-rata			(9)
(10)	Personal property tax			(10)
(11)	Loan Trust Fund			(11)
(12)	Commission paid to: Granada Realty	1,080.00		(12)
(13)				(13)
(14)				(14)
(15)	Revenue Stamps	19.80		(15)
(16)	Recording Fees	2.00		(16)
(17)	Reconveyance Fee			(17)
(18)	Bonds, Special Assessments			(18)
(19)	Taxes, ☐ Co., ☐ City, ☐ Tax Sale(s)			(19)
(20)	Notary Fees to: Drawing Fees to:	3.50		(20)
(21)	Demand of: DVA			(21)
	Principal $14,885.18			
	Int. @ $1.80 from 8/31 to rec. 3.60			
	Prepayment charge 304.08	15,192.86		
(22)	Loan Discount Fee	258.00		(22)
(23)	Termite Repair Work	pay if any		(23)
(24)	Held in escrow for:			(24)
(25)	Balance due this escrow (Estimated)			(25)
(26)	Balance Due Seller (Estimated)	1,395.04		(26)
	TOTALS	$ 18,000.00	$ 18,000.00	

I hereby agree to pay all my proper costs and fees, including any adjustments, and authorize you to deduct same from funds due me

and remit balance to me at the address shown below or to:

Received , 19

Sellers *Luther C. Miller* (signature)
Luther D. Miller
Address *Lillian G. Miller* (signature)
Lillian G. Miller

By
City Phone No.

Form No. CC-820 · Revised 7-59

PLEASE GIVE FORWARDING ADDRESS

Exhibit B-49
Seller's Instructions to Title Company

THIS BOX FOR EXCLUSIVE USE OF COUNTY RECORDER

GRANT DEED
(Individual Grantor)

Order No._____

For value received

BESSIE B. BENNETT, a widow,

GRANT 8to

ALVIN A. APPLEY and ROBERTA S. APPLEY, as Joint Tenants

*
all that real property situate in the **City of Concord**   County of
Contra Costa   State of California, described as follows:

Lot 38, Block 12, as designated on the map entitled "Map No. 1,
Wildwood Acres", which map was filed in the office of the
Recorder of the County of Contra Costa, State of California, on
January 10, 1917 in Volume 11 of Maps, at page 662.

WITNESS **my** hand this **3rd**   day of **September**   . 19--

* *For joint tenancy deed add after grantee names:–"as joint tenants"*

Bessie B. Bennett

STATE OF CALIFORNIA
County of Contra Costa   } ss.
County in which acknowledgement is taken
On_____ September 3 ____ 19-- ___ before me, _____
Write or type name of notary
a Notary Public, in and for said:*_____County and State, personally appeared_____
Bennett
known to me to be the person____whose name____ is ___subscribed to the within instrument, and acknowledged to me that she_____executed
the same.

**If notary is commissioned in another County
strike "said" and name County.   GAEL C. HIMMAH, Notary Public   In addition to signature type or print name of notary
My Commission Expires September 15, 1967   Notary Public.

Form No. 8-9-59

GRANT DEED (Individual) -*Tenancy in Common or Joint Tenancy*

Exhibit B-50
Grant Deed

APPENDIX C

A VISUAL LISTING PRESENTATION BOOK

When you use the following VISUAL LISTING PRESENTA-
TION BOOK, sit next to the homeowners and open your book so
they may see the pages. Then read each page, letting them follow
your finger as you casually point to the words as you read.

As you read along, you will bring out scores of motivating points
which will cause the homeowners to want to list their home with
you. The more you use the VISUAL LISTING PRESENTATION
BOOK, the more your listing skills will develop for soon you will
have memorized the wealth of information on the pages.

A VISUAL LISTING PRESENTATION BOOK such as the one
I offer in this text benefits both the newly licensed salesman and the
"old timer" alike. Read it carefully, then use it. You'll get results!

FOR
SALE

ABC REALTY

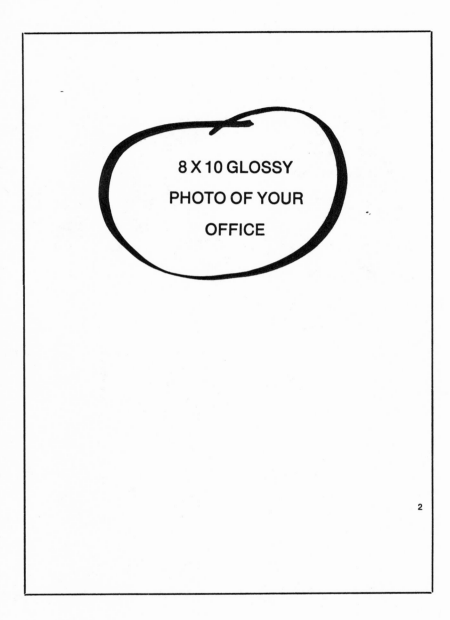

2

ABC REALTY

126 OAK ST.,   ORINDA, CALIFORNIA 94549   (415) 282-1211

IF YOUR FIRM IS LARGE, USE THIS LETTERHEAD FORMAT

1. We have 46 skilled salespeople ready to work for you.

2. We have been in business 15 years.

3. We have 6 offices to serve you.

4. We sold $1,000,000 worth of properties like yours last year.

5. The executives of our company have 125 years of experience selling real estate.

6. We average 20 newspaper ads per week.

7. Our staff is highly trained and thoroughly professional.

8. We have a proven method to sell your home.

4

ABC REALTY

126 OAK ST.,   ORINDA, CALIFORNIA 94549   (415) 282-1211

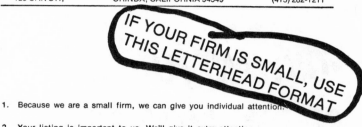

1. Because we are a small firm, we can give you individual attention.

2. Your listing is important to us. We'll give it extra attention.

3. We have been in business 20 years.

4. We sold $200,000 worth of properties like yours last year.

5. The executives of our company have 50 years of experience selling real estate.

6. We average 6 newspaper ads per week.

7. Our staff is highly trained and thoroughly professional.

8. We have a proven method to sell your home.

5

Because

YOU WANT TO
SELL YOUR HOUSE....

—At the best possible price

—As quickly as possible

YOU NEED....

6

ABC REALTY

AS YOUR

AGENT

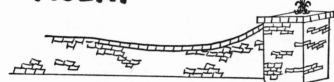

THE DICTIONARY SAYS

AN AGENT IS:

One who has the authority to
act for another

AS YOUR AGENT . . .

7

ACTING FOR YOU . . . .

WE WILL DO MANY THINGS

FOR YOU

THAT YOU CANNOT DO YOURSELF

WE WILL DO THE THINGS FOR YOU
THAT WILL GIVE YOU THE

RESULTS

YOU WANT

WE WILL SAVE YOU...

8

THE EXPENSE OF

WASTEFUL

ADVERTISING

HOUSES

DO NOT SELL

FROM THEIR OWN AD *!*

(Less than 1 out of 500 by actual survey.)

WE CAN-AND DO...

9

SPEND MANY MORE

ADVERTISING DOLLARS FOR YOU

Than you could possibly spend for yourself

DON'T WASTE YOUR

$

WE SPEND OUR ADVERTISING MONEY

FOR YOUR BENEFIT

Because we are professionals....

10

1. WE USE ONLY THE BEST MEDIA.
2. WE KNOW WHEN AND WHERE TO PLACE ADS THAT

PACK A PUNCH!

OUR ADS GET RESULTS BECAUSE THEY ARE WRITTEN BY EXPERTS.

WE KNOW

-A GOOD HOUSE MAY NOT MAKE A GOOD AD
-THE BEST PROSPECT FOR YOUR HOUSE MAY RESPOND TO AN AD ON A DIFFERENT KIND OF HOUSE.
-WE RUN MANY TYPES OF ADS TO ATTRACT THE BEST BUYERS.

BECAUSE WE RUN

MANY ADS..

1. We reach many more buyers.
2. We reach buyers who are qualified to buy your home

when you let us ....

11

WORK FOR YOU —

YOU CAN BE CERTAIN

We will continually run
ads which will produce
buyers interested in
your type of home.

THAT MEANS — — —

MORE MONEY FOR YOU!

We Know....

12

THAT THE BUYER MUST SEE THE

INTERIOR of your home.

GIVING HIM THE ADDRESS (As a FOR-SALE-
BY-OWNER must do when someone calls)

MEANS

A ## LOST SALE

because he will cruise by
and not come in.

WE NEVER GIVE

AN ADDRESS!

IN ADDITION . . . .
we show BOTH the **interior** and
the **exterior** only to those buyers who
are interested, and financially able to
buy your home.

THEN, WHEN WE HAVE . . .

13

FOUND THE

RIGHT BUYER

WE
PROTECT YOU

BY:
1. Having the buyer sign a binding legal contract.
2. Insisting on a substantial deposit.
2. Obtaining the best possible financing.
4. Working closely with the buyer and the lender throughout the escrow period.

WE WILL FIND....

14

THE **RIGHT BUYER**

FROM ONE OF OUR MANY SOURCES

REFERRALS FROM PAST CLIENTS

OUR PRESENT PROSPECTS

OUR MANY ADVERTISEMENTS

OUR OPEN HOUSES

A 'FOR SALE' SIGN ON ANOTHER HOUSE

A 'WALK IN' AT OUR OFFICE

A BUYER FROM ONE OF OUR 'SOLD' LISTINGS

IT'S A FACT....

15

THE RIGHT BUYER
WILL PAY
MORE For your home

THAN ANY OTHER BUYER

The buyer who is expertly matched to your home, the one whose needs it fits, who likes it, who has an enthusiastic reaction to it, will pay more money than anyone else.

WE WILL FIND THE
RIGHT BUYER FOR YOU!

HERE'S HOW . . .

16

WHEN WE REPRESENT YOU AS

YOUR EXCLUSIVE AGENT

YOU RECEIVE
THE BENEFIT

OF MANY SPECIAL
SERVICES

AT NO COST TO YOU

INCLUDING...

17

ALL THIS

1.	We carefully qualify buyers before we call for an appointment to show your property. This saves you time and inconvenience.
2.	We prepare a listing form describing your property to the best advantage.
3.	We prepare a special sales management folder on your house.
4.	I will feature your home at office sales meetings.
5.	We will hold your home open for inspection by real estate salesmen and brokers so they will add it to their inventory.
6.	Periodically we will hold you home open for inspection by the public.
7.	We will take colored photos of your home, both exterior and interior, for our office bulletin boards.
8.	We have an attorney and accountant on retainer to assist in the sale of your property.
9.	I will 'plug' your house at our Multiple Listing Service meetings.
10.	I will get the lowest 'point' quotes possible on your house. This saves you money!
11.	I will submit all purchase contracts to you and explain the details of each.
12.	I will prepare a list of 'comparable properties sold' for you.- You can compare their sales prices with your own.

WE WILL DO EVEN MORE....

18

SUCH AS

13.	I won't allow you to be 'pressured' by other salesmen.
14.	We will help a 'marginal' buyer qualify for a loan on your home through our financial sources.
15.	We will keep the attention of our sales force focused on your home.
16.	We will immediately advise all other brokers in this area about your home - and keep them advised.
17.	We will obtain marketing information for your home from these cooperating brokers.
18.	We will keep in touch with salesmen members of our real estate board to be sure they are working on your property.
19.	We will continually advise you of broker, salesmen, and client reactions to your property and the progress of our marketing efforts.
20.	We assist other brokers in securing the best possible financing for you.
21.	We pay a full selling commission to cooperating brokers.
22.	We 'follow up' prospects who show interest in your property.
23.	We protect you from the danger of opening your home to complete strangers.
24.	I work without pay until I bring you a contract at a price and terms acceptable to you.

THIS WILL BE THE RESULT.....

19

20

IT'SAFACT

BUYERS WILL DEDUCT A REAL ESTATE
COMMISSION FROM A HOMEOWNER'S
ASKING PRICE (they know it's not listed
with an agent — they will deduct it anyway.)

IT'SAFACT

BUYERS WORKING WITH OUR OFFICE
WILL PAY MORE FOR YOUR HOME
FOR THE SECURITY OF BUYING
THROUGH AN AGENT.

YOU REAP THE PROFIT!

21

IT'S A FACT

ABC REALTY

CAN GET YOU THE

MOST

MONEY

FOR YOUR HOME

22

LET

ABC REALTY

WORK

FOR

YOU!

23

INDEX